LABORATORY MANUAL

Chemistry

EXPERIMENTAL FOUNDATIONS

Chemistry: Experimental Foundations, Third Edition

Student Text

Laboratory Manual

Laboratory Notebook

Teachers Guide

Achievement Tests

LABORATORY MANUAL

Third Edition

Chemistry

EXPERIMENTAL FOUNDATIONS

PHYLLIS MERRILL

Chemistry Teacher
Fountain Valley High School
Fountain Valley, California

ROBERT W. PARRY

Professor of Chemistry
University of Utah
Salt Lake City, Utah

ROBERT L. TELLEFSEN

Chemistry Teacher
Vintage High School
Napa, California

HERB BASSOW

Chemistry Teacher
Germantown Friends School
Philadelphia, Pennsylvania

PRENTICE-HALL, INC., ENGLEWOOD CLIFFS, NEW JERSEY

LABORATORY MANUAL
CHEMISTRY: EXPERIMENTAL FOUNDATIONS
Third Edition

Phyllis Merrill, Robert W. Parry, Robert L. Tellefsen, and Herb Bassow

ISBN 0-13-129270-6

10 9 8 7 6 5 4 3 2 1

Prentice-Hall International, Inc., London
Prentice-Hall of Australia, Pty. Ltd., Sydney
Prentice-Hall of Canada, Ltd., Toronto
Prentice-Hall of India Private Ltd., New Delhi
Prentice-Hall of Japan, Inc., Tokyo
Prentice-Hall of Southeast Asia, Pte. Ltd., Singapore
Whitehall Books Limited, Wellington, New Zealand

Contents

APPENDIXES

Those sciences are in vain and full of errors which are not born from experiment, the mother of all certainty. LEONARDO DA VINCI

Preface

The authors hope that this laboratory manual will be useful in a variety of ways. Primarily, of course, it is a manual of experiments. The 43 main experiments and 11 supplementary experiments are closely tied to the text of the third edition of *Chemistry: Experimental Foundations*. Many of the experiments provide the basis for discussions in the text. As you learn to recognize and use important chemistry principles in the lab, you will gain appreciation and understanding of the theories that have been proposed to explain the regularities observed in nature.

The experiments in this manual are designed to

1. help you form good habits for working safely with laboratory apparatus and chemicals
2. enable you to discover for yourself the regularities and principles that unify chemistry and make it easier to understand
3. encourage careful observation and measurement under controlled conditions
4. foster the preparation of well-organized tables for recording data and results of calculations so that you can readily make deductions and recognize regularities
5. stimulate discussion by posing challenging questions to help you apply the principles observed in experiments to new situations

In addition, you will gain self-reliance by working alone on some experiments. And when you work with a partner, you will work as part of a team in which both partners contribute to as well as benefit from the investigation at hand. You will be called upon to apply your common sense and your ingenuity, for there is ample opportunity for both logical and imaginative thinking in the lab. Finally, you may wish to extend your knowledge beyond that provided by the experiments outlined in this manual. For that reason, many of the experiments end with suggestions for additional investigations that you may undertake with the permission of your teacher.

The introductory sections of this manual are devoted to helping you do a good job in the laboratory. Before beginning your first experiment, read pages 6–18 carefully. They contain general laboratory instructions and information on preparing for the laboratory, writing lab reports, and using proper experimental technique. The eight appendixes at the back of the manual will help you with your calculations and results. Appendixes 1 and 2 discuss how to express your data and answers properly. Appendixes 3 through 6 contain useful tables. Answers to the exercises in Appendixes 1 and 2 appear in Appendix 7, and Appendix 8 is the periodic table.

Remember, your laboratory work is the heart of your chemistry course. In the lab, you will have a unique and challenging opportunity to observe first-hand many of the facts and regularities that comprise the study of chemistry. From just such observations, scientists have developed the principles that unify chemistry and the theories that provide the current explanations of the regularities in nature. This is the scientific method in action.

Laboratory instructions

1. Remember at all times that the laboratory is a place for serious work.
2. Always prepare for an experiment by reading the directions in the manual before you come to the lab. Follow the directions implicitly and intelligently, noting carefully all precautions. Make no changes in the directions without consulting your teacher.
3. **Do only the experiments assigned or approved by your teacher. Unauthorized experiments are prohibited.**
4. If an acid or other corrosive chemical is spilled, wash it off immediately with water.
5. Do not touch chemicals with your hands unless directed to do so.
6. Never taste a chemical or solution unless directed to do so.
7. When observing the odor of a substance, do not hold your face directly over the container. Fan a little of the vapor toward you by sweeping your hand over the top of the container.
8. Allow ample time for hot glass to cool. Remember, hot glass looks like cool glass.
9. Smother any fires with a towel. Be sure you know the location of the fire extinguisher in the laboratory.
10. **Report any accident or injury, however minor, to your teacher.**
11. **Wear safety goggles at all times in the laboratory. Use the fume hood when directed.**
12. Discard solids and paper in a waste jar or wastebasket. Never discard matches, filter paper, or slightly soluble solids in the sink.
13. Check the label on a reagent bottle carefully before removing any of its contents. Read the label twice to be sure you have the right bottle.
14. Never return unused chemicals to the stock bottles. Do not put any object into a reagent bottle except the dropper with which it may be equipped.
15. Keep your apparatus and desk top clean. Avoid spillage, but if you do spill something, clean it up immediately. Store your own equipment in your drawer and return all special apparatus to its proper place at the end of the period.

Laboratory preparations

Read the complete experiment—introduction, procedure, and calculations and results—*before* coming to the laboratory. This is a must! You are not expected to memorize the procedures to be followed but, rather, to study them thoroughly enough to understand what you will be doing in the experiment and to summarize the overall plan of attack.

1. Each experiment begins with an introduction that outlines the purpose of the experiment. Read it carefully. Make sure that you can summarize the ideas in your own words before doing the experiment.
2. Each experiment has a detailed procedure to be followed. Any deviation from or extension of the procedure should be approved by your teacher. It is important that you have the procedure clearly in mind before coming to the laboratory. This will cut down on wasted time and motions during the laboratory period. Understanding the procedure thoroughly keeps you from having to ask "What do I do next?"
3. Many experiments involve calculations as well as questions. A look at both beforehand will not only help you understand the experiment but also aid you in preparing your data table.

Laboratory reports

1. Record all data in your laboratory notebook as soon after making the observations as possible. Make no erasures. Instead, cross out any errors with a single line. Always record your name, the date, and the title of the experiment.
2. Enter all data and observations neatly. Use tabular form when appropriate. If possible, design a data table before coming to the laboratory.
3. Indicate the operations used in making calculations by including an orderly sample calculation in your report. Do not clutter the calculations section with arithmetic details. Indicate the units used for all measurements. Normally, calculations should not be made during the laboratory period.
4. Answer the numbered questions in each experiment as part of your laboratory report. Use concise statements.
5. Do not include written answers to questions that appear in the introduction and procedure sections. Some are intended to direct your attention to problems that will be investigated. Others point out the reasons for certain procedures or controls.

Laboratory apparatus

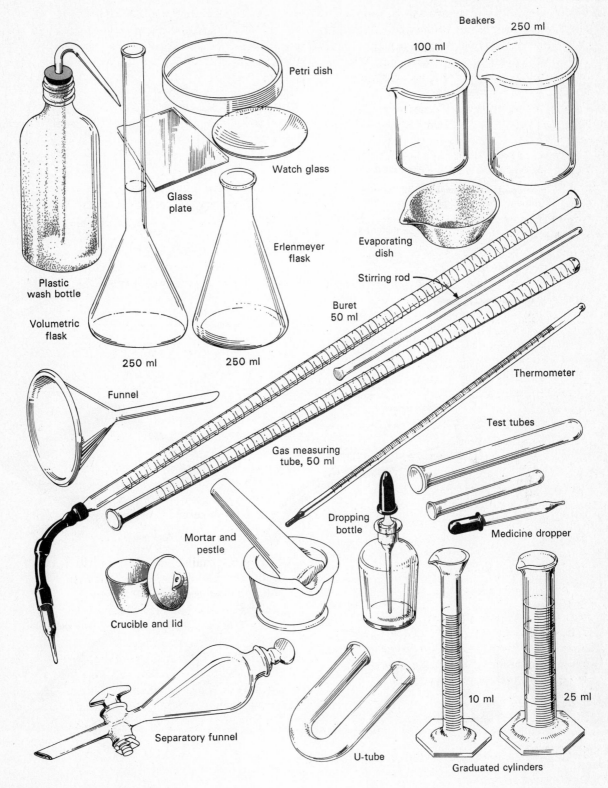

Petri dish

Watch glass

Glass plate

Erlenmeyer flask

Beakers

100 ml   250 ml

Evaporating dish

Stirring rod

Buret 50 ml

Plastic wash bottle

Volumetric flask

250 ml   250 ml

Funnel

Gas measuring tube, 50 ml

Thermometer

Test tubes

Dropping bottle

Medicine dropper

Mortar and pestle

Crucible and lid

Separatory funnel

U-tube

10 ml   25 ml

Graduated cylinders

Figure 1 Glass and porcelain.

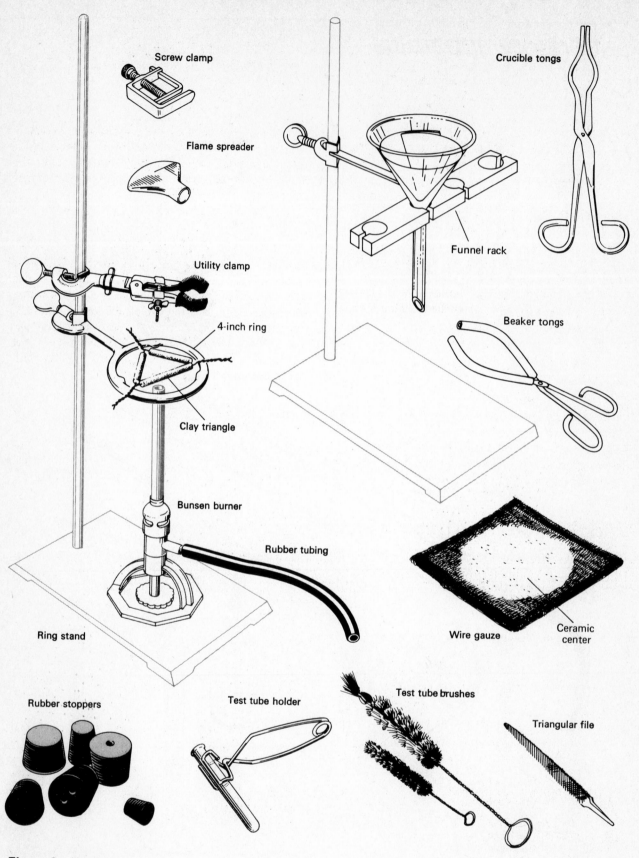

Screw clamp

Flame spreader

Utility clamp

4-inch ring

Clay triangle

Bunsen burner

Rubber tubing

Ring stand

Crucible tongs

Funnel rack

Beaker tongs

Wire gauze

Ceramic center

Rubber stoppers

Test tube holder

Test tube brushes

Triangular file

Figure 2 Hardware.

Experimental techniques

Chemistry is an experimental science. To a large extent, your success in chemistry will depend on how well you perform in the laboratory. During this course, you will learn many basic skills that will enable you to work in the laboratory with minimum fuss and maximum enjoyment.

The following is an outline of the basic operations you will perform and the reasons for their use. It is impossible to cover every process and detail here, but with frequent reference to this section and attention to specific instructions in this manual and from your teacher, you will quickly master the techniques necessary for good laboratory work.

Using a gas burner

Two commonly used laboratory gas burners are illustrated in Figure 3. While details of construction vary among burners, every burner has four main parts: a base, a vertical tube or barrel, a gas inlet near the base, and adjustable openings at the bottom of the barrel to introduce air to the gas stream.

Compare the parts of your burner with Figure 3, noting in particular how to control the amount of air admitted. After examining your burner, study the following. Make sure you can operate your burner effectively.

LIGHTING

To light your gas burner, hold a lighted match a little to one side and above the barrel of the burner. Turn on the main gas supply. If your burner is equipped with a gas adjustment, as is the one on the left in Figure 3, turn the main gas supply on full and adjust the gas flow with the control on the burner. If the burner is not equipped with a gas control, adjust the gas flow with the main gas valve.

ADJUSTING AIR FLOW

Adjust the air flow until you have a quiet, steady flame with a sharply defined inner cone. This adjustment gives the highest possible flame temperature. In gener-

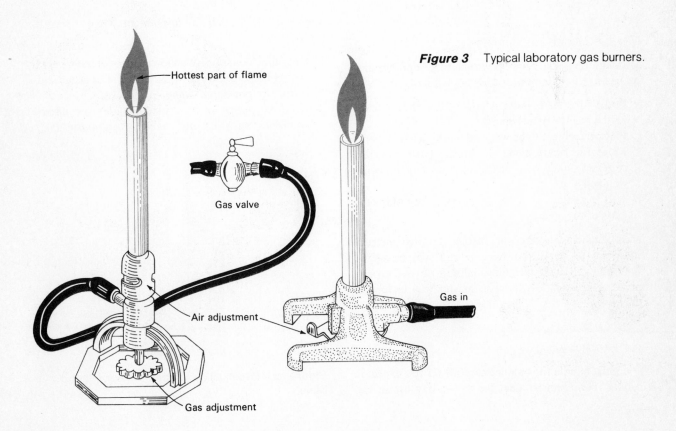

Figure 3   Typical laboratory gas burners.

al, when the gas is on low, less air is needed, and the opening is partially closed. When the gas is on full, more air is needed, and the opening will usually be completely open. Following are the most common adjustment problems and how to solve them:

1. A smoky yellow flame is due to insufficient air (see Figure 4). Increase the air opening.
2. If the flame rises off the burner, the gas pressure is too high (see Figure 4). Reduce the gas flow.
3. If the flame "strikes back" and burns inside the barrel, the air flow is too high for the gas pressure. Turn the gas off for a moment. **Do not touch the hot barrel.** Allow the burner to cool, reduce the air intake, and relight the burner.

HEATING

When heating glassware, always use a wire screen between the flame and the glassware. This procedure spreads the heat evenly over the bottom of the apparatus and avoids concentrating a large amount of heat at one point on the glass.

Exercise

If you have some extra time, try the experiment shown in Figure 5. Suspend a wooden match in the barrel of an unlighted burner. Light the burner. What can you conclude about this zone of the flame from the experiment?

Weighing solids and liquids

Although balances come in various sizes and designs, the basic principles of operation apply to all:

1. Make sure the balance is adjusted so that it reads zero when the pan is empty.
2. Place the object to be weighed on the balance pan.
3. Move the riders along the beams until they just counterbalance the mass of the object being weighed.
4. Add the values of the rider positions to obtain the mass of the object.

Your teacher will give you further detailed instructions for the particular balance you will be using. Since you will make weighings in most of your experiments, it is essential that you master this technique quickly.

CARING FOR A BALANCE

You must handle the balance carefully if you expect it to be a reliable instrument for day-to-day use in the

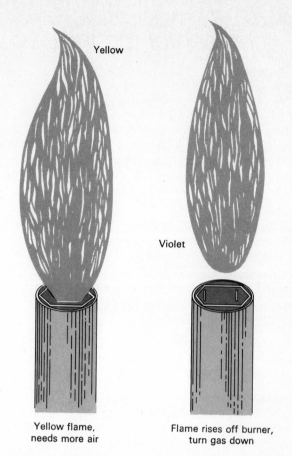

Yellow

Violet

Yellow flame, needs more air

Flame rises off burner, turn gas down

Figure 4 Flames resulting from improper gas-air adjustment.

laboratory. It is a delicate instrument. Treat it accordingly.

1. Only dry, nonreactive solids such as glass or metal should be placed directly on the balance pan. *Crystalline or powdered chemicals must be placed on weighing paper or in a suitable glass or plastic container such as a beaker or weighing boat.*

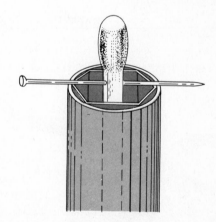

Figure 5 Investigation of one zone of the burner flame.

Liquid chemicals are *never* placed directly on the pan. If liquid or solid reagents are spilled on the pan, clean them up immediately. Get help if needed.

2. Extremely hot objects should not be put on the balance. They may damage the pan, and they may cause convection currents in the air above the pan. Such currents result in an incorrect reading.

3. When you are finished weighing, remove all objects from the pan and return all riders to their zero positions. If the balance has a balance-arrest lever, it should be engaged to lift the beam off the knife edge when masses or objects are being added to the pan, riders are being moved, or the balance is not in use.

USING A BALANCE

Before placing anything on the pan and with all the riders at zero, check to see that the balance is properly adjusted. To be properly adjusted, the balance must be on a level surface. Use the leveling bubble if your balance has one. If not, level your balance by eye. The pointer should swing an equal distance on either side of the zero mark. If the balance is *not* adjusted, do not attempt to fix it. Notify your teacher immediately. Balance adjustment should be checked before every use.

After the balance is properly adjusted, place the object to be weighed on the pan. Move riders along their beams to counterbalance the mass of the object. If the beam is notched, the rider *must* be in the notch when making a reading. Determine that the object mass has been counterbalanced while the pointer is still moving. It is impractical and less reliable to wait for the pointer to stop moving. Observe the values of the maximum upward and downward swings, and mentally calculate the midpoint. The midpoint (also called the *rest point*) should not be more than 0.5 division on either side of zero. To avoid an incorrect reading, you must have your eye at the exact level of the zero point.

The mass of the object is represented by the sum of the readings indicated by the positions of the riders. Make sure to remove the object and return all riders to zero when you are through weighing.

Exercises

1. Examine your centigram balance. Answer the following questions as you examine the characteristics of the balance. (a) What is the maximum mass that can be weighed on this balance? (b) Where must the riders be placed on the rear and middle beams? (c) Note the zero position of the rider on the front beam. Which part of this rider should be used for making the reading? (d) Place the riders in their proper places for balancing a mass suggested by your partner, and have him or her check them. (e) Into what numbered units is each beam divided? (f) What unit of mass does each of the smallest divisions on the front beam represent?

2. Check the sensitivity of your balance by doing the following. (a) Weigh a nickel, noting the rest point. (b) Now move the front rider half of the smallest division to the left or right. Is there a detectable change in the rest point? (c) Move the rider another half of one division in the same direction. Note the rest point. (d) Keep repeating this procedure until you have determined the minimum amount the rider must be moved before *you* can detect a change in the rest point. This is the sensitivity of your balance, which represents the uncertainty in the reading of *that* balance for *you*.

Measuring the volume of liquids

Much of the glassware used in the laboratory is marked with a graduated scale for volume readings. Erlenmeyer flasks and beakers have approximate graduations (± 5 percent) for rough estimates. Most of the volume measurements will be made with a graduated cylinder, but you will have occasion to use a pipet or buret for more precise work (see Experiments 9, 13, and 25 for specific instructions on the use of these pieces of apparatus). A 50-ml graduated cylinder has a precision of 1 percent (50 ± 0.5 ml), while a buret can easily be read to a precision of 0.1 percent (50 ± 0.05 ml).

READING A VOLUME

With each piece of graduated apparatus, the process of volume measurement is the same. Liquid is placed in the apparatus and its level is compared with the graduations etched in the side of the vessel.

Read the markings at the level of the *bottom* of the meniscus, the lens-shaped surface of the water. Your eye must be at the same height as the bottom of the meniscus if the reading is to be correct (see Figure 36, in Experiment 9). If your eye is at the correct height, you will see only one curved surface.

No matter which piece of graduated glassware you are going to use, make it a habit to look at the graduations *before* using it. Note the smallest division that is marked; note whether you can divide the smallest division into tenths, fifths, or halves with your eye; and note in which direction the scale runs. For example, 10-ml graduated cylinders are usually marked every 0.2 ml (but some are marked every 0.1

ml), whereas 250-ml graduated cylinders are commonly marked every 2 ml. By eye you can easily estimate half a division on both the 10-ml and 250-ml cylinders. The estimate represents 0.1 ml in the first case and 1 ml in the second. Scales on graduated cylinders commonly start with 0 at the bottom and have the highest value at the top. But some cylinders also have a second scale that goes in the reverse direction. Look first before reading.

Exercises

1. Have your partner put water into a graduated cylinder to a given level. Practice reading the volume with different amounts.
2. You are asked to transfer 2.0 ml of water from a graduated cylinder. On reading the initial volume, your eye is exactly at the level of the bottom of the meniscus. On reading the final volume, your eye is considerably *above* the meniscus level. Will you have transferred more or less than 2.0 ml?

Filtering

Filtering, a method of separating solid particles from a liquid, is one of the most common laboratory operations. Filtering can be accomplished in a variety of ways. The method discussed here consists of pouring the solid-liquid mixture into a filter-paper cone supported by a funnel. The liquid, or *filtrate*, passes through the paper while the solid, or *precipitate*, is retained on the paper. The precipitate is then washed several times to rinse any remaining filtrate from the solid.

PREPARATION OF THE FILTER CONE

Fold a piece of circular filter paper in half once (Figure 6) and then in half again (Figure 7). Note that the second fold is made unevenly so that the top half of the original fold is *not* directly over the bottom half. This allows the resulting cone to fit snugly into the

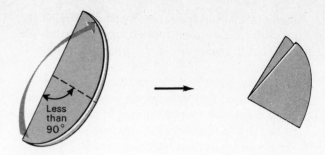

Figure 7 The second fold in a piece of filter paper.

funnel. Tear a small triangular piece from the top fold (Figure 8). This reduces the bulk of the fold so the paper can adhere to the funnel. Open the cone-shaped pocket thus formed, with the torn fold on the outside, and place it in the filter funnel (Figure 9).

Next, moisten the paper so that it will stick firmly to the sides of the funnel. This is easily accomplished by directing a stream of water from a wash bottle onto the paper. If correctly done, a continuous stream of water will form in the stem of the funnel and the water will pour quickly through the system (Figure 9). If improperly done, air will leak through the seal along the folded seam and the water will drip through very slowly (Figure 10). *Slight* adjustments may be made to overcome this, but be very careful because the paper tears easily when wet. Place the funnel in a holder, and position a container (usually a beaker or test tube) beneath the funnel to catch the filtrate.

THE FILTERING PROCESS

A general rule for filtering is to retain as much precipitate as possible in the beaker or flask until most of the filtrate and some of the washings have passed through the filter paper. The reason for this is twofold: the presence of the precipitate on the paper tends to clog the surface, which in turn slows the rate of filtering; and the precipitate is more easily washed in the beaker than on the filter paper (see the section of this outline on "Transferring Materials").

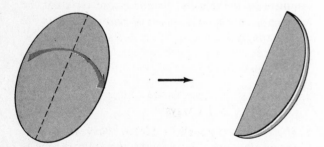

Figure 6 The first fold in a piece of filter paper.

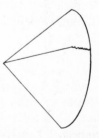

Figure 8 Filter paper cone with triangular tear.

Figure 9 Funnel with filter paper cone correctly fitted.

If the precipitate is fine enough, it may go through the paper, causing the filtrate to appear cloudy. The mixture of filtrate and precipitate may be heated (*digested*) at about 85°C for 10 to 15 minutes. This digestion promotes the growth and clumping of the smaller particles into large crystals.

If the solid continues to pass through the filter paper upon refiltering, a less porous paper must be used. There are many grades of filter paper available. By selecting the proper grade for the precipitate involved, you can avoid cloudy filtrates.

WASHING

In washing a precipitate, there is always the decision of how much wash solution (usually water) to use. The

Figure 10 Funnel with filter paper cone incorrectly fitted.

decision should be based on two factors: solubility of the precipitate and cleaning efficiency. Two examples from the experiments in this manual will illustrate the problem.

In Experiment 8, lead metal is separated from a solution containing several dissolved materials. In that case, the solubility of the precipitate is *not* a factor. The solubility of lead in water is negligible. Therefore, use enough water to completely remove the dissolved materials.

In Experiment 13, solid lead iodide is separated from a solution of sodium nitrate. Since lead iodide is soluble to the extent of 0.063 g per 100 ml of water, excess washing must be avoided. However, insufficient washing will leave some sodium nitrate with the lead iodide. Based on the solubility given above, 15 ml of water will dissolve 0.0094 g of lead iodide, an amount just outside the limit of the centigram balance. Thus, three 5-ml washes might be appropriate. (See "Transferring Materials" for a discussion of the efficiency of one 15-ml wash compared with three 5-ml washes.)

Transferring materials

All your efforts to gather precise data will be wasted unless you follow careful handling procedures. The two enemies of good results are *contamination* and *lack of quantitative transfer*. Correct interpretation of experimental data is based on the assumptions that only the reactants under study are present (contamination has not been introduced through poor handling) and that in transferring reagents from one container to another, *all* the measured material has been transferred.

CONTAMINATION OF REAGENTS

Since most of the reagents for your laboratory work will be stored in small glass or plastic bottles, the main reasons for contamination are

1. not reading the label on the bottle and therefore having the wrong material to begin with
2. putting a dirty spoon, rod, or spatula into the bottle
3. setting a lid down on the counter top
4. putting the wrong lid on the bottle (this can be avoided by not having several bottles open at the same time)

TRANSFERRING SOLIDS

Small amounts of solids should be taken from a bottle in one of the following ways:

1. *Use a clean, dry spatula.* Ideally there should be a spatula for every bottle. If this is not the case, you must clean the spatula thoroughly before each use.

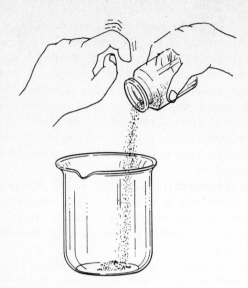

Figure 11 Pouring a solid directly into a container.

2. *Pour the solid directly into a container.* If you tap the bottle gently with one finger while tilting it over a container, there will be less chance of the solid's coming out all at once (see Figure 11).
3. *Pour the approximate amount of material onto a small piece of creased paper* by method 2. Then pour the solid from the paper to the desired container (see Figure 12).

TRANSFERRING LIQUIDS

For liquid reagents that come in plastic bottles with medicine dropper tops, there should be little if any problem with contamination or incomplete transfer of materials. However, you will probably observe early in your laboratory work that pouring a water solution

from a glass container—even a beaker with a pouring spout—usually results in droplets running down the side of the container. A better transfer can be obtained if a glass stirring rod is used to direct the flow of the solution.

If both of your hands are free, use one to hold a stirring rod pointed toward the container into which the solution is being poured, and with the other hand pick up the vessel containing the solution. Touch the rim or spout to the rod and pour carefully (see Figure 13). The solution will cling to and flow down the rod instead of the container side. If you have to stop pouring before all the solution is transferred, tilt the vessel back and *then* take it away from the rod.

Sometimes you have only one hand available for pouring. In this case, if the container is small enough, place the stirring rod across the top of the container and hold it there with your forefinger while using the rest of your hand to grasp the container. Tilt both stirring rod and container (see Figure 14).

USE OF THE WASH BOTTLE

When rinsing precipitates out of a beaker, first make sure you have an idea of how much wash water is to be used (see "Washing" under 'Filtering'). Then, while tilting the beaker, direct a stream of water from your wash bottle over all the inner surface (see Figure 15). If you direct the stream of water toward the back of

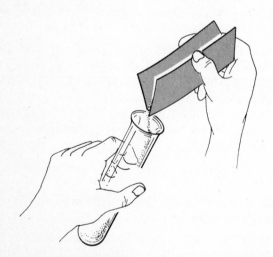

Figure 12 Transferring a solid with a creased paper.

Figure 13 Transferring a liquid.

the beaker, the natural flow of the water will tend to flush the solid particles down and out.

You cannot pour out 100 percent of an aqueous solution from any piece of glassware. Some droplets remain behind no matter how clean the glass is. Therefore, a *single* rinse is less than 100-percent efficient. But several rinses can approach 100-percent efficiency.

Assume that you can rinse out 95 percent of the solution from a beaker in any one wash. If you limit yourself to one wash, 5 percent of the original solution remains. If you do two washes with the same efficiency, you can expect to have only 5 percent of 5 percent, or 0.25 percent, of the original solution left.

As a general rule, several small rinses are much more efficient than one large one.

Exercises

1. How many washes are needed (at 90-percent efficiency) to leave no more than 0.5 percent of the original solution?
2. What percentage of the original solution remains after five washes (each with 75-percent efficiency?
3. Practice rinsing solids from containers: (a) Add 10 ml of a 0.1 M solution of $Ba(NO_3)_2$ to 10 ml of a 0.1 M solution of K_2CrO_4 in a 100-ml beaker. Swirl the solution to mix thoroughly. (b) Let the precipi-

Figure 14   Transferring a liquid when only one hand is free.

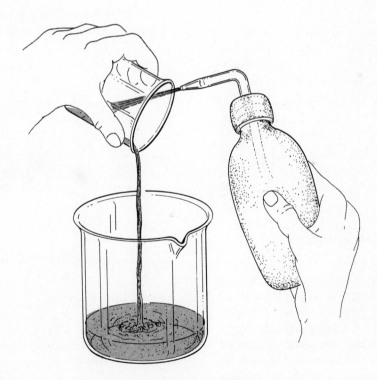

Figure 15   Rinsing a precipitate from a beaker with a wash bottle.

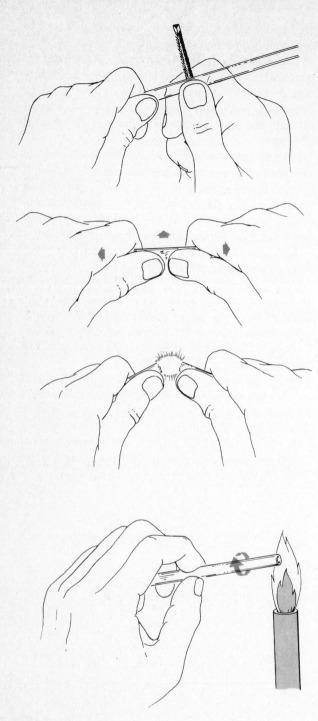

from the beaker onto the paper as outlined above. Collect all the washes in the graduated cylinder. (d) Measure the total volume of wash water used to remove all the solid from the beaker. If you used over 10 ml, you need more practice. If you used between 5 ml and 10 ml, it was a good washing, but more practice is in order. If you used less than 5 ml, you understand the technique of washing.

4. Practice rinsing solutions from containers: (a) Put 10.0 ml of 0.5 M Na_2SO_4 into a 100-ml beaker. Now pour out all you can. (b) Add 9.0 ml of distilled water to the beaker. Rotate the beaker so that the wash water rinses the entire inner surface. Pour the wash water into a clean 18 × 150 mm test tube. (c) Now add 2.0 ml of a 0.2 M $Ba(NO_3)_2$ solution to the test tube and note the results. Save the test tube and contents for comparison in step (e). (d) Repeat the procedure for steps (a) and (b), but substitute three 3.0-ml washes for the single 9.0-ml wash. Collect each of the washes in a separate 18 × 150 mm test tube. (e) Now add 2.0 ml of the 0.2 M $Ba(NO_3)_2$ solution to each of the three test tubes and compare with the test tube from step (c).

Working with glass

HOW TO CUT, FIRE-POLISH, AND BEND GLASS TUBING

Hold the glass tubing firmly between your thumb and an edge of a triangular file, as shown in Figure 16.

Figure 16 Cutting and fire-polishing glass tubing.

tate settle slightly while you prepare a filtration setup, as described under "Filtering." Swirl the mixture and pour it onto the filter paper. Try to get as much of the solid as possible onto the paper. Ignore any precipitate that may come through the paper. After all the filtrate has passed through the filter paper, put a dry, 10-ml graduated cylinder under the funnel. (c) Now wash the remaining solid

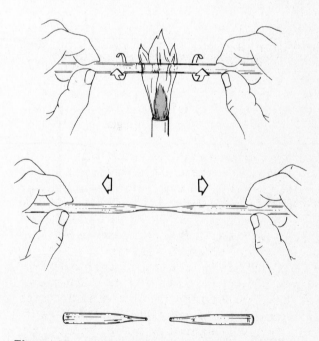

Figure 17 Drawing glass tubing to form a jet tip.

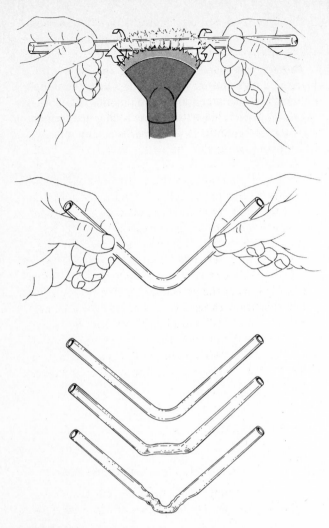

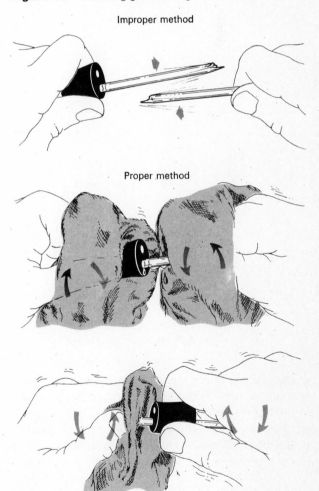

Figure 18 Making a smooth 90-degree bend in glass tubing.

remove it from the flame and pull the tubing until the desired diameter (jet tip) is obtained. Place the hot glass on wire gauze to cool. Cut the glass in the middle of the drawn-out portion and fire-polish the sharp ends.

To bend glass tubing, heat it by rotating it back and forth in a flat burner flame, using a wing top as shown in Figure 18. Continue heating the tubing until the glass becomes quite soft and is just beginning to sag as it is rotated. Remove the tubing from the burner flame and bend it by raising the ends to obtain the desired angle. Since hot glass tends to sag, bending it in this manner will produce a more uniformly smooth bend. Figure 18 also illustrates the difference between a "good" bend (at top) and two "bad" bends. The middle bend resulted from holding the glass too low in the flame so that the middle of the tubing was in the cool portion of the flame. The bottom bend was produced by concentrating the flame on too narrow a portion of the glass tubing. This problem frequently

Figure 19 Inserting glass tubing into a stopper.

Improper method

Proper method

Rotate the glass about one fourth of a turn to make a short, sharp scratch on the glass tubing.

Place your thumbs together opposite the scratch. Pull and bend quickly to snap the glass tubing at the mark.

To fire-polish the freshly cut edges, hold one end of the glass tubing in the hottest part of the burner flame and rotate the tube back and forth until the edges are rounded. Do not fire-polish so long that the end of the tube begins to close. (**Caution: hot glass looks like cool glass.**) Put the hot glass on wire gauze to cool, then fire-polish the other end of the tubing.

To make a jet tip, heat the glass tubing in a burner flame in the position shown in Figure 17, rotating the glass in the hottest part of the flame. Allow the tubing to become slightly shorter as the glass melts and the walls increase to about twice their original thickness. After the glass becomes quite soft and thickened, results when a wing top is not used to spread the flame.

INSERTING GLASS TUBING OR A THERMOMETER INTO A RUBBER STOPPER

Before attempting to insert glass tubing or a thermometer into a rubber stopper, be sure that the hole in the stopper is large enough so it will stretch easily to accommodate the tubing (Figure 19). Place a drop of glycerine or some water in the hole of the stopper or on the tip of the glass to serve as a lubricant.

Protect your hands by wrapping the glass with a piece of cloth or towel. Hold the glass near the stopper and push it with a gentle twisting motion. Do not use excessive force to insert the glass tubing or thermometer. **Be very careful.** If you experience any difficulty, consult your teacher.

LABORATORY MANUAL

Chemistry

EXPERIMENTAL FOUNDATIONS

Scientific observation and description

We all think of ourselves as good observers. Yet there is much more to observation than meets the eye. It takes concentration, alertness to detail, ingenuity, and patience. It also takes practice. Try it yourself. See how complete a description you can write about a familiar object—a burning candle, for example. Be "scientific" about this and start with an experiment. This means you should observe a burning candle in a laboratory, because the laboratory is a place where conditions can be controlled.

But how do we know what conditions should be controlled? Sometimes the important conditions are difficult to discover, but an experiment can be meaningless unless the *conditions that matter* are controlled. Here are some conditions that might be important in *some* experiments but are not important in this one:

1. The experiment is done on the second floor.
2. The experiment is done in the daytime.
3. The room lights are on.

Here are some conditions that *might* be important in your experiment:

1. The lab bench is near the door.
2. The windows are open.

3. You are standing close enough to the candle to breathe on it.

Why is this second set of conditions important? It is important because all three conditions relate to a common factor: a candle does not burn well in a draft.

Important conditions are often not as easily recognized as these. A good experimentalist pays much attention to the discovery and control of conditions that are important.

PROCEDURE

First examine the candle carefully. Then light it. Record in your notebook as many observations as you can make during a short period (10 to 15 minutes).

Do *not* write these observations in paragraph form. Simply list the observations. Be sure to number them. Leave space at the left margin of your paper before each of the observations. Additional information can be recorded there if needed.

One of the many qualitative observations that could be made in Experiment 1 is that in the complex process of burning, a liquid, presumably molten wax, accumulates in the bowl at the base of the candle flame. Apparently, solid wax will melt to a clear liquid as heat is applied. In Experiment 2 you will observe various other substances as they are heated in a candle flame and in a burner flame. Many kinds of observations are possible and useful, but at this time we are particularly interested in the *melting behavior* of these substances. In Experiment 3, you will make your observations quantitative by studying the melting of a single solid.

You will probably find it useful to take notes on the class discussion following this experiment. Do not hesitate to contribute your ideas to the class discussion.

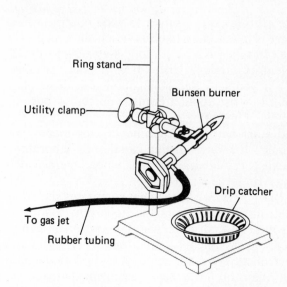

Figure 20 Bunsen burner mounted at a slant with a utility clamp and drip catcher under the burner flame.

PROCEDURE

1. Using a pair of tongs, hold each of the materials listed below in the flame of a candle. Write down what you see in each case. Use

1. a piece of candle wax (a dripping from the side of a candle works well)
2. a piece of sulfur
3. a piece of lead foil
4. a piece of iron wire
5. a small piece of metallic tin foil or wire
6. a piece of standard aluminum kitchen foil
7. a piece of no. 22 copper wire
8. a piece of fine platinum wire

2. Repeat step 1, but use the flame of a Bunsen burner instead of a candle flame. Use a utility clamp to mount the burner on a ring stand at a slant, as shown in Figure 20. This will prevent the melted material from clogging up the burner.

3. With a pair of tongs, hold a piece of steel wool (finely divided iron) in the burner flame. Record what you see. Are your observations the same as those made on iron wire in steps 1 and 2?

4. Wind a copper wire (no. 22) around a pencil about ten times to form a coil. Leave enough wire to serve as a handle. Slip the wire off the pencil, then lower the coil into the candle flame. (See Figure 21) Record what you see.

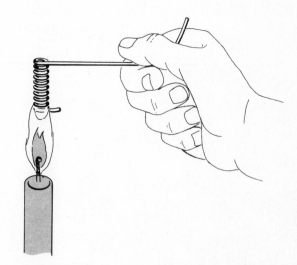

Figure 21 Lowering a copper wire into a flame.

Questions and regularities

1. In what ways, if any, were tin and lead changed by placing them in the candle flame?
2. Which materials in step 1 change at a temperature that is clearly *lower* than the temperature reached in the *candle* flame?
3. Which materials in step 2 change at a temperature that is *lower* than the temperature reached in the *burner* flame?
4. Using your observations as a guide, arrange the materials studied in order of *increasing melting temperature*. If you have no basis for deciding between two materials, place them together in your list.

FOR FURTHER THOUGHT

1. What further experiments would enable you to distinguish between the melting points of those substances for which you were unable to reach a decision?
2. Can you suggest a possible explanation for the observations made with steel wool in step 3? This kind of observation will be considered again when we reach Chapter 15 of the textbook.
3. Can you suggest a model to explain what you saw in step 4? A number of factors are involved, so feel free to guess. Wondering why and proposing an explanation are the lifeblood of science. Even Einstein was wrong on occasion.

Our data from Experiment 2 suggest that some substances melt more easily than others. Candle wax melts easily. Iron wire melts with great difficulty. How can we describe these qualitative observations in more detail? Numbers help. Let us be quantitative in our study of the melting of solids by measuring the melting temperature (or melting point) of a pure solid taken from the stockroom shelf. Information about the melting point of a substance has many uses in chemistry.

We shall consider a few of these at the end of the experiment.

A test tube containing a solid will be supplied by your teacher. This will be heated until the solid melts. The resulting liquid will then be allowed to cool, and the temperature of the substance will be recorded at regular time intervals until all of the liquid has resolidified. The solid will then be reheated gradually, and temperature readings will be taken at regular time

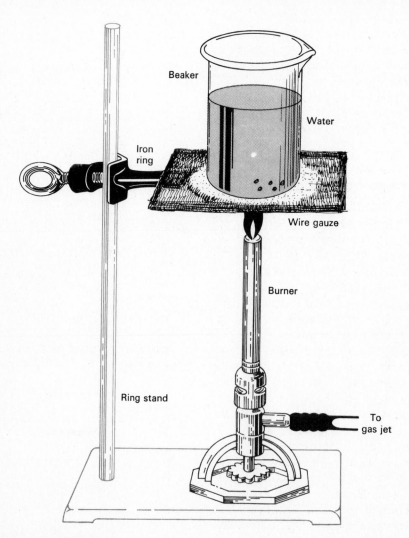

Figure 22   Use of the ring stand and burner.

intervals during the heating process. Such time-temperature readings are valuable in determining the melting and freezing points of substances.

PROCEDURE

PART 1

The cooling behavior of a pure substance

1. Obtain a test tube containing an unknown solid from your teacher. Fill a 400-ml beaker about three-fourths full of hot tap water and add four or five boiling chips to the beaker. Place it on top of the wire gauze and iron ring combination above the burner and heat the water in the beaker. (See Figure 22). When the water boils, turn off the flame. Use beaker tongs around the beaker of hot water to remove it from the burner and set it on the desk top.

2. Place the test tube containing the unknown solid in the hot water; *carefully* stir the solid-liquid mass in the test tube with a thermometer until all the sample has melted. After all the solid has melted, remove the tube containing the melted unknown and clamp it into position *above* a second 400-ml beaker containing about 250 ml of cool tap water. (See Figure 23.)

3. Now clearly divide the labor between you and your partner. One partner will stir and make thermometer readings while the other partner will time and record temperature readings and other observations.

4. When all is ready, check the temperature of the *liquid substance* and record it to the nearest 0.2 °C. Immediately immerse the lower half of the test tube in the cool water and clamp the test tube in place. The water level should be *above* the level of the substance in the test tube. Now move the thermometer *gently* and *continuously* up and down, **without hitting the bottom of the test tube.** Record the temperature indicated by the thermometer in the tube every 30 seconds, even though the thermometer eventually sticks in the frozen substance and cannot be moved. *Continue until a temperature in the middle thirties is reached.* Note this temperature. Note also when solidification starts and when it is completed. It is convenient to record your data in a table similar to the one shown here. (Be sure to leave space for 8–10 minutes of readings.) You will need one table for recording warming behavior and one for cooling behavior.

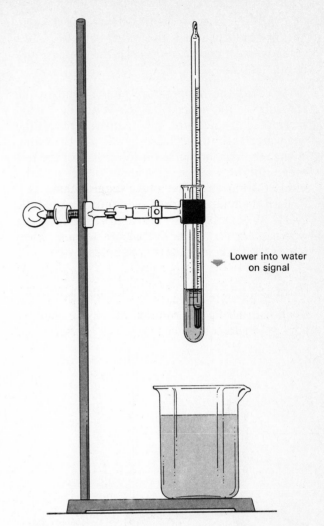

Figure 23 Apparatus for observing cooling behavior.

PART 2

The warming behavior of a pure substance

1. The observer and recorder should exchange duties at this time.

2. Place a 400-ml beaker, three-fourths full of hot tap water, on the wire gauze and iron ring combination used in Part 1. Adjust the water temperature to 65 °C, unless your teacher speci-

Table 1

Time (min)	Temperature (°C)	Observations
0		
½		
1		
1½		
2		

fies a different temperature. Have the Bunsen burner ready to warm the water bath for a few seconds when necessary to keep the temperature between 60 and 65 °C.

3. Record the temperature of the solid in the test tube to the nearest 0.2 °C. With the second thermometer measure the temperature of the hot-water bath to the nearest 1 °C. On the signal of the recorder, immerse the lower half of the test tube until the water level is above the level of the solid. Clamp the tube into place (Figure 24). Record the temperature of the sample in the tube every 30 seconds and the temperature of the water every 60 seconds. You are to note when melting starts and when it is completed.

4. As soon as the solid comes free from the walls of the test tube, move the thermometer gently but continuously up and down. It may be necessary to put the lighted burner under the beaker for a few seconds at intervals in order to keep the temperature of the water bath about 8–10 °C above the melting point of the solid. Continue to move the thermometer up and down and record temperatures until the temperature of the solid is about 5 °C above the point at which all the solid was just melted.

5. Your table of data should now include the temperature of the bath as well as the temperature of the solid.

Calculations and results

1. A graph is a very useful device for finding trends and regularities in data. It is helpful to use one here. Use a full page of graph paper. Show time on the horizontal axis (increasing from the origin to the right) and temperature on the vertical axis (increasing from the origin upward). Start the time scale at "0," but use any convenient temperature as the origin of the vertical scale.

   Plot heating and cooling temperatures on the same graph. For each cooling temperature and its corresponding time, make a small cross. Use small circles for the heating data. Draw a continuous curve to represent the heating of the solid. Draw a smooth dashed curve for the cooling process. Be sure the graph has a title and the axes are labeled (see Appendix 2, page 143). At the top of the graph paper put your name, your partner's name, the date, and the name of the experiment.

2. Study the experimental results as shown on the graph. Write a one-paragraph summary describing the graph.

3. What effect would increasing the amount of solid have on the shape of the melting or cooling curves?

4. From your graph, what is the melting temperature of the solid you used?

5. From your graph, what is the freezing temperature of the solid you used?

6. Your teacher will give you a list of materials and their melting points. Use answers to calculations 4 and 5 to suggest the possible identity of your own solid.

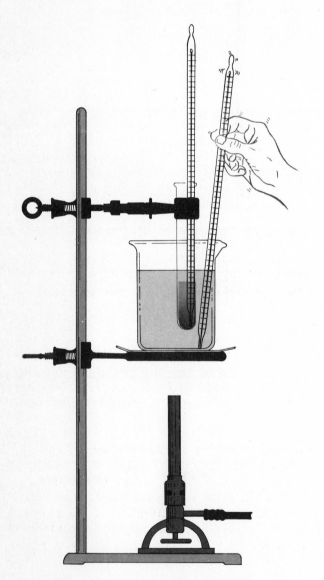

Figure 24 Apparatus for observing warming behavior.

FOR FURTHER THOUGHT

Why do the heating curve and the cooling curve have the shapes shown by your graph?

Is there a relationship between the pressure applied to a gas and the volume it occupies? In this experiment, a given *quantity* of gas will be trapped in a syringe. The pressure on this gas will then be increased by placing weights (books) on top of the plunger of the syringe. The total pressure acting on the gas consists of the weight of the books plus the weight of the atmosphere. Symbolically we write

$$\left\{\begin{array}{c}\text{total}\\\text{pressure}\end{array}\right\} = \left\{\begin{array}{c}\text{pressure}\\\text{due to}\\\text{books}\end{array}\right\} + \left\{\begin{array}{c}\text{pressure}\\\text{due to}\\\text{atmosphere}\end{array}\right\}$$

The volume of the gas will be recorded for each of the pressures used. The data (values for pressure and volume) will be plotted on a graph in several ways in order to find a simple mathematical relationship between pressure and volume.

PROCEDURE

PART 1

Qualitative observations on compressibility

Each student should make the qualitative observations of this part individually. We hope that in doing this you come to realize that gases are real materials and a syringe full of air is not empty.

1. Take the barrel of the syringe in one hand and the plunger in the other. Place the plunger in the syringe and push as hard as you can. You are exerting pressure on the gas in the syringe. Record *all* your observations.

2. Now place a thin piece of copper wire alongside the plunger and push the plunger to the bottom of the syringe. Remove the copper wire and attempt to remove the plunger from the syringe. Record your observations.

Questions and regularities

1. What is "pressure" as observed in this experiment?

2. Suggest a simple model that might explain what you felt in Part 1, step 1.
3. In Part 1, step 2, where is the pressure being exerted that opposes movement of the plunger? Explain.

PART 2

The quantitative relationship between gas pressure and gas volume

In this part of the experiment you will work in pairs.

1. Set the plunger at the highest mark of a dry syringe by inserting a strip of paper alongside the plunger as before. Remove the strip of paper and place the sealed tip of the syringe into a large rubber stopper with one hole bored in it. Clamp the syringe-stopper arrangement in an upright position, as shown in Figure 25.

2. Carefully center a textbook on top of the plunger. (Any textbook will do, but you will need six more copies of the *same* textbook to complete the experiment.) Read as precisely as possible the volume of gas trapped in the syringe when a load of one book is on the plunger. Be sure to record the uncertainty that you estimate is associated with each reading. Record the pressure in books and the volume of gas in millilitres. Repeat this procedure twice by removing the book and replacing it. Read and record the volume each time the book is replaced.

3. Now add another textbook and carefully determine the volume three times. (Do not worry if the syringe does not return to the original volume when the books are removed. This is not due to air loss, but to friction between the plunger and the syringe. Do not attempt to correct for it.) Continue in this manner until a pressure of 6 or 7 books is obtained.

4. Starting with one book, repeat the entire procedure to check your results.

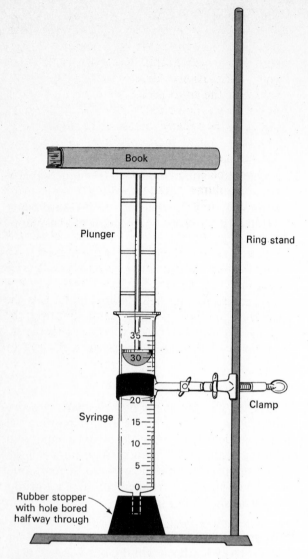

Figure 25 Apparatus for pressure-volume measurements.

Labels on figure: Book, Plunger, Ring stand, Syringe, Clamp, Rubber stopper with hole bored halfway through. Syringe scale: 35, 30, 20, 15, 10, 5, 0

Calculations and results

GRAPHICAL RELATIONSHIPS BETWEEN
PRESSURE AND VOLUME

We now have several sets of numbers. What regularities can we find in them? Let us do as we did in Experiment 3 and plot our data in various ways. From such plots, regularities may become clear.

1. Construct a graph of pressure against volume in the following manner: (a) Using the data from the various trials at each pressure, calculate the *average* gas volume associated with each pressure in books. Record these average values in a column in your calculations table. (b) To find the experimental uncertainty for each average volume, find the average of the absolute differences of the individual readings from the *average* volume. Record these experimental uncertainties in your calculations table. (c) On a graph, plot the pressure (in books) on the vertical axis and the average volume (in ml) on the horizontal axis. Use only the upper two-thirds of a piece of graph paper to do this. Through each point, draw a horizontal line that extends as far to the left and right of each point as the experimental uncertainty in that measurement indicates. Draw the best smooth curve through these lines.

2. Find the reciprocal of volume, $1/V$, in the following manner: (a) For each of the values of *average* volume (calculation 1a), find the value for the reciprocal of volume ($1/V$). Record these values of $1/V$ in your calculations table.* (b) To find the uncertainty in $1/V$, take each value for average volume and *add* the uncertainty value to it. Find the reciprocal of the resulting number and record it in your calculations table. This is the *lowest* value $1/V$ can have. Then take each value for average volume, *subtract* the uncertainty and find the reciprocal of the resulting number. This is the *highest* value for $1/V$.

3. Graph pressure against $1/V$ in the following manner: Now use a different color to plot P against $1/V$ on the same graph used in calculation 1c. You will need to mark off a new horizontal scale, but the original vertical scale can be used for pressure. *Be sure that your new horizontal scale starts with $1/V = 0$ at the y-axis.* As in calculation 1c, draw a horizontal line through each point that extends as far to the left and right as the uncertainty in $1/V$ (calculation 2b) dictates.

Draw the best straight line through these $1/V$ plots, making sure that it extends down to the horizontal axis.

A MATHEMATICAL RELATIONSHIP BETWEEN *P* AND *V*

The plot of calculation 3 shows a straight-line relationship between pressure (in books) and

---

*A simple way to determine how many decimal places are appropriate in recording this number is with significant figures. When one number (*A*) is divided by another number (*B*), the quotient must have the same number of significant figures as whichever of *A* or *B* has the *least* number of significant figures.

In this case, where we are calculating a reciprocal, the 1 in $1/V$ is not a measurement number, and thus has an infinite number of significant figures. It is the number of significant figures in the average volume, then, that determines the number of significant figures retained in the quotient. Remember that zeros between the decimal point and the first other number are *not* significant. (See Appendix 1, page 132.)

$1/V$. However, this line does not pass through the origin of the graph. How can this be? Surely a gas under zero pressure should occupy an infinite volume. The value of $1/V$ should be zero when no pressure is being exerted on the gas. The answer, of course, is that in addition to "book pressure," atmospheric pressure is also pushing on the gas.

1. Determine the value for atmospheric pressure in the following manner:

    Extend the plotted straight line on your graph until it intersects the y-axis. (You may have to extend your graph to do this.) Also extend the pressure scale (in books) downward as far as is necessary to read the value of the y-intercept. The difference between the y-intercept and $y = 0$ is the value for the atmospheric pressure pushing on the gas in addition to the "book pressure" that you measured. (Don't worry that the value for atmospheric pressure appears to have a negative sign. This simply means that the entire scale of "book pressure" needs to be shifted downward so that $1/V = 0$ when there is no pressure on the gas.)

2. Find the mathematical relationship between pressure and volume in the following manner: (a) Determine the value of atmospheric pressure from your graph. Record this value in your calculations table. (b) Calculate the value for the *total* pressure for each pressure in books you have recorded. This is done by adding atmospheric pressure to each "book pressure." Enter these values in your calculations table. (c) Find the product of pressure and volume by multiplying the *total* pressure by the volume the gas occupied under that pressure. (The same rules of significant figures apply in multiplication as in division. Whichever of the numbers A or B in the expression $A \times B$ has *fewer* significant figures determines the number of significant figures you may retain in the product.) Enter the $P \times V$ products in your calculations table. Use the correct number of significant figures. (d) What relationship is there between the arithmetic products of total pressure $\times$ volume obtained in the last calculation?

In Experiment 4 you investigated some of the properties of gases. You now know that an "empty" container on the shelf with an open top is actually full of air. Perhaps these gas molecules have mass. If gases have mass, do different gases have the same or different masses? Experimentation will provide the answer.

In this experiment you will find the mass of equal volumes of some gases: oxygen, carbon dioxide, and perhaps another gas. Care must be taken to avoid sources of error. A few greasy finger marks or a moisture droplet can interfere with the experiment.

Before coming to the laboratory, read the experimental directions carefully and organize a table for recording the data.

PROCEDURE

PART I

The mass of oxygen gas

1. Obtain a one-hole rubber stopper, plastic bag, and medicine dropper. Gather the plastic bag (in small pleats) around the large end of the stopper. Hold it very firmly in place with a rubber band. Push the tapered end of the glass dropper into the hole of the stopper until it is held firmly (see Figure 26).

2. Press out any air in the bag by smoothing it flat. Put the rubber bulb on the glass dropper, and weigh this assembly to the nearest 0.01 gram (g). (See pages 10–11 for proper use of the balance.)

3. Remove the rubber bulb and connect the assembly to an oxygen source. Allow the bag to be fully inflated (see Figure 27). (**Caution: wear safety goggles when working around compressed gas cylinders.**) Hold the bag assembly by the stopper and disconnect the rubber tubing from the medicine dropper. Allow any excess gas to escape (so that the gas in the bag will be at room pressure), but do not squeeze the bag. Then

replace the rubber bulb to close off the opening in the medicine dropper.

4. Determine the mass of the bag assembly containing the oxygen gas (at room temperature and pressure) to the nearest 0.01 g. Make sure that the bag assembly does not rub against any *stationary* part of the balance (see Figure 28).

PART 2

The mass of carbon dioxide

Be sure that the bag and stopper assembly is empty and dry. Fill it with carbon dioxide gas, using the source supplied by your teacher. Repeat steps 3 and 4 of Part 1. Try to have the same volume of gas as before.

PART 3

The mass of another gas (*optional*)

Determine the mass of a bag filled with another gas.

PART 4

Obtaining the volume of the bag

1. Empty the bag, then fill it with air from a compressed air source or a hand pump. Do not blow into the bag. Use the same volume of gas as you used in each of the previous parts of the experiment.

2. Measure the volume of air in the bag by the method shown in Figure 29. Completely fill a large bottle or jug (½-gal size) with tap water. Cover with a small glass plate or your hand and invert it in a large container of water. Remove the plate or your hand under water. Fasten a pinch clamp near one end of a length of rubber hose. Push the other end up into the bottle.

3. Remove the bulb from the medicine dropper and in its place attach the free end of the rubber hose. Remove the clamp and *gently* press on the bag so that the gas will displace the water in the bottle. Finally smooth out the bag to remove all

Figure 26 The plastic bag assembly.

the gas. Hold the plastic bag higher than the level of the water, otherwise water may siphon back into the bag.

4. Pinch the tubing closed and remove it from the water container. Replace the glass plate or your hand over the top of the bottle. Remove the bottle from the water and set it upright on the table.

5. Measure the amount of water required to refill the bottle, using the largest graduated cylinder available to you. Record *each* measurement taken and its uncertainty.

6. Record the room temperature and pressure.

Calculations and results

THE EFFECT OF BUOYANCY OF AIR

Since we live in an atmosphere of air, we usually do not consider its effects on measurements. Any object that is surrounded by air when its mass is determined is buoyed up by a force equal to the mass of the volume of air it displaces. We usually neglect this fact since the effect is relatively small.

Suppose the medium surrounding us were water. You have probably noticed that objects are easier to lift when they are submerged in water than when they are in air. The water buoys up the

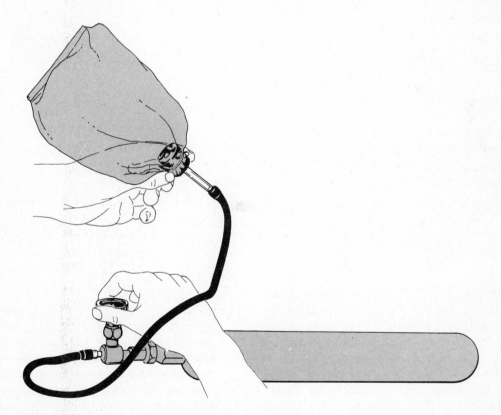

Figure 27 Filling the plastic bag with a gas.

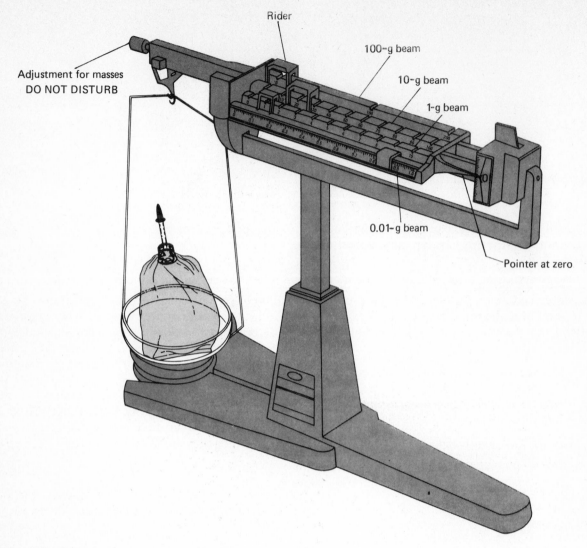

Rider

100-g beam

10-g beam

1-g beam

Adjustment for masses
DO NOT DISTURB

0.01-g beam

Pointer at zero

Figure 28   Determining the mass of a bag filled with gas. The masses on the balances are set at 21.81 g.

submerged object with a force equal to the mass of the volume of water that the object displaces. For example, an object with a volume of 1 litre (1,000 ml) displaces 1 litre of water when submerged in water, so it is buoyed up with a force of 1,000 g, the mass of 1 litre of water. The same object in air is buoyed up with a force of about 1.2 g, the mass of the litre of air it displaces.

In this experiment the apparent mass that you recorded for the mass of the gas did not allow for the buoyant effect of the air. The mass of the volume of air displaced must be added to obtain the actual mass.

The mass of the volume of air displaced can be computed by using the experimentally determined volume of the bag in litres and the mass of

a litre of dry air at the appropriate temperature and pressure. See Table 2.

1. (a) What is the apparent mass of oxygen in the bag? (Subtract the mass of the empty bag from the mass of the bag full of oxygen.) (b) Determine the apparent mass of the other gases used.

2. Calculate the mass of the air displaced by the bag filled with gas.

3. (a) What is the actual mass of oxygen in the bag? (Add the mass of the air displaced to the apparent mass of the oxygen.) (b) In a similar way, determine the actual mass of carbon dioxide and any other gas used in the bag.

4. Compare the mass of each gas measured to that of oxygen by dividing each mass by the

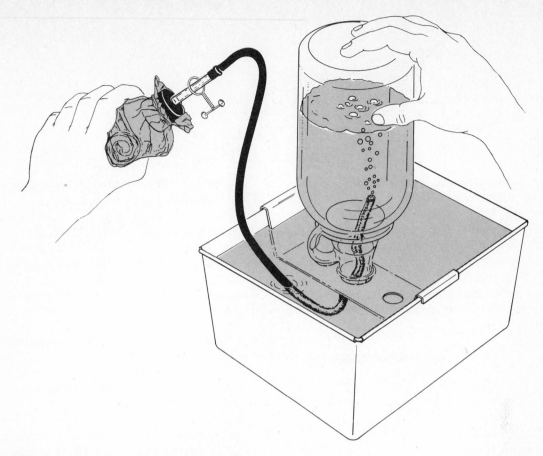

Figure 29 Measuring the volume of the plastic bag.

mass of the comparable volume of oxygen. Express each ratio as a decimal fraction.

Table 2 Mass of a litre of air in grams per litre, ±0.01 g, at various temperatures and pressures

Pressure (mm)	Temperature			
	15°C	20°C	25°C	30°C
600	0.97	0.95	0.94	0.92
610	0.98	0.97	0.95	0.93
620	1.00	0.98	0.97	0.95
630	1.02	1.00	0.98	0.97
640	1.03	1.01	1.00	0.98
650	1.05	1.03	1.01	1.00
660	1.06	1.05	1.03	1.01
670	1.08	1.06	1.04	1.03
680	1.10	1.08	1.06	1.04
690	1.11	1.09	1.07	1.06
700	1.13	1.11	1.09	1.07
710	1.14	1.12	1.10	1.09
720	1.16	1.14	1.12	1.10
730	1.18	1.16	1.14	1.12
740	1.19	1.17	1.15	1.13
750	1.21	1.19	1.17	1.15
760	1.23	1.21	1.19	1.16
770	1.24	1.22	1.20	1.18

FOR FURTHER THOUGHT

Is there any relation between the comparative masses of equal volumes of gases and the relative masses of molecules?

ADDITIONAL INVESTIGATIONS

(To be undertaken as extracurricular experiments. Consult your teacher before proceeding.)

1. How do the masses (of equal volumes) of gases at atmospheric pressure but at higher than ordinary temperatures compare with those at room temperature?
2. The burner gas in the laboratory is ordinarily natural gas, which is mostly methane, CH_4, and small amounts of other compounds. Determine the mass of a sample of burner gas. Calculate the percentages of methane and ethane, C_2H_6, assuming that they are the only gases present.

How are atoms arranged in molecules? The properties of substances are dependent upon the number and kinds of atoms present and upon their arrangement. The detailed information required to build accurate models has been obtained by complicated experiments that do not concern us at this point. We can, however, learn a lot about molecules by looking at models that can be assembled from expanded polystyrene spheres.

PROCEDURE

PART 1

Models for methane and related molecules

The methane molecule has the formula CH_4. Let us see what kind of "molecules" can be built from one carbon and four hydrogen "atoms."

1. To construct a planar model of methane, first place one black sphere on the table. This represents a carbon atom. Now take four white spheres to represent hydrogen atoms. Construct a planar model that is consistent with the following observations: (1) the hydrogen atoms are *all* alike, and (2) the hydrogen atoms are as close to the carbon atom as possible and as far from each other as possible.

Use toothpicks to fasten this "molecule" together. Each toothpick represents a *bond* between two atoms.

Draw a picture of your planar molecule, letting C represent the carbon atom and H represent each hydrogen atom.

2. We live in a three-dimensional world. Molecules, like everything else, are not necessarily planar but can be three-dimensional. Construct a three-dimensional model of methane that is consistent with the observations given in step 1. Use toothpicks to fasten this "molecule" together.

Construct an *imaginary* three-dimensional CH_4 "molecule" that would have the following properties: (1) two hydrogen atoms are positioned differently from the other two; (2) there are two bonds, each joining two hydrogen atoms in the molecule; and (3) two hydrogen atoms are joined directly to the carbon atom and are as far apart as possible. (Experiments show that this model does *not* have the properties of methane.)

3. Now, you will construct three-dimensional models made from overlapping spheres. These are called Stuart models. First, obtain six "carbon atoms," 12 hydrogen atoms," and one "oxygen atom" of the truncated-sphere type.

Build a methane "molecule" and a C_2H_6 "molecule" using "atoms" of this type. Then, build a model of the compound H_3COCH_3. Now, use the six "carbon atoms" and the twelve "hydrogen atoms" to construct a "molecule" of formula C_6H_{12}. Finally, use the "oxygen atom" and two "hydrogen atoms" to build a "water molecule."

Questions and regularities for part 1

1. In what ways is the planar structural formula, implied by the model of step 1, misleading?
2. Consider the three-dimensional model of step 2. What is the name of the geometric figure that results when each hydrogen atom is connected to the other three hydrogen atoms by a line?
3. Where is the carbon atom in the figure of question 2?
4. Is the "water molecule" constructed in step 3 different than the one that would have been built had you used a spherical "oxygen atom" and two spherical "hydrogen atoms?" Explain.

(In Chapter 12 we shall consider a set of rules that will help us to decide between various molecular models for a given compound. Water has a structure close to that indicated by the overlapping-sphere model.)

PART 2

Models of elements and compounds and balancing equations

1. Elements are substances made from only one kind of atom. Use Stuart-type models and toothpicks to put together a "molecule" of H_2 (white spheres) and a "molecule" of Cl_2 (green spheres).

2. Compounds are substances containing two or more kinds of atoms. With your models, show the bond-breaking and molecule-altering that is needed to change one "hydrogen molecule" and one "chlorine molecule" into two "hydrogen chloride molecules."

Repeat the above process, but show the reaction of "hydrogen molecules" and "oxygen molecules" to give "water molecules."

Questions and regularities for part 2

1. For each of the chemical reactions considered in step 2, write the chemical equation. Make sure that the number of "atoms" and "molecules" used in the equation agrees with what is shown by the models.

PART 3

Relative masses, atomic weights, and molecular weights

1. Find the mass of one orange sphere and of one blue sphere.

2. Find the mass of one dozen each of the orange and blue spheres.

Questions and regularities for part 3

1. From your data in step 1, calculate the ratio

$$\frac{\text{mass of 1 blue sphere}}{\text{mass of 1 orange sphere}}$$

2. From your data in step 2, calculate the same ratio as in question 1.
3. Calculate the ratio

$$\frac{\text{mass of 1 mole blue spheres}}{\text{mass of 1 mole orange spheres}}$$

4. If each of your "hydrogen atoms" has a mass of 1 g, and each "carbon atom" has a mass of 12 g, (a) What is the mass of 1 mole of "hydrogen atoms"? (b) What is the mass of 1 mole of "carbon atoms"? (c) What is the ratio of

$$\frac{\text{mass of 1 mole "carbon atoms"}}{\text{mass of 1 mole "hydrogen atoms"}}$$

(d) How does the ratio in the last question compare to the ratio of the atomic weight of carbon to the atomic weight of hydrogen?

Mass relationships accompanying chemical changes

When a chemical reaction occurs, how do the masses of reactants and products compare? In this experiment, you will use the same number of *moles* of two reactants, lead nitrate, $Pb(NO_3)_2$, and potassium chromate, K_2CrO_4, and allow them to react with each other. You will be making a comparison between the *masses* of reactants and products and the *number of moles* of reactants and products.

You will review one technique—careful use of the balance—and learn some new ones—decanting, filtering, washing, and drying. Carry them out well, for it will be assumed in future work that you are able to follow these procedures. If you have any questions about these techniques, refer to Experimental Techniques on pages 9–18.

Record your data carefully and neatly. Take special care to show the units used in your measurements. Include the uncertainty in each measurement. Before you come to the lab to do an experiment, you should plan what you are going to do. This preparation will free your mind from mechanical details and allow you to concentrate on making the required observations in the allotted time.

PROCEDURE

PRELAB ASSIGNMENT

Determine the mass in grams of 0.00500 mole of potassium chromate, K_2CrO_4, and of 0.00500 mole of lead nitrate, $Pb(NO_3)_2$ (see Figure 30).

IN THE LABORATORY

1. Find the mass of a clean, dry 250-ml beaker to the nearest 0.01 g.

2. Find the mass of a piece of weighing paper. Next, move the riders on the balance arm so that they are set at the number of grams the weighing paper *with* K_2CrO_4 on it must equal. (This is the mass of the weighing paper plus the mass of 0.00500 mole of K_2CrO_4, which you calculated as

part of your prelab assignment.) Your data table should look like this:

mass of weighing paper $\pm$ 0.01g + K_2CrO_4
mass of weighing paper $\pm$ 0.01g
  mass of K_2CrO_4 $\pm$ 0.02g

3. Carefully tap out crystals of K_2CrO_4 onto the weighing paper until the balance arm is again centered (see Figure 30).

4. Transfer the K_2CrO_4 to the 250-ml beaker.

5. Find the mass of a clean, dry Erlenmeyer flask (125 ml or 250 ml) to the nearest 0.01 g.

6. Using the procedure in steps 2 and 3, obtain the correct mass of $Pb(NO_3)_2$ crystals and transfer it to the Erlenmeyer flask.

7. Dissolve each of the solids in about 25 ml of distilled water. Warm the solutions if desired to increase the rate of dissolving.

8. Add about 1 ml of the lead nitrate solution from the flask to the potassium chromate solution

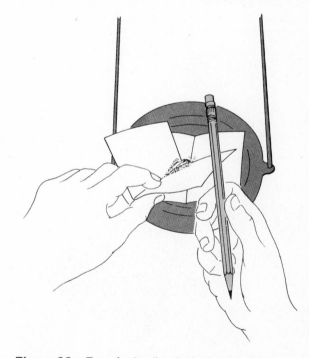

Figure 30 Transferring the desired amount.

in the beaker and stir about 1 minute. Avoid splashing.

9. While continuing to stir the solution, add the rest of the lead nitrate, a few millilitres at a time. Rinse the last traces of lead nitrate from the flask into the beaker with some distilled water, using a wash bottle. *Use as little water as is practical.* Several rinses of small volume are more effective than a single one of larger volume. Heat the solution for about five minutes, but do not let it boil vigorously. Allow the precipitate to settle.

10. Determine the mass of a piece of filter paper to the nearest 0.01 g. See page 12 for directions on folding the filter paper, or ask your teacher to demonstrate this. After folding the paper, fit it into a funnel and moisten it with some distilled water from a wash bottle. Set up the funnel for filtering as shown in Figure 31.

11. Put the flask under the funnel. Decant the clear liquid from the beaker into the funnel.

Retain as much of the precipitate as possible in the beaker.

12. Wash the precipitate in the beaker by adding about 20 ml of distilled water and warming the mixture again. Let the precipitate settle and decant the liquid into the funnel, leaving as much of the precipitate as possible in the beaker. Wash the precipitate in the beaker with another 15 ml of distilled water.

13. Again decant the wash water into the filter paper in the funnel. Wash the sides of the beaker with 10 ml of distilled water (see Figure 32) and pour this also into the filter paper. It is not necessary to attempt to transfer all of the precipitate, since you will later place the filter paper and its contents in the beaker to be dried.

14. When the filtering is complete, remove the flask and begin to evaporate the filtrate over a very low burner flame. Your teacher may suggest an alternate method of evaporating the solution to obtain the dry crystals overnight.

15. Remove the filter paper from the funnel. Unfold it to expose as much of the precipitate as possible to the air and place it loosely into the beaker. Dry the precipitate overnight as directed by your teacher.

16. When the residue in the flask is dry, determine the total mass of flask and residue.

17. When the precipitate in the beaker is dry, find the total mass of beaker, filter paper, and precipitate.

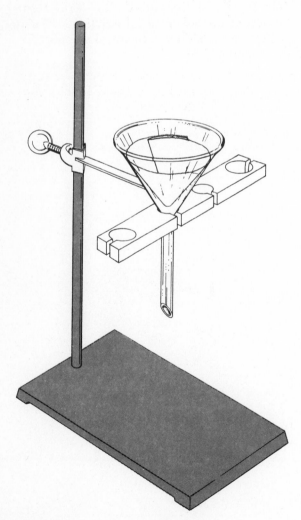

Figure 31 Apparatus for filtering.

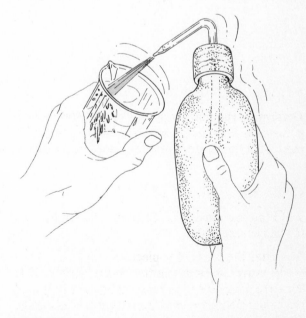

Figure 32 Washing the sides of the beaker with a wash bottle.

Calculations and results

1. Determine the mass of each product. The yellow precipitate is lead chromate, $PbCrO_4$. The dry residue from the filtrate is potassium nitrate, KNO_3.
2. Copy the following table and make the necessary calculations to fill in the entries.

Table 3

	Mass	Number of moles
$Pb(NO_3)_2$		0.00500
K_2CrO_4		0.00500
$PbCrO_4$		
KNO_3		

3. Compare the sum of the masses of the reactants to the sum of the masses of the products by finding the ratio

$$\frac{\text{mass of products } [PbCrO_4 + KNO_3]}{\text{mass of reactants } [Pb(NO_3)_2 + K_2CrO_4]}$$

Express your answer as a decimal and use the correct number of significant figures.

4. What is the significance of the ratio calculated in question 3?
5. Write the formulas for the two reactants on the left of an arrow sign and the formulas for the two products on the right side of the same arrow. Below each substance, write the number of moles used or formed.
6. Use the information from question 5 to balance the following equation:

   1 mole of $Pb(NO_3)_2$ (*in solution*)

   $+$ 1 mole of K_2CrO_4 (*in solution*)

   $\rightarrow$ _____ mole(s) of $PbCrO_4$ (*solid*)

   $+$ _____ mole(s) of KNO_3 (*solid*)

7. When a quantity does not change during a chemical reaction, we say that it is *conserved*. Use your answers to questions 3 and 6 to answer the following: (a) Is mass conserved in this chemical reaction? (b) Are atoms conserved in this chemical reaction? (c) Are moles conserved in this chemical reaction?

What mass and mole relationships are there in chemical reactions? In this experiment, you will find the mass of a sample of solid lead acetate and prepare a water solution of it. You will also find the mass of a zinc strip, place it in the solution, and observe its behavior. By finding the mass of the zinc strip at the close of the experiment, you will be able to investigate quantitatively any changes that occur.

In keeping with chemical practice, we shall refer to the chemical substances by using appropriate symbols. Zinc is an element; it contains only one kind of atom. The symbol for zinc is Zn. Lead acetate, $Pb(CH_3COO)_2 \cdot 3H_2O$, is a compound. The formula identifies it by having the symbol Pb for the lead part and the symbols CH_3COO for the acetate part. The group CH_3COO—consisting of two carbon atoms, three hydrogen atoms, and two oxygen atoms—is often found in chemical compounds and has the name acetate. The subscript "2" following the parentheses indicates that two acetates combine with one lead atom. The "$3H_2O$" in the formula indicates that there are three water molecules for every molecule of lead acetate in the crystals.

PROCEDURE

1. Obtain a strip of zinc. If it has been used before, clean it with emery paper until a shiny surface is obtained.

2. As precisely as possible, find the mass of the zinc strip, a clean, dry 250-ml beaker, and a piece of weighing paper.

3. With the weighing paper on the pan of the balance, its mass recorded, and the masses still in place on the balance arm, add exactly 2.00 grams to the arm of the balance. Then open the vial of lead acetate, $Pb(CH_3COO)_2 \cdot 3H_2O$, and tap out crystals until exactly 2.00 g have been added to the weighing paper. **If you should touch any of the crystals, be sure to wash your hands.**

4. Transfer the solid lead acetate to the 250-ml beaker. Add 200 ml of distilled water to the lead acetate and swirl gently until all the solid dissolves. Add a few drops of concentrated acetic acid, CH_3COOH, to clarify the solution.

5. Place the zinc strip in the beaker containing the lead acetate solution.

6. Observe for several minutes and record any changes that take place. Cover the beaker with a watch glass and place it in your locker until the next laboratory period.

7. At the beginning of the next laboratory period, very carefully open your locker and lift the beaker to the desk top. Observe what has happened in the beaker. Record *all* your observations in your laboratory notebook.

8. Remove the watch glass. Shake the lead off the zinc strip into the beaker and remove the strip from the beaker. Use your wash bottle to rinse into the beaker any lead that tends to adhere to the strip. (See Figure 33.) Set the strip aside. When it is dry, find its mass.

9. Let the lead settle in the beaker. Carefully decant the solution. Decant means to pour off liquid, leaving a solid behind, as shown in Figure 34. Wash the residue with 10 ml of water and

Figure 33 Rinsing with a wash bottle.

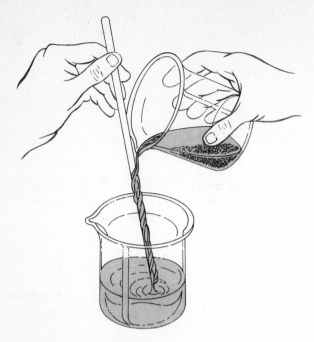

Figure 34 Decanting the supernatant liquid from the residue.

carefully decant. Wash and decant at least three more times. Finally, wash the lead with 10 ml of acetone and decant once again.

10. After the final acetone washing, the residue must be dried. Your teacher will suggest a suitable method.

11. Allow the beaker and contents to cool before finding their mass. Use the same balance you did previously and record the mass together with the uncertainty.

Your data table should include the following:

1. Numbers that permit you to calculate the mass of $Pb(CH_3COO)_2 \cdot 3H_2O$ used, such as the mass of the weighing paper and $Pb(CH_3COO)_2 \cdot 3H_2O$, and the mass of the weighing paper alone.
2. Numbers that permit you to calculate the mass of zinc metal used, such as the mass of the zinc strip before and after the reaction.
3. Numbers that permit you to calculate the mass of lead produced, such as the mass of the empty beaker and the mass of the beaker with the dried lead in it.

Calculations and results

1. Calculate the change in mass of the zinc strip.
2. Calculate the mass of lead obtained.
3. Calculate the number of moles of zinc reacted. Remember that the mass of a substance divided by the mass per mole equals the number of moles. Express the uncertainty in your answer as directed by your teacher.
4. Calculate the number of moles of lead produced. Express the uncertainty as directed by your teacher.
5. Determine the ratio moles Pb/moles Zn. Express your answer as a decimal to the proper number of significant figures.
6. (a) Calculate the mass of $Pb(CH_3COO)_2 \cdot 3H_2O$ used in the experiment. (b) Calculate the number of moles of $Pb(CH_3COO)_2 \cdot 3H_2O$ used in the experiment. Express the uncertainty as you did in calculations 3 and 4 above.
7. Determine the ratio moles Pb/moles $Pb(CH_3COO)_2 \cdot 3H_2O$. Express your answer as a decimal to the proper number of significant figures.
8. Using the results of calculations 5 and 7, write *whole number* coefficients in the following statement:

   _____1____ mole of Zn (*solid*) + _____ mole(s)

   of $Pb(CH_3COO)_2 \cdot 3H_2O$ (*solution*) →

   _____mole(s) of Pb (*solid*)

   + _____mole(s) of $Zn(CH_3COO)_2$ (*solution*)

9. Collect the results obtained by other members of your class. Make a graph of these results. Plot the ratio of moles Pb/moles Zn along the horizontal axis and the number of groups obtaining a particular ratio along the vertical axis.
10. Considering only the middle two-thirds of the data plotted, estimate the range of the values obtained. How does this compare with the uncertainty you considered justifiable from your measurements?
11. How many individual atoms of zinc metal were involved in *your* experiment?
12. How many individual atoms of lead metal were produced in *your* experiment?

Heat of combustion

In this experiment you will determine the amount of energy (heat) involved in a chemical change. Experiments with candles have shown that during burning the candle changes into at least three substances (finely divided carbon, carbon dioxide, and water). The products are strikingly different from the starting materials. Recall that the type of change in which new products are formed is called a *chemical change*. Let us determine the amount of heat (in calories) liberated when a candle burns. The heat obtained when a known mass of candle burns will be used to warm a measured volume of water. (We shall assume that 1 ml of water has a mass of 1 g.)

PROCEDURE

1. Attach a candle to a tin lid or index card. Find the mass of the combination on a suitable balance to the nearest 0.01 g. Record the mass and its uncertainty.

2. Set up the apparatus as shown in Figure 35 such that the flame of the candle when lit (do *not* light it yet) will almost, but not quite, touch the bottom of the can.

3. Using a 250-ml graduated cylinder, obtain *approximately* 200 ml of cold tap water, and put it into the can, which will be the calorimeter.

4. Cool the water with ice, if necessary, so that its temperature is about 10 °C–15 °C below room temperature. Add the ice directly to the water. Remove any remaining ice when the desired temperature has been reached.

5. Read and record the temperature of the water to the nearest 0.2 °C. Light the candle and heat the water. Stir *gently* until the water reaches a temperature as much above room temperature as it was below at the start. Carefully blow out the candle, but continue to stir the water and watch the thermometer reading. Record the highest temperature that is reached.

6. Determine the mass of the candle and lid or index card on the same balance as before. Make certain that any drippings from the candle are weighed with it. Remember, you want to find out how much candle was actually burned.

7. Measure the volume of the water to the nearest 1 ml. In measuring the volume of a liquid in any graduated container, always have your eye at the same level as the bottom of the *meniscus* (the lens-shaped surface the liquid forms in the container). See Figure 36.

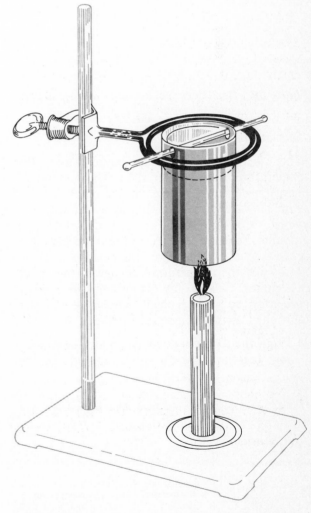

Figure 35 Apparatus for determining the heat of combustion.

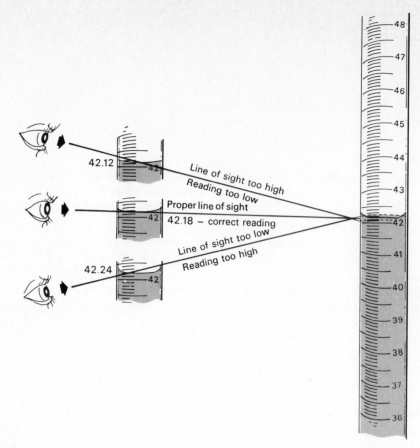

Figure 36 Read bottom of meniscus with eye at proper level.

Calculations and results

When heat is absorbed by liquid water, the temperature of the water rises. The amount of energy necessary to raise the temperature of 1 gram of water 1 degree Celsius is defined as 1 calorie. Consequently, we can calculate the amount of energy released or absorbed during a process. We have measured the mass of water in grams and the temperature change of the water in degrees Celsius. By definition, the energy gained by the water is equal to the mass of water multiplied by the temperature change.*

1. From the data obtained, calculate the following: (a) the mass of candle burned (b) the mass of water heated (c) the temperature change of water (ΔT) (d) the quantity of heat absorbed by the water (assume that all the heat from the burning candle went into the water) (e) the heat of combustion per gram of candle material.

2. Compare your results with those of other members of your class. Considering the assumptions made in the calculations for the experiment, would you expect your results to be lower than or higher than the *accepted* value? Explain.

ADDITIONAL INVESTIGATION

(To be undertaken as extracurricular experiment. Consult your teacher before proceeding.)

Devise suitable refinements in the experimental procedure to eliminate the major sources of error that you encountered. Determine the heat of combustion of a pure substance, such as stearic acid, and then compare the results with the literature.

*In the general case, the heat associated with a temperature change for a substance is

$$\left\{\begin{array}{l}\text{heat associated with} \\ \text{temperature change} \\ \text{of substance}\end{array}\right\} =$$

$$\left\{\begin{array}{l}\text{mass of} \\ \text{substance}\end{array}\right\} \times \left\{\begin{array}{l}\text{change in} \\ \text{temperature} \\ \text{(°C)}\end{array}\right\} \times \left\{\begin{array}{l}\text{calories to} \\ \text{change temperature} \\ \text{of 1 g by 1 °C}\end{array}\right\}$$

Reaction of a metal with hydrochloric acid

How many litres of dry hydrogen gas at room temperature and 1 atmosphere (atm) can be produced per mole of magnesium metal? In this experiment you will determine the volume of hydrogen gas that is produced when a sample of magnesium metal reacts with hydrogen chloride dissolved in water. The volume of hydrogen gas will be measured at room temperature and pressure, conditions that are important for a gas.

PROCEDURE

1. Obtain a piece of magnesium (Mg) ribbon approximately 5 cm long.* Measure the length of the ribbon carefully and record this to the nearest 0.05 cm. Your teacher will give you the mass of 1 metre (m) of the ribbon. Since it is uniform in thickness, you can calculate the mass of the magnesium used.

2. Fold the magnesium ribbon so that it can be encased in a small spiral cage made of fine copper wire. Let enough copper wire serve as a handle so that the cage can be put up to the 50-ml mark in the gas measuring tube (see Figure 37).

3. Set up a ring stand and utility clamp in position to hold a 50-ml gas measuring tube that has been fitted with a one- or two-hole rubber stopper, as shown in Figure 38a. Place a 400-ml beaker about two-thirds full of tap water near the ring stand.

4. Tilt the gas measuring tube slightly and pour in 3-*M* hydrochloric acid (HCl) to about the 15-ml mark.

5. With the tube still tilted, slowly fill it with tap water from a beaker. While pouring, rinse any acid that may be on the sides of the tube, so that the final liquid in the top of the tube will contain very little acid. Try to avoid stirring up the acid layer in the bottom of the tube.

6. Holding the copper coil by the handle, insert it into the tube until the case is positioned at about the 50-ml mark. Hook the copper wire over the edge of the tube and clamp it there by inserting the rubber stopper. When properly set up, the tube will contain no air bubbles, and the water will completely fill the hole(s) in the stopper as well as the tube.

7. Cover the hole(s) in the stopper with your finger, and invert the tube in the container of water, as shown in Figure 38b. Clamp the tube in place. The acid, being more dense than water, will stream down through the water and eventually react with the metal.

8. After the reaction stops, wait about 5 minutes to allow the tube and its contents to come to room temperature. Bubbles clinging to the sides of the tube can be dislodged by tapping the tube gently.

9. Cover the hole(s) in the stopper with your finger and transfer the tube to a large cylinder or battery jar that is almost filled with water at room temperature. See Figure 39. Raise or lower the tube until the level of the liquid inside the tube is the same as the level of the water outside the tube. This permits you to measure the volume of the gases in the tube (hydrogen and water

Figure 37 Copper cage containing magnesium ribbon folded in thirds.

---

*If atmospheric pressure is usually about 760 mm, use 5.0 cm; if it is usually about 700 mm, use 5.0 × 700/760 cm; and so on.

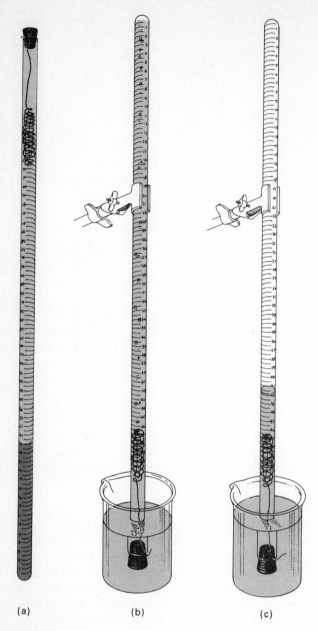

(a)   (b)   (c)

Figure 38   Manipulating the gas measuring tube.

vapor) at the air pressure of the room. Read the volume with your eye at the same level as the bottom of the *meniscus* (the lens-shaped surface formed by the water in the tube). See Figure 36. Record the volume of the gas to the nearest 0.05 ml.

10.   Remove the gas measuring tube from the water and pour the acid solution it contains down the sink. Rinse the tube with tap water.

11.   Record the room temperature. Your teacher will give you the air pressure in the room or will assist you in reading the barometer.

Calculations and results

1. Determine the mass of the magnesium you used from the grams-per-metre relationship and the length of your piece of ribbon.
2. Determine the number of moles of magnesium used.
3. Determine the partial pressure of the hydrogen gas. Since the hydrogen gas was collected over water, the gas in the tube consists of a mixture of hydrogen gas and water vapor. The total pressure caused by these two gases is equal to the room pressure. See the hypothetical case illustrated in Figure 40a. Mathematically this can be expressed as

$$P_{H_2} + P_{H_2O} = P_{room}$$

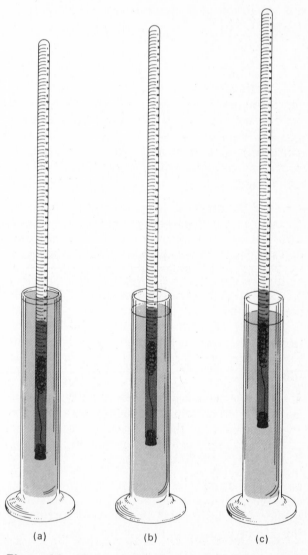

(a)   (b)   (c)

Figure 39   Measuring the volume of gas. In (b), room pressure is just equal to the combined pressure of $H_2(g)$ and $H_2O(g)$.

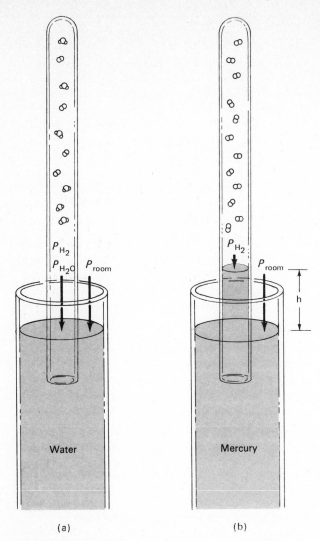

(a)   (b)

Figure 40 Correcting for the vapor pressure of water. (a) The pressure in the tube is equal to the combined pressures of $H_2O(g)$ and $H_2(g)$. This total pressure is equal to the room pressure. (b) The pressure of $H_2(g)$ alone.

The pressure of the room may be determined by reading the barometer. The pressure of the water vapor, P_{H_2O}, can be determined from Table 4. The values in the table were obtained by measuring the pressure of water vapor above liquid water at various temperatures. The partial pressure of the hydrogen can then be calculated as:

$$P_{H_2} = P_{room} - P_{H_2O}$$

See Figure 40b for an illustration of the pressure due to the hydrogen alone.

Table 4 Vapor pressure of water at various temperatures

Temperature (°C)	Pressure (mm)	Temperature (°C)	Pressure (mm)
15	12.8	23	21.0
16	13.6	24	22.4
17	14.5	25	23.7
18	15.5	26	25.2
19	16.5	27	26.7
20	17.5	28	28.3
21	18.6	29	30.0
22	19.8	30	31.8

4. Determine the volume of the hydrogen gas at 1 atm (760 mm). You have learned that for a given temperature the product of the pressure and volume of a gas is constant, $PV = k$. To calculate the new volume, V_{new}, at 760 mm pressure, the following mathematical relationship can be stated:

$$V_{(at\ original\ H_2\ pressure)} \times P_{H_2(measured)} =$$
$$V_{(at\ 760\ mm)} \times P_{(760\ mm)}$$

Rearranging this equation, we get

$$V_{(at\ 760\ mm)} = \frac{V_{(at\ original\ H_2\ pressure)} \times P_{H_2(measured)}}{760\ mm}$$

5. Calculate the volume of dry hydrogen that would be produced by 1 mole of magnesium at 1 atm pressure and the temperature of your laboratory.

6. Calculation 5 represents the volume of hydrogen (measured at 1 atm pressure and at laboratory temperature) produced when 1 mole of magnesium reacts with an acid. What additional information is needed in order to say that this answer also represents the volume of 1 mole of hydrogen gas (measured at 1 atm pressure and at room temperature)?

ADDITIONAL INVESTIGATION

(To be undertaken as an extracurricular experiment. Consult your teacher before proceeding.)

Determine the volume of hydrogen gas produced when a mole of another metal reacts with an acid.

In Experiment 4 we saw that gas volume decreases as pressure is applied. Is this a property characteristic of all matter, or is it specific for gases? Experimentation provides the answer.

PROCEDURE

Part 1

Compressibility of liquids

How do liquids behave when pressure is applied? Fill the syringe with water to the 25-ml mark. Make sure that there are no bubbles of gas in the syringe. Put your finger over the tip and push the plunger.

Questions and regularities

1. How does a liquid differ from a gas in compressibility?
2. Interpret this fact by a modification of the model used to describe gases.

PART 2

The solubility of a gas in a liquid

How much gas dissolves in a given quantity of liquid? A number of factors are involved. We shall determine how many millilitres of carbon dioxide gas dissolve in 1 ml of water if the pressure of carbon dioxide is always 1 atm.

1. Fill a *dry* syringe to the 25-ml mark with carbon dioxide gas. Your teacher will show you how to fill the syringe.

2. Place the tip of the syringe under the surface of approximately 250 ml of water in a 400-ml beaker. The tip should be immersed to its juncture with the body of the syringe. Slowly pull out the plunger so that water is drawn up to the 5-ml mark.

3. Place your finger over the tip of the syringe, remove it from the water, and shake it. With your finger still over the tip, leave the plunger free to seek its own level to equalize the pressure. Place the tip back under water (to the same depth) before removing your finger. Repeat this procedure at least once to see if there is any change.

4. Repeat step **3** until no further changes are noticed.

5. *(Optional)* Other gases may be used.

Calculations and results

1. How many millilitres of carbon dioxide gas, measured at 1 atm, dissolved in the water?
2. What was the volume of water that was finally used?
3. Calculate the number of millilitres of carbon dioxide dissolved per millilitre of water.

Heat of solidification

What energy changes occur when a liquid solidifies? In Experiment 3 we discovered two characteristic properties of substances: the temperature of melting is different for different pure substances, and the temperature of a melting solid or freezing liquid remains constant as long as both liquid and solid phases are present. The energy that was required to change the solid to a liquid was released when the substance changed from a liquid to a solid. Remember that the change that occurs when a solid melts or a liquid freezes is called a *phase change*.

In this experiment, you will use the same solid that you used in Experiment 3. The heat given off as the substance turns from a liquid to a solid will be used to change the temperature of a measured amount of water.

PROCEDURE

1. Obtain an 18 × 150 mm test tube partially filled with the same solid that you used in Experiment 3. Find the mass of the test tube containing the solid to the nearest 0.01 g, and record the mass and its uncertainty.

2. Record the mass of the empty tube. This information will either be marked on the tube or given to you by your teacher.

3. Using a 250-ml graduated cylinder, obtain approximately 125 ml of cold tap water and put it into the 7-oz expanded polystyrene cup that is to be used as the calorimeter. The level of the water in the cup should be above the level of the solid tube when the latter is in the cup. Read the temperature of the water, and if it is not 1°C to 2°C below room temperature, add an ice cube to the water and stir until the temperature has been sufficiently lowered, as you did in Experiment 9. Remove any remaining ice.

4. Make a bath of boiling water by putting about 125 ml of water into a 250-ml beaker and heating the water to boiling. Place the test tube containing the solid material into the boiling water until the material is *just melted. Avoid overheating.*

5. Using a test tube holder, remove the test tube containing the melted material from the hot water. Allow the liquid material to cool until the first trace of solid is seen on the bottom of the test tube. If you miss this observation and more than a trace of solid is present, place the test tube back in the boiling water for just a moment until the solid melts. Then let it cool again until the first trace of solid appears.

6. While the liquid is cooling, measure and record the temperature of the cold-water bath to the nearest 0.2 °C. Place the test tube containing the liquid and trace of solid into the plastic cup and stir gently with the test tube (see Figure 41). Note the temperature of the water as you stir and continue to observe the temperature until no further increase is noted. (When reading the thermometer, immerse it in the cup midway between the tube and the side of the plastic cup.) Record the maximum temperature to the nearest 0.2 °C.

Figure 41   Determining the heat of solidification.

7. Pour the water from the expanded polystyrene cup into a graduated cylinder. Measure the volume of water to the nearest millilitre.

Calculations and results

1. Calculate the following: (a) the mass of solid, (b) the mass of water in the plastic cup, (c) the temperature change of the water, ΔT, (d) the quantity of heat (number of calories) used in effecting the temperature change (neglect the heat required to change the temperature of the plastic cup itself), (e) the heat of solidification per gram of solid.
2. Compare the heat of solidification value you obtained with those of your classmates—both those who had the same substance and those who used different substances. Is the heat of solidification a characteristic property that might help identify the substance? (Be sure you note the uncertainties involved when answering this.) Reread the discussion on uncertainty in Chapter 1 of your textbook if you have questions about the way uncertainty of measurement influences a conclusion.
3. The heat of solidification of a substance is the heat released as a given quantity of the substance changes from liquid to solid. The heat of fusion is the heat absorbed when a solid substance changes to a liquid. What is the heat of fusion of your substance?
4. Compare the heat of solidification value you obtained with the heat of combustion obtained in Experiment 9. Propose a model to account for any differences observed.
5. *(Optional)* Obtain the molecular weight of the substance you used, and calculate the heat of solidification in calories *per mole* of substance.

ADDITIONAL INVESTIGATION

(To be undertaken as an extracurricular experiment. Consult your teacher before proceeding.)

Devise an experiment to measure the energy effect for the phase change gas to liquid, or liquid to gas, for some suitable substance.

Production of a precipitate from solutions of sodium iodide and lead nitrate

How is the chemical formula for a substance determined? In this experiment you will prepare solutions of lead nitrate, $Pb(NO_3)_2$, and sodium iodide, NaI, of known concentration, 0.500 M. You will observe the results when various volumes of these solutions are mixed. From the relative volumes of the solutions used and their molar concentrations, and from the masses of the precipitate formed, it will be possible to determine the number of moles of the substances involved and the formula for the precipitate.

P R O C E D U R E

PART 1

Preparation of the solutions

In this experiment you will work with a partner. Each will prepare *one* of the 0.500 M solutions that will be shared as the experiment is performed.

PRELAB ASSIGNMENT

Before coming to the laboratory, each partner will calculate the mass of lead nitrate and of sodium iodide needed to make 25.0 ml of a 0.500 M solution of each. Check your answers with those of your partner and your teacher before proceeding to step 1.

IN THE LABORATORY

1. In the laboratory each partner will weigh out the calculated amount of one solid. First find the mass of a clean, dry 50-ml beaker. Then adjust the mass by adding or subtracting solid until the desired mass is measured. Figure 11, on page 14 shows the technique for transferring a solid a little at a time from a bottle. If you should transfer too much, discard the excess. *Never return it to the bottle.*

2. Add about 20 ml of distilled water to the beaker. Swirl the solution or stir it with a glass

rod until the solid disappears. Pour the resulting solution into a clean 25-ml or 50-ml graduated cylinder and add just enough distilled water with a squeeze bottle to make the volume 25.0 ml. (Refer to Figure 36 on page 40 for the proper method of reading a meniscus.) *Pour the solution back* into the same beaker used to dissolve the solid, and *stir the solution* gently until it is *uniformly mixed.* If you or your partner must reuse the graduated cylinder for the second solution, rinse it well. Label each solution.

PART 2

A study of the amounts of precipitate formed when various volumes of the solutions are mixed

Table 5 gives the volumes that are to be carefully measured into clean 18 × 150 mm test tubes by either the technique described in Part 2 Method 1 or Method 2. You will do only one set. Your teacher will tell you and your partner which assignment is yours.

MEASURING VOLUMES: METHOD 1

1. One technique for measuring volumes of solution is with a pipet. Practice with the 10-ml pipet by measuring out distilled water a few times. In using a pipet, the tip of the pipet is inserted *well below* the surface of the liquid in the container. Pull liquid up into the pipet with a

Table 5

Assignment	Test tube	0.500 M sodium iodide	0.500 M lead nitrate
1	1	9.0	1.0
2	2	8.0	2.0
3	3	7.0	3.0
4	4	6.0	4.0
5	5	5.0	5.0
6	6	4.0	6.0
7	7	3.0	7.0
8	8	2.0	8.0
9	9	1.0	9.0

Figure 42 Using a pipet to measure the volume of a solution.

syringe or rubber bulb until the level is *above* the highest graduated marking. Then place your forefinger over the top of the pipet to keep the liquid at that level (see Figure 42). Wipe the outside of the pipet with a piece of tissue.

Carefully let air into the pipet, a little at a time, until the bottom of the meniscus is at the zero mark. Touch the tip of the pipet to the side of the beaker to drain for a moment. Be careful not to dip it into the liquid. Then place the pipet over a test tube and slide your finger to one side to allow the proper amount of liquid to drain into the test tube. When the bottom of the meniscus is at the proper mark, replace your finger and touch the tip of the pipet to the side of the test tube. Following the trials with water, rinse the pipet with two or three small portions of the sodium iodide solution, *which you then discard.* Now use the pipet to measure the proper volume of sodium iodide solution into a clean 18 × 150 mm test tube.

2. Carefully rinse the pipet with water before measuring the lead nitrate solution. Rinse with two small portions of the lead nitrate (which are discarded) before measuring the required amount of lead nitrate solution into the test tube.

MEASURING VOLUMES: METHOD 2

An alternative method for measuring the volume of the solutions is to use two burets (see Experi-

ment 25 on the use of the buret). After the solutions are made, obtain for each one a buret that has been cleaned, well rinsed with distilled water, and labeled. Use about 3 ml of the solution to rinse the inside of the buret in which it will be used. Discard the rinsing solutions.

Now pour the rest of the solutions into the appropriate burets. Make sure that air is eliminated from each tip by running out a little of the solutions. Dispense the required amounts of the two solutions into your test tube.

DETERMINING THE AMOUNT OF PRECIPITATE

1. Place a clean stopper on the test tube and mix the solutions by shaking the tube. Let the precipitate settle for a few minutes. Your teacher may want you to compare the amount of precipitate you obtained with what other members of the class obtained.

2. In *pencil,* label the edge of a piece of filter paper with your name or locker number, plus your assignment number. Find the mass of the filter paper, and place it in a funnel as shown in Figure 31. Have a small beaker under the funnel.

3. Shake the test tube once again, then remove the stopper and quickly pour the precipitate and solution into the filter cone. Place the *same* test tube under the funnel tip and collect several millilitres of the filtrate. Rinse the walls of the test tube with this filtrate and quickly pour the contents into the filter to remove the remaining precipitate from the test tube. Catch the final filtrate in a beaker.

4. When the filter has drained, direct a small stream of distilled water from a wash bottle over the filter paper to rinse away the soluble sodium nitrate. (Since the precipitate is slightly soluble in water—0.063 g/100 ml at 20 °C—you will not want to use a large quantity of water. Three 5-ml washings are sufficient.) Discard the filtrate and washings.

5. Remove the filter paper carefully and place it on a paper towel. Gently blot out some of the moisture. Place the labeled filter cone in your desk and allow it to dry overnight. In some climates it may be necessary to dry the precipitates with heat lamps or by another method suggested by your teacher.

6. Determine the mass of the dry filter cone containing the lead iodide precipitate.

Calculations and results

1. Obtain the mass of the precipitate by subtracting the mass of the filter paper from the mass of filter paper plus precipitate recorded in Part 2, step 6.
2. Prepare a summary table for recording the masses of precipitates obtained for assignments 1 through 9 by you and your classmates. Exchange data with your classmates, and record the results in the summary table.
3. Make a graph for plotting the information tabulated in question 2. Use the number of millilitres of lead nitrate solution (including 0 and 10) for the horizontal axis, and the number of grams of precipitate formed for the vertical axis. You may assume that no more than 1 g of precipitate will be precipitated. Plot the data obtained by you and your classmates.
4. How do you explain the shape of the curve obtained when you connect the plotted points on the graph?
5. Calculate the number of moles of lead nitrate and of sodium iodide used in each of the test tubes, and the ratio of moles of lead nitrate to moles of sodium iodide for each tube. Tabulate your answers. Such a table with two entries is shown on this page.

Table 6

Test tube	Moles of NaI	Moles of $Pb(NO_3)_2$	Ratio $\dfrac{\text{moles } Pb(NO_3)_2}{\text{moles NaI}}$
1	0.0045	0.00050	1:9
2	0.0040	0.0010	1:4

6. On the horizontal axis of your graph, record the ratio of moles of $Pb(NO_3)_2$ to moles of NaI for each set of data.
7. Refer to the graph and select the combination or combinations in which there was apparently just enough of the lead nitrate solution to react with all of the sodium iodide and just enough of the sodium iodide to react with all of the lead nitrate.
8. What ratios of moles $Pb(NO_3)_2$ to moles NaI correspond to the combinations selected in question 7? What small whole-number ratio is nearest to the ratios you selected?
9. Use the ratio selected in question 8 to determine the formula of the precipitate. You may assume that the precipitate is composed of lead atoms and iodine atoms.

How can the identity of a precipitate be determined? Each of the compounds used in this experiment is an ionic solid. The aqueous solution of each contains positive and negative ions in such proportion that their net electric charge is zero. The actual manipulation of the solutions is quite simple. You are to mix every different combination of a set of six solutions and record the cases where a precipitate is formed. Also include a description of the precipitate.

PROCEDURE

PRELAB ASSIGNMENT

Number each solution that you will use, and write the ionic equation for the dissolving of each compound. If you do not know the charge associated with an ion, refer to Appendix 3.

Organize a table for your observations. In the left column write the formulas for the pair of ions present in each solution. Write the pairs of formulas again in the top horizontal row, but in reverse order. Note in the partial sample table (Table 7) that only the *kinds* of ions are indicated, not how many of each are present. The entries shown are not necessarily the ions you will encounter in your set of solutions.

With six different solutions, how many combinations of solutions will you need in order to study all of the different combinations, using two solutions at a time?*

IN THE LABORATORY

1. Obtain a square of thin plastic sheet or a spot plate. Place a drop of one solution on the plastic

*Count them as follows:

Combinations	Total
1-2, 1-3, 1-4, 1-5, 1-6	5
2-3, 2-4, 2-5, 2-6	4
3-4, 3-5, 3-6	3
and so on	

and add a drop of a second solution to it. Be sure that the dropper from the second solution does not touch the first drop, or contamination will result. Continue until you have tried all the different pairs of solutions from the six provided.

2. In your data table, describe the results in those combinations in which a precipitate formed (see sample table). Write "NR" when no apparent change is observed.

3. If time permits, you may wish to repeat the above procedure with a different set of solutions.

Questions and regularities

Since the pairs of ions listed in your data table were present in solution, you may assume that each precipitate was formed because of a *new* combination of ions. For example, if you mix aqueous solutions of $AgNO_3$ and $NaCl$, the ions initially present are $Ag^+(aq)$, $NO_3^-(aq)$, $Na^+(aq)$, and $Cl^-(aq)$. From the new combination of ions, it is possible to form $AgCl$ and $NaNO_3$. Note that in each case a precipitate could result from either or both of the new combinations.

1. For each case in which a precipitate was formed, list the ions present in the two solutions that were mixed.
2. Combine the ions in each case in question 1 to write possible formulas for the precipitate observed.
3. For each of the formulas listed in question 2, identify which are present in combinations in

Table 7

	6	5	4
	Na^+, S^{--}	Na^+, SO_4^{--}	and so on
1 Cu^{++}, SO_4^{--}	fine black ppt	NR	
2 Na^+, NO_3^-	NR	NR	
3 and so on			

which no precipitate was formed. Use this information to decide which formulas represent soluble compounds.

4. Write net ionic equations to indicate what you consider to have happened in each case where there was a reaction. Use ions to represent the species in the reacting solutions; but for products that were precipitates, write a formula for the compound. Place "(aq)" after the species in solution and "(s)" after the precipitates. Be sure to write the equations so that both atoms and charges are conserved. For example,

$$2\,Ag^+(aq) + SO_4^{--}(aq) \rightarrow Ag_2So_4(s)$$

How can a model be developed for something one cannot touch or see? How are theories about the nature of the atom obtained? In the first part of this experiment, you will attempt to determine the nature of an object that is concealed from view. The goal is not to guess what specific object is concealed, but to describe it sufficiently to make a drawing or model of its general appearance.

In the second part of the experiment, you will use a thin metal probe to determine the internal nature of an expanded polystyrene sphere. This sphere can be thought of as a model of an atom.

PROCEDURE

PART 1

Determining the internal nature of a sealed container

1. Obtain a sealed box that contains an object. Without breaking the seal make all the observations you can by carefully shaking, tilting, or otherwise manipulating the box. Record the observations made each time a given manipulation of the box is performed.

2. After obtaining data that will enable you to make closer approximations of the size, shape, and some of the physical properties of the object, make a drawing of your conception of that object.

Include a short description of the main characteristics of your drawing.

3. (*Optional*) After completing the drawing, open the box and look at the object. Write a two-paragraph summary of the similarities and differences between the real object and your conception of it. In the first paragraph, list the characteristics that you were successful in determining. In the second paragraph, list the characteristics that you were unable to determine.

4. (*Optional*) List any regularities that exist in the pattern of your successes and failures. (Is there any reason why you were successful for certain characteristics and not for others?)

PART 2

Determining the internal nature of an "atom"

1. Obtain an expanded polystyrene sphere representing an atom. Take the thin metal probe and carefully insert it into the sphere. Make a systematic series of probings. Record your observations each time a probing is made.

2. After obtaining your data, make a drawing that will answer the question: what is inside the "atom"?

3. (*Optional*) After completing your drawing, open up the "atom" and determine the actual nature of the inside. Make the same summary and listings as in Part 1, steps 3 and 4.

What is a chemical reaction? A chemical change is one in which the atoms are rearranged, by the breaking and reforming of bonds, to form substances whose empirical formulas differ from those of the reactants. Since these processes are not directly observable, how do we know when a chemical change has occurred? You note that a new substance has been formed by the appearance of

1. a precipitate
2. a gas
3. a change of color

In addition, to break bonds requires energy, and to form bonds releases energy. The amounts of energy used in these two processes are usually not the same. Thus the overall reaction is either *exothermic* (releasing energy) or *endothermic* (absorbing energy).

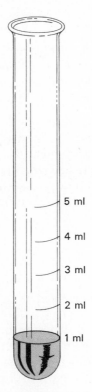

Figure 43 A full-scale drawing of a calibrated 13 × 100 mm test tube.

Besides looking for evidence of a chemical change, you should observe the rate of chemical reactions. You will study some of the factors that affect the rate: temperature, concentration, and catalysts.

Refer to items 5, 6, and 7 of the Laboratory Instructions (page 6) regarding the precautions to be observed in handling, tasting, and smelling chemicals.

Make a table for your data. The table should include the following:

1. a description of the reactants involved in each reaction
2. a rather detailed observation of each reaction
3. your reasons for believing a chemical reaction has or has not taken place

Quantities are to be *estimated* in this experiment. Do *not* use a graduated cylinder. Use 13 × 100 mm test tubes (see Figure 43). **Wear safety goggles at all times during this experiment.**

PROCEDURE

PART 1

Reactions

1. To 5 ml of tap water in a test tube add 15 drops, one at a time, of 18 *M* sulfuric acid, H_2SO_4. Record your observations. *Always add concentrated acid to water.* Never add water to concentrated acid. Save the diluted acid (about 2 *M*) for use in steps 4 and 5.

2. To 2 ml of tap water in a test tube add 3 small pellets of solid potassium hydroxide, KOH(*s*). *Do not handle potassium hydroxide pellets with your fingers.* Place a stopper in the test tube and shake it gently. Record your observations. Save the solution for step 3.

3. Add 5 ml of tap water to the potassium hydroxide solution prepared in step 2. Add a few drops of a solution of phenolphthalein (an indicator). Stopper the tube and shake it gently.

4. Repeat the test of step 3 with 1 ml of the sulfuric acid solution prepared in step 1, in place of the potassium hydroxide solution.

5. Set up four test tubes, each containing 5 ml of 0.1 M sodium oxalate, $Na_2C_2O_4$. Acidify each by adding about 1 ml of 2 M H_2SO_4 (prepared in step 1).

Place *two* of the test tubes in a hot water bath (40 °C to 50 °C) so that both will be at the same temperature. To *one* of these test tubes add 5 drops of 0.1 M manganese(II) sulfate, $MnSO_4$. Next add 2 drops of 0.1 M potassium permanganate, $KMnO_4$, to each of the two test tubes. Shake each test tube to mix, and note the reaction time for each to reach the same end products.

To *one* of the *other* two test tubes (at room temperature) add 5 drops of 0.1 M $MnSO_4$. Then to each of these two test tubes add 2 drops of 0.1 M $KMnO_4$. Shake each test tube to mix, and compare the reaction time for each as in 1 above.

PART 2
Reactions

1. To 1 ml of solid ammonium chloride, $NH_4Cl(s)$, in a test tube add 5 ml of tap water. Stopper the test tube and shake it. Record your observations.

2. Repeat step 1, using 1 ml of solid sodium acetate, $NaCH_3COO(s)$.

3. Place a *small* amount (about ¼ ml) of solid sodium sulfite, $Na_2SO_3(s)$, in a test tube. Cautiously add about 3 ml of dilute hydrochloric acid, 3 M HCl. (This can be conveniently made by diluting, in another test tube, 6 M HCl 1 to 1 with tap water.)

4. Place about 5 ml of acidified 0.1 M iron(II) sulfate, $FeSO_4$, in a test tube. Add 10 drops of 0.1 M $KMnO_4$, one drop at a time, shaking the test tube after the addition of each drop.

5. Add 1 ml of 0.1 M sodium chloride, NaCl, to 1 ml of 0.1 M potassium bromide, KBr.

6. (*Optional*) Place about 1 ml of 0.1 M NaCl in one test tube and 1 ml of 0.1 M potassium chromate, K_2CrO_4, in *another* test tube. Add a few drops of 0.2 M silver nitrate, $AgNO_3$, to each. Note the results.

7. (*Optional*) Mix in a single test tube about 1 ml of 0.1 M NaCl and 1 ml of 0.1 M K_2CrO_4. Add 0.2 M $AgNO_3$, one drop at a time, shaking the test tube after the addition of each drop.

Continue to add $AgNO_3$ solution until no further change is noted.

PART 3
Reactions

1. Label five test tubes 1, 2, 3, 4, and 5, and arrange them in a test tube rack. To each tube add the following, as shown in Table 8:

Table 8

Test tube	Add 5 ml of
1	6 M hydrochloric acid, HCl
2	6 M acetic acid, CH_3COOH
3	1 M HCl
4	1 M CH_3COOH
5	0.1 M HCl

The 1 M and 0.1 M HCl solutions can be made from the 6 M HCl by:

Mixing 1 ml of 6 M HCl with 5 ml of tap water. Add 5 ml of this solution (1 M HCl) to tube 3.

Mixing 1 ml of 1 M HCl (left over from above) to 9 ml of water. Add 5 ml of this (0.1 M HCl) to tube 5.

The 1 M CH_3COOH can be prepared in the same way as the 1 M HCl.

To each test tube add a small chip of calcium carbonate, $CaCO_3(s)$. Record the relative rates of reaction observed.

2. Heat about ¼ ml of powdered lead nitrate, $Pb(NO_3)_2$, in a Pyrex test tube. If a reaction occurs, remove the burner and observe what happens. After the material has cooled, reheat it.

3. Place about ½ ml of powdered lead dioxide, PbO_2, in a dry Pyrex test tube. Heat over a burner flame and note any changes. Light a wood splint, blow out the flame, and quickly put the glowing splint into the test tube so that its tip is just above the solid. How do you account for the results? Set the test tube aside to cool before you rinse it out.

PART 4
Teacher's Demonstration

(To be done in a fume hood.)

A small pile of ammonium dichromate, $(NH_4)_2Cr_2O_7$, on a transite board will be ignited with a burner. When the reaction starts, the burner will be removed. Describe what you see. Avoid inhaling the product.

Questions and regularities

1. In which of the experiments was there no evidence of chemical reaction?
2. Which chemical reactions produced a new phase?
3. Which reactions in this experiment were exothermic? Which were endothermic?
4. In which reactions did an increase in *temperature* alter the rate?
5. In which reactions did an increase in *concentration* alter the rate?

6. In Part 1, step 5, what effect did the $MnSO_4$ solution have on the rate of the reaction?
7. What evidence did you observe to indicate that in some of the reactions parts of the reactants were not used up?

FOR FURTHER THOUGHT

Why was there a difference in rate when solutions of hydrochloric acid and acetic acid—at the same concentration—reacted with $CaCO_3(s)$?

The crystalline state of matter consists of a regular arrangement of atoms, molecules, or ions. If we represent each building block as a point, then the crystal structure can be represented by a regularly repeating pattern called the *space lattice.*

In this experiment you will use *uniform* expanded polystyrene spheres as the building blocks to study some of the ways in which *uniform* metal atoms can be packed into typical metallic crystals. Three types of packing arrangements will be investigated:

1. hexagonal close-packing
2. cubic close-packing (also called face-centered cubic packing)
3. body-centered cubic packing

You will observe the number of nearest neighbors (the *coordination number*) of the particles in each of these structures.

In addition, you will investigate one way of packing spheres of *different radii* into lattices that represent ionic crystals, such as the crystals of NaCl or CsCl.

PROCEDURE

Obtain 27 2-inch and 13 1-inch expanded polystyrene spheres. Use toothpicks to connect the spheres.

PART 1

Some general considerations on packing of spheres

1. Determine how many 2-inch spheres you can pack around a marked 2-inch sphere in the same plane. Do you think this number is dependent on the size of the sphere? Check your prediction.

2. Place additional loose spheres above and below the marked sphere so that they all touch it. How many nearest neighbors does it have? In other words, what is the coordination number for this type of close packing?

3. Note that the three spheres in the top layer can occupy a position directly above the comparable bottom layer, or they can be rotated through an angle of 60° and still have the same coordination number.

PART 2

Model A: Hexagonal close-packing

1. Connect the groups of spheres you used in Part 1 with toothpicks to obtain the layers shown in Figure 44.

2. Place the layer of 3 spheres on the desk with the apex of the triangle facing you.

3. Now place the layer of 7 spheres over the 3 spheres in such a way that the center sphere fits closely into the depression of the bottom layer.

4. Place the other layer of 3 spheres over the center sphere of the second layer in such a way that they are oriented directly over those in the bottom layer.

If a pattern such as this were expanded into space until billions of atoms were involved, one would have a model of a very small crystal of a metal such as magnesium, zinc, or many other metals. Note the coordination number. Retain this model for use in Part 4.

PART 3

Model B: Cubic close-packing or face-centered cubic packing

1. Construct the layers illustrated in Figure 45 using 2-inch spheres and toothpicks as before.

Figure 44 Layers for hexagonal close packing.

Figure 45 Layers for cubic close packing.

Figure 46 Layers for body-centered cubic packing.

2. Place the first layer flat on the desk. Place the second layer on it in such a way that the spheres rest in the spaces between the corner spheres of the first layer. Now add the third layer in such a way that its spheres are directly over those in the first layer. Study the structure of this model carefully. Why is it called face-centered cubic? This is the packing that is found in copper, silver, aluminum, and many other metals.

PART 4
Comparison of hexagonal close-packing with cubic close-packing

1. Return to the hexagonal close-packing model A. Rearrange it in such a way that the top layer is not directly over the first layer but is rotated 60° with respect to it.

2. Rotate this model slightly and look for 4 spheres forming a square facing you. Now take the top layer from model B and place it on the 4 spheres you located on model A. Note that this new model contains a face-centered cube just like model B, but tilted toward you.

3. In light of the above comparison, is there a difference in coordination number in the two types of close packing? Is there a difference in density when spheres of comparable size and mass are involved in each of these types of packing? Most metals crystallize in only one, not both, of these forms. What does this indicate about the directional nature of bonds between atoms of these metals?

PART 5
Model C: Body-centered cubic packing

1. Construct the layers shown in Figure 46 using the 2-inch spheres from model A. Be sure to leave space of about ¼ inch between the spheres, as indicated.

2. Place the single sphere in the center of the first layer, and then place the third layer such that its spheres are directly over the first layer.

Study the symmetry of this model and justify its name. This type of packing is typical of the alkali metals, such as sodium and potassium. Can you suggest any reason, in terms of numbers of valence electrons, why Na and K crystallize in this form, while most other metals crystallize in a close-packed form?

3. Metallic iron crystallizes in the body-centered cubic form called α-ferrite below 906 °C. Above this temperature the stable form is γ-ferrite, which is face-centered cubic. At 1401 °C the crystal form changes back to a body-centered cubic solid called δ-ferrite. What is the coordination number of iron in each of these forms?

PART 6
The sodium chloride lattice

1. Ionic crystals are formed by packing positive and negative ions alternately into a lattice. The positive and negative ions usually differ in size. Sodium ions have a diameter of 1.90×10^{-10} metre while that of the chloride ions is 3.62×10^{-10} metre. We shall use 1-inch spheres for Na^+ and 2-inch spheres for Cl^- in our model, thus approximating their relative sizes.

2. Use model B from Part 3 with its 2-inch spheres for the face-centered cubic arrangement of the chloride ions. Now insert 13 1-inch spheres, representing sodium ions, into the holes between the chloride ions in each layer. Note that the Na^+Cl^- lattice is an interpenetrating set of face-centered cubes—one involving Na^+ and one involving Cl^-.

3. What type of ion surrounds each Na^+? Each Cl^-? What is the coordination number of the spheres representing Na^+, and of those representing Cl^-?

4. Note that in order to achieve this type of lattice, there must be a favorable relation between the relative radii of the two spheres that will permit a given sphere to fit into a given hole in the lattice. What is the radius ratio for Na^+/Cl^- ions? Can you account for the stability of this type of packing in terms of inter-ionic forces?

1. Write a brief description of each type of packing of metallic crystals that you studied.
2. Answer all questions raised in the Procedure section. Label them by parts and sections.
3. In one type of cubic packing, the spheres occupy about two-thirds of the space. In the other, they fill about three-fourths of the space available. Identify which type is which. Which is more dense? Which has the larger number of bonds?
4. Suppose you have a crystal XY, with the sodium chloride packing, in which each of the ions is the same size as the Na^+ and Cl^-, respectively. However, each ion is doubly charged, X^{++} and Y^{--}. Would XY have a higher or lower melting point than NaCl? Suggest a real pair of ions whose crystal meets the above criteria, and look up its melting point to check your prediction.
5. Suppose you have a crystal AB, with the sodium chloride packing, in which each of the ions has the same charge, A^+ and B^-, as Na^+ and Cl^-. The radii of A and B are proportionately larger, however. Would AB have a higher or lower melting point than NaCl? Suggest a real pair of ions whose crystal meets the above criteria, and look up its melting point to check your prediction.

The strong dipole of water, which causes it to be an excellent solvent for ionic substances, also causes water molecules to attach themselves to ions in solution. Such ions are called *hydrated ions*. When some solutions of hydrated ions are evaporated, the water molecules are so strongly attracted to the ions in solution that they remain attached as crystallization occurs. Water molecules are incorporated into the crystal structure. This water is called *water of hydration*.

Crystals that have formed in this way appear to be perfectly dry, yet when heated yield large quantities of water. The crystals change form, sometimes, even color, as the water is driven off. This indicates that the water was present as an integral part of the crystal structure. Such compounds are called *hydrates*. The number of moles of water present per mole of anhydrous salt is usually some simple number.

In this experiment you will be given an appropriate hydrate selected by your teacher. You will find the mass of water driven off by heating and the amount of anhydrous salt that remains. Your teacher will give you the formula of 1 mole of the anhydrous salt so you can find the empirical formula of the hydrate.

PROCEDURE

1. Place a clean, dry crucible with cover in a triangle mounted on an iron ring. Heat with a nonluminous flame for two or three minutes.

2. When the crucible and cover are cool enough to touch, transfer them to a balance. Find their mass to the nearest 0.01 g.

3. Put enough of the hydrate crystals in the crucible to fill it one-fourth to one-third full. Replace the cover and find the mass.

4. Place the covered crucible on the triangle and heat gently until most of the water has been driven off. Then increase the heat until the crucible bottom is at most a dull red. Maintain this temperature for five minutes. Allow the covered crucible to cool (in a desiccator if available).

5. When the covered crucible is cool enough to touch, transfer it to the balance and find the mass.

6. To make sure all the water is driven off, heat the crucible and cover to dull redness again. Cool and find the mass. If your results do not agree within 0.02 g, consult your instructor concerning further heating and weighing.

Your data should include the following information:

1. mass of crucible and cover
2. mass of crucible, cover, and hydrate
3. mass of crucible, cover, and anhydrous salt after first heating
4. mass of crucible, cover, and anhydrous salt after second heating
5. mass of 1 mole of anhydrous salt

Calculations and results

1. Calculate the number of moles of the anhydrous salt you prepared.
2. How many moles of water were associated with 1 mole of anhydrous salt?
3. Write the empirical formula for the hydrate.
4. Suggest reasons for weighing the crucible and anhydrous salt each time just as soon as the crucible has cooled, not before and not after.
5. Do your results agree exactly with those for a definite hydrate? If not, what are some plausible explanations for the deviation?
6. Suggest reasons why the above method might not be suitable for all hydrates.

In this experiment you will measure and compare the quantity of heat involved in three chemical reactions. As in Experiment 12, you will calculate the amount of energy after measuring the temperature change of a known quantity of water. An expanded polystyrene cup will serve as the calorimeter in this experiment. We will assume that the heat of reaction is used to change the temperature of the aqueous solution only. Any small heat losses to the surroundings will be neglected. We will also assume that the aqueous solution has the same heat capacity as water. That is, it takes 1 calorie to change the temperature of 1 g of solution 1°C.

You do not need to find the mass of the water used since 1.0 ml of water has a mass of 1.0 g (within experimental uncertainty), and you will measure the volume of water to the nearest millilitre. The reactions to be compared are:

1. Solid sodium hydroxide dissolves in water to form an aqueous solution of ions.

$$NaOH(s) \rightarrow Na^+(aq) + OH^-(aq) + x_1 cal$$

$$\Delta H_1 = -x_1 cal$$

2. Solid sodium hydroxide reacts with an aqueous solution of hydrogen chloride to form water and an aqueous solution of sodium chloride.

$$NaOH(s) + H^+(aq) + Cl^-(aq) \rightarrow$$

$$H_2O + Na^+(aq) + Cl^-(aq) + x_2 cal$$

$$\Delta H_2 = -x_2 cal$$

3. An aqueous solution of sodium hydroxide reacts with an aqueous solution of hydrogen chloride to form water and an aqueous solution of sodium chloride.

$$Na^+(aq) + OH^-(aq) + H^+(aq) + Cl^-(aq) \rightarrow$$

$$H_2O + Na^+(aq) + Cl^-(aq) + x_3 cal$$

$$\Delta H_3 = -x_3 cal$$

Note that the energy term is shown both as part of the equation and separately with the ΔH notation.

PROCEDURE

PART 1

Determination of the heat of reaction 1

Caution: Sodium hydroxide is extremely corrosive to the skin and may cause blindness if it gets into your eyes.

1. Put 200 (± 1) ml of cool tap water into an expanded polystyrene cup. Stir *carefully* with a thermometer until a constant temperature is reached (about room temperature). Measure this temperature as precisely as possible, and record it.

2. Obtain a sample of about 4 g of sodium hydroxide, NaOH(s), and determine its mass to the nearest ± 0.01 g. **Do not handle sodium hydroxide pellets with your fingers.** Since sodium hydroxide becomes moist in contact with the open air, your teacher will tell you how many pellets to use to get a sample of about 4 g (between 3.9 and 4.1 grams).

3. Pour the NaOH(s) into the water in the expanded polystyrene cup. Place the thermometer into the solution and stir *gently but continuously* until the sodium hydroxide is dissolved. Record the extreme temperature reached. Before proceeding to reaction 2, discard the solution and rinse the cup thoroughly with water.

PART 2

Determination of the heat of reaction 2

1. Repeat steps 1, 2, and 3 of Part 1, but substitute 200 ml of 0.50 *M* HCl for the tap water in step 1.

2. Discard the solution and rinse the cup before proceeding to reaction 3.

PART 3

Determination of the heat of reaction 3

1. Measure 100 ml of 1.0 *M* HCl into the expanded polystyrene cup and 100 ml of 1.0 *M* NaOH into a 250-ml beaker. Both of these solutions should be at, or slightly below, room temperature. Check this with the thermometer (rinse and dry the thermometer before changing from one solution to the other). Record the temperatures.

2. Add the sodium hydroxide solution to the hydrochloric acid solution in the expanded polystyrene cup. Mix quickly and record the extreme temperature reached.

Calculations and results

1. For each reaction, calculate: (a) the change in temperature; (b) the amount of heat absorbed by the solution; (c) the number of moles of NaOH used; and (d) the amount of heat evolved *per mole of NaOH*.

2. Express the above results as heats of reaction: ΔH_1, ΔH_2, and ΔH_3.

3. Write the net ionic equations for reactions 2 and 3.

4. In reaction 1, ΔH_1 represents the heat evolved as solid NaOH dissolves. Look at the net ionic equations for reactions 2 and 3 and make similar statements as to what ΔH_2 and ΔH_3 represent.

5. (a) Compare ΔH_2 with $(\Delta H_1 + \Delta H_3)$ and explain in terms of your answer to question 4. (b) Calculate the percentage difference between ΔH_2 and $(\Delta H_1 + \Delta H_3)$, assuming ΔH_2 to be correct (see Appendix 1, page 139).

6. Suppose you had used 8 g of NaOH(*s*) in reaction 1. (a) How would this have affected the change in temperature? (b) What would have been the number of calories evolved in your experiment? (c) What effect would this have had on your calculations of ΔH_1, the heat evolved *per mole*?

A study of reaction rates: The "clock reaction"

Do temperature and concentration changes alter the rate of chemical reaction? If so, to what extent? In this experiment you will investigate the role of concentration and temperature in the rate of a chemical reaction. You will perform some experiments with an interesting reaction called the "clock reaction." You will appreciate the significance of the name after you have completed your first determination. (An additional study of reaction rates is Experiment S-7, or pages 125–127.)

In order to determine the role of each factor independently, you will vary the concentration of one of the reacting species in Part 1 and vary the temperature in Part 2. In each case you will keep other possible variables—that is, "conditions that matter"—constant.

The clock reaction is performed by mixing the two solutions described below:

1. Solution A is a dilute solution of potassium iodate, KIO_3. This is the source of the iodate ion, $IO_3^-(aq)$.
2. Solution B contains some starch and the other reacting species, the hydrogen sulfite ion, $HSO_3^-(aq)$.

When the two solutions are thoroughly mixed, the ions of the resulting solution proceed through the following reactions:

$$IO_3^-(aq) + 3HSO_3^-(aq) \rightarrow$$
$$I^-(aq) + 3SO_4^{--}(aq) + 3H^+(aq) \quad (1)$$
$$5I^-(aq) + 6H^+(aq) + IO_3^-(aq) \rightarrow$$
$$3I_2(dissolved) + 3H_2O(l) \quad (2)$$
$$I_2(dissolved) + HSO_3^-(aq) + H_2O(l) \rightarrow$$
$$2I^-(aq) + SO_4^{--}(aq) + 3H^+(aq) \quad (3)$$
$$I_2(dissolved) + starch \rightarrow blue\ solution \quad (4)$$

The reactions take place in the manner outlined in the flow chart shown in Figure 47. Only when the $HSO_3^-(aq)$ has been entirely consumed in reactions 1, 2, and 3 will the $I_2(dissolved)$ react with the starch in reaction 4. The appearance of

the blue color indicates that all the $HSO_3^-(aq)$ has been consumed and I_2 remains in the solution.

PROCEDURE

PART 1

The effect of concentration changes

In order to study the effect on the reaction time of changing the concentration of one of the reactants, you will prepare dilutions of solution A to vary the concentration of the $IO_3^-(aq)$ ion. In each case the concentration of the $HSO_3^-(aq)$ ion will be kept constant. The temperature of the solutions should be that of the room. Your teacher will assign you certain concentrations. By exchanging results with other members of the class, you will be able to draw some conclusions about the effect of $IO_3^-(aq)$ ion concentration on reaction rate.

1. Use a clean, graduated cylinder to measure 10.0 ml of solution A. Pour it into a clean test tube (18 × 150 mm). Rinse the graduated cylinder and in a similar manner place 10.0 ml of solution B into another test tube. If the solutions have been in the laboratory for some time, you may assume that they are at room temperature. Otherwise, you should put the test tubes containing the solutions into a 250-ml beaker about two-thirds full of water at room temperature and let them stand for several minutes.

2. Using a watch with a second hand, record the time to the nearest second as you pour solution A into solution B. Pour them back and forth *quickly* three times to insure uniform mixing. Time should be recorded from the instant both solutions are in contact.

3. Watch the solution in the test tube carefully. Record the time at the first sign of a reaction.

4. Repeat the experiment to check your results, if directed to do so by your teacher.

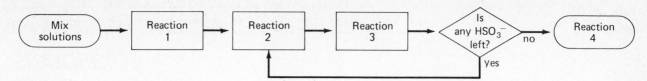

Figure 47 A flow chart for the "clock reaction."

Prepare different concentrations of the KIO_3 solution by diluting solution A as shown in Table 9. Do as many dilutions as your teacher directs. Note that the total volume is always 10.0 ml. Mix each of the diluted solutions well.

Repeat the procedure by adding one diluted solution of KIO_3 to 10.0 ml of solutions B, both at room temperature.

PART 2

The effect of temperature

In order to investigate the effect of changes in temperature, you will determine the time required for this reaction at room temperature and at other temperatures within a range of ±20 °C. Your teacher will assign particular temperatures for you and your partner to use.

By exchanging results with other members of the class, you will be able to draw some conclusions about the effect of temperature on the time of reaction.

1. Put 10.0 ml of solution A (labeled for Part 2) into one test tube (18 × 150 mm) and 10.0 ml of solution B into another. These solutions must be brought to the desired temperature before they are mixed. Put both test tubes into a 250-ml beaker about two-thirds full of water and adjusted to the temperature you were assigned to investigate. Let them stand for about 10 minutes so the solutions will come to the temperature of the water bath. If the same thermometer is used for measuring the temperatures of the two solutions, be sure to rinse it carefully between uses.

2. Using a watch with a second hand, record the time to the nearest second as you pour solution A into solution B. Immediately mix the solutions by pouring them back and forth *quickly* three times. Time should be recorded from the instant both solutions are in contact.

3. Place the test tube back in the water bath and observe it carefully. Record the time at the first sign of a reaction.

4. Repeat the experiment at the same or another temperature if directed to do so by your teacher.

Calculations and results for part 1

1. Your teacher will tell you the concentration of solution A. Calculate the concentration of KIO_3 in moles per litre in each of the solutions after all the components (A + B + H_2O) have been mixed.
2. Why is it important to keep the total volume at 10 ml during the dilutions of solution A?
3. Plot a graph of the concentration-time data with time on the vertical axis and the concentration of the KIO_3 on the horizontal axis. Use the data of other members of the class also.
4. What generalizations can you make concerning the effect on the time of the reaction resulting from varying the concentration?
5. How is the time of the reaction related to the rate of the reaction?

Calculations and results for part 2

1. Using your data and that of other members of the class, plot a graph of the temperature-time data with temperature on the horizontal axis and time on the vertical axis.
2. What general relationships can you derive from the graph of calculation 1?
3. Make a prediction of the time of the reaction at 0 °C and at 50 °C, assuming that the other variables in the experiment are held constant.

Table 9

Solution A	Distilled water
9.0 ml	1.0 ml
8.0 ml	2.0 ml
7.0 ml	3.0 ml
and so on	

This experiment is a short introduction to the qualitative aspects of chemical equilibrium. Starting with a reaction at equilibrium, you will change the concentrations of various ions that are present and note the effect on the state of equilibrium. The equilibrium reaction chosen for study has a colored product, so changes in its concentration can be readily detected by a corresponding change in color intensity.

PROCEDURE

1. Put about 25 ml of 0.0020 *M* potassium thiocyanate solution, KSCN, and 25 ml of distilled water into a beaker. Obtain a solution of 0.20 *M* ferric nitrate, $Fe(NO_3)_3$, in a dropper bottle. Describe each solution.

2. Add 5 to 6 drops of the $Fe(NO_3)_3$ solution to the beaker. Swirl the mixture and describe the results.

3. Obtain a bottle containing a solution of potassium nitrate, KNO_3. Describe the appearance of the solution.

4. Pour equal amounts of the solution from the beaker into four numbered Petri dishes. Place the dishes over a piece of white paper.

The solution in the first dish will be the reference solution. To the second dish add 2 to 3 small crystals of solid KSCN. Describe the results.

5. To the third dish add 3 drops of the $Fe(NO_3)_3$ solution. Stir and describe the results.

6. To the fourth dish add 5 to 10 small crystals of Na_2HPO_4, a few at a time. Stir between additions and describe the results.

Questions and regularities

1. For *each* solution in step 1, what ions are present?
2. What *possible* combination of ions could account for the results in step 2?
3. What ions are present in the potassium nitrate solution?
4. Could the ions in potassium nitrate be responsible for the change noted in step 2? Explain.
5. Considering your answer to question 4, what ions must be responsible for the change noted in step 2?
6. Other experiments have shown that the formula for the colored complex ion is $FeSCN^{++}(aq)$. Use your answer to question 5 to write the equation for its formation.
7. How does the addition of the KSCN in step 4 affect the concentration of the $SCN^-(aq)$ ion?
8. What effect does the addition of KSCN in step 4 have on the concentration of the $FeSCN^{++}(aq)$ ion?
9. How does the addition of $Fe(NO_3)_3$ solution in step 5 affect the concentration of the $Fe^{+++}(aq)$ ion?
10. What effect does the addition of $Fe(NO_3)_3$ solution in step 5 have on the concentration of the $FeSCN^{++}(aq)$ ion?
11. Other experiments have shown that the $Fe^{+++}(aq)$ ion can readily combine with $HPO_4^{--}(aq)$ ions. This combination usually appears as a very slightly milky solution. (a) What effect does addition of $HPO_4^{--}(aq)$ ions (from the Na_2HPO_4) in step 6 have on the concentration of the $Fe^{+++}(aq)$ ion in the solution? (b) What effect does it have on the concentration of the $FeSCN^{++}(aq)$ ion?

Chemical equilibrium: Quantitative aspects

In this experiment you will take a *quantitative* look at the reaction of Experiment 21:

$$Fe^{+++}(aq) + SCN^-(aq) \rightleftharpoons FeSCN^{++}(aq)$$

This time you will determine the concentration of each of the ions at equilibrium, and then seek a mathematical expression that relates these quantities in a simple, convenient manner.

The initial concentrations of the reacting ions will be calculated from dilution data, and the equilibrium concentrations of $FeSCN^{++}(aq)$ ion will be determined colorimetrically. If you have ever looked critically at a glass full of a colored liquid, such as cherry soda or iced tea, you know that the color intensity as viewed through the sides of the glass is much less than the color intensity as viewed from the top. This is because the color intensity depends upon the concentration of the colored substance and the depth of the solution. Thus, a 1-cm depth of a 1 *M* colored solution will appear to have the same color intensity as a 2-cm depth of a 0.5 *M* solution of the same material.

The concentration of two such solutions may be compared by altering their relative depths until the color intensity appears the same. The ratio of the concentrations is found to be the inverse of the ratio of the depths. Note that this procedure gives only relative values for the concentrations. To get absolute values a standard solution of known concentration must be used.

In preparing the standard solution in step 2 of this experiment, you will use a low, known concentration of thiocyanate ion, $SCN^-(aq)$, and add a large excess of iron(III) ion, $Fe^{+++}(aq)$. You can assume that essentially all of the thiocyanate ion will be used in forming the complex thiocyanato iron(III) ion, $FeSCN^{++}(aq)$, and that the equilibrium concentration of the $FeSCN^{++}(aq)$ ion will be essentially the same as the concentration of the $SCN^-(aq)$ ion with which you started. This is true only in solution 1, however.

PROCEDURE

PRELAB ASSIGNMENT

Before coming to the laboratory, study the dilution procedure outlined in steps 1, 2, and 3 of the procedure. The flow chart shown in Figure 48 may be helpful in understanding the dilution scheme. Calculate the following concentrations:

1. The concentration of the $SCN^-(aq)$ ion in each of the vials *before any reaction takes place*. Each vial has 5.0 ml of 0.00200 *M* KSCN diluted by an equal volume of $Fe(NO_3)_3$ solution.
2. The concentration of $Fe^{+++}(aq)$ ion in each of the vials *before any reaction takes place*. Make sure you distinguish between the $Fe^{+++}(aq)$ ion concentration in the beaker and the $Fe^{+++}(aq)$ ion concentration in the vial. They are not the same.

Arrange your data sheet so that as you match the color intensities of the standard solution with each of the other four solutions, you can record the depth of the standard solution and of the solution in the other vial.

IN THE LABORATORY

1. Line up five dry, flat-bottomed vials and label them 1, 2, 3, 4, and 5. To each vial add 5.0 ml of 0.00200 *M* potassium thiocyanate, which is written as 2.00×10^{-3} *M* KSCN.

2. To vial 1 add 5.0 ml of 0.200 *M* iron(III) nitrate, which is written as 2.00×10^{-1} *M* $Fe(NO_3)_3$. This vial will be used as the standard.

3. Measure 10.0 ml of 0.200 *M* $Fe(NO_3)_3$ in your graduated cylinder and fill to the 25.0-ml mark with distilled water. Pour the solution into a clean, dry beaker to mix it. Measure 5.0 ml of this solution and pour it into vial 2. Save the remainder of the $Fe(No_3)_3$ solution for step 4.

4. Pour 10.0 ml of the solution from the beaker into your graduate. Discard the rest. Fill the graduate to the 25.0-ml mark with distilled water, and pour the solution into a clean, dry

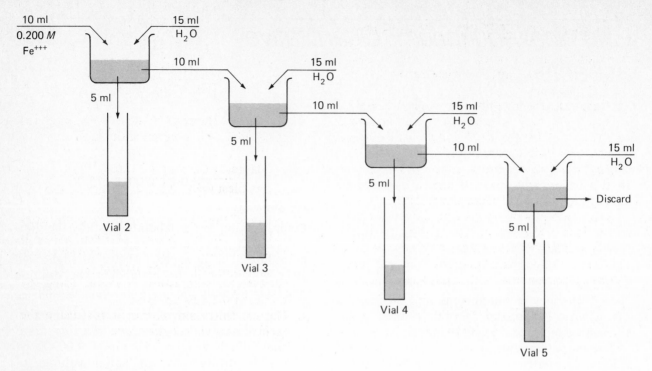

Figure 48 Dilution scheme for Fe^{+++} solution. Each vial contains 5 ml of 0.00200 M KSCN already.

beaker to mix. Pour 5.0 ml of this solution into vial 3.

5. Continue dilution in this manner until you have 5.0 ml of successively more dilute solution in each vial.

6. The problem is to compare the color intensity of the solutions in each of the vials with that of the solution in the standard vial (vial 1) in order to determine the concentration of the thiocyanato iron(III) ion, $FeSCN^{++}(aq)$.

Wrap a strip of paper around vials 1 and 2 to block out light entering from the side. Look vertically down through the solutions toward a diffused light source. Even if the color intensities appear the same, remove some of the solution from the standard vial (into a clean, dry beaker) with a medicine dropper until the color intensity of the standard vial is definitely less than that of vial 2.

Now put some of the solution back into the *standard vial*, drop by drop. When the color intensities are the same in both vials, measure and record the depth of both solutions as precisely as possible.

7. Repeat the procedure with vials 1 and 3, 1 and 4, and finally 1 and 5.

Calculations and results

1. Assume in your calculations that: (a) The iron(III) nitrate and the potassium thiocyanate exist in their respective solutions entirely as ions. (b) In the standard vial No. 1, essentially all the thiocyanate ions have reacted to form thiocyanato iron(III) complex ions. Also remember that *both* solutions are diluted on mixing.

2. The symbol [ ] will be used to represent the equilibrium concentration in moles per litre. The formula within the bracket denotes the species. Thus, the notation $[Fe^{+++}]$ stands for the equilibrium concentration of iron(III) ion, $Fe^{+++}(aq)$, in moles per litre.

3. Do all the calculations for each vial through 5 as follows: (a) Calculate the ratio of the depths in the color comparison. For example:

$$\text{ratio} = \frac{\begin{array}{c}\text{depth of liquid in standard vial}\\\text{(matched with vial 2)}\end{array}}{\text{depth of liquid in vial 2}}$$

(b) From each ratio, calculate the equilibrium concentration of the thiocyanato iron(III) ion, $[FeSCN^{++}]$:

$$[FeSCN^{++}] = \left\{\begin{array}{c}\text{ratio}\\\text{of depth}\end{array}\right\} \times \left\{\begin{array}{c}\text{concentration}\\\text{of standard}\end{array}\right\}$$

4. Calculate the equilibrium concentration of $Fe^{+++}(aq)$ ion, $[Fe^{+++}]$, by subtracting the equilibrium concentration of $FeSCN^{++}(aq)$ ion from the initial concentration of the $Fe^{+++}(aq)$ ion.

5. Calculate the equilibrium concentration of the $SCN^-(aq)$ ion, $[SCN^-]$, in the same manner as for the $Fe^{+++}(aq)$ ion. Subtract the equilibrium concentration of $FeSCN^{++}(aq)$ ion from the initial concentration of the $SCN^-(aq)$ ion.

6. Now try to find some constant numerical relationship between the equilibrium concentrations of the ions in each vial by multiplying and dividing the values obtained for each vial in various combinations. For example, for each of the vials 2 through 5 calculate:

(a) $$\frac{[Fe^{+++}]\,[FeSCN^{++}]}{[SCN^-]}$$

(b) $$\frac{[FeSCN^{++}]}{[Fe^{+++}]\,[SCN^-]}$$

(c) $$\frac{[FeSCN^{++}]}{[Fe^{+++}] + [SCN^-]}$$

7. For each of the combinations (a) through (c) of calculation 6, determine the ratio

$$\frac{\text{largest value (vials 2 through 5)}}{\text{smallest value (vials 2 through 5)}}$$

8. Which of the combinations of concentrations (a), (b), or (c) gives the most constant numerical value? This form is known as the equilibrium constant expression.

9. Restate this expression in words, using the names of the ions involved.

10. Restate this expression in words, using the terms reactants and products.

Solubility product constant of lead chloride

In this experiment, you will determine the equilibrium concentration of lead ions in a saturated solution of lead chloride at room temperature. From this data, you will then calculate the K_{sp} of lead chloride.

The reaction between $Zn(s)$ and $Pb^{++}(aq)$ is the same one that you studied in Experiment 8. In a saturated solution, the ions in solution are in equilibrium with the solid. The rate at which ions are leaving the solid crystal is equal to the rate at which they are returning to the crystal.

$$PbCl_2(s) \rightleftharpoons Pb^{++}(aq) + 2Cl^-(aq)$$

The concentrations of the ionic species, $Pb^{++}(aq)$ and $Cl^-(aq)$, when no net change is taking place, determine the equilibrium solubility. The equilibrium constant expression for this reaction is

$$K_{sp} = [Pb^{++}] [Cl^-]^2$$

If pure lead chloride is dissolved, the concentration of chloride ions is twice the concentration of lead ions. Thus, the solubility product constant can be calculated after experimentally determining the equilibrium concentration of either ion.

PROCEDURE

1. In a 100-ml graduated cylinder, carefully measure 100 ml of saturated lead chloride solution. Pour the solution into a clean, dry 250-ml beaker.

2. Obtain a zinc strip, approximately 10 cm × 1 cm. Clean the surface of the strip with emery paper, and find its mass to the nearest 0.01 g.

3. Place the zinc strip in the beaker containing the lead chloride solution. Allow the system to stand overnight so that all of the lead ions will have an opportunity to react.

4. Shake the lead particles free from the zinc strip by tapping the zinc strip against the side of the beaker. Wash off any lead particles that adhere to the zinc strip by using a stream of distilled water from your wash bottle. Use a spatula to loosen any particularly difficult lead deposits.

5. Finally, wash the zinc strip in a stream of water from the tap. Then rinse the zinc strip with acetone, and find its mass when it is dry.

Calculations and results

1. Calculate the number of moles of $Zn(s)$ that reacted with the lead ions in solution.
2. Recall the relationship between $Zn(s)$ and $Pb^{++}(aq)$ obtained in Experiment 8. How many moles of lead ions were present in the 100-ml sample?
3. What is the concentration of the lead ions in moles per litre?
4. What is the concentration of the chloride ions in moles per litre?
5. Calculate the value of K_{sp} for lead chloride at room temperature.
6. If 100 ml of 0.02 M $Pb(NO_3)_2$ is mixed with 100 ml of 0.02 M NaCl, would a precipitate of $PbCl_2$ be expected to form? In your calculations, use the value of K_{sp} you obtained in question 5.
7. If some solid NaCl is added to a saturated solution of $PbCl_2$, what will be the effect of the increased concentration of the chloride ion on the equilibrium?

$$PbCl_2(s) \rightleftharpoons Pb^{++}(aq) + 2Cl^-(aq)$$

8. Calculate the $[Pb^{++}]$ if the $[Cl^-]$ in question 7 is 1.0 M.

Le Chatelier's principle

In this experiment you will study some reactions in which there is appreciable reversibility and in which the presence of the reactants and products can be readily observed by noting color changes or the formation of a precipitate. Most of the chemical reactions you have observed in the laboratory seem to have gone to completion—that is, all the reactants appear to have been used up to form the products. Actually, all chemical reactions are reversible, even though the extent of reversibility may sometimes be very small. In many reactions that you will encounter in the laboratory you must concern yourself with their reversibility and the possibilities of controlling the extent of reversibility.

In an aqueous solution the chromate ion, $CrO_4^{--}(aq)$, can be converted to the dichromate ion, $Cr_2O_7^{--}(aq)$. Conversely, the $Cr_2O_7^{--}(aq)$ ion can be converted to the $CrO_4^{--}(aq)$ ion. The extent to which these reactions occur is dependent upon the concentration of the hydrogen ion, $H^+(aq)$, in the solution. The $H^+(aq)$ concentration can be increased by adding a source of $H^+(aq)$—hydrochloric acid, HCl. The $H^+(aq)$ concentration can be decreased by adding a solution of sodium hydroxide, NaOH, which contains the hydroxide ion, $OH^-(aq)$. The $OH^-(aq)$ reacts with the $H^+(aq)$ to form H_2O.

PROCEDURE

PART 1

The chromate-dichromate equilibrium

1. A 0.1 M potassium chromate (K_2CrO_4) solution and a 0.1 M potassium dichromate ($K_2Cr_2O_7$) solution will serve as sources for the ions, $CrO_4^{--}(aq)$ and $Cr_2O_7^{--}(aq)$. Record the color of each solution.

2. Place 10 drops (about 1/2 ml) of each solution into separate 13 × 100 mm test tubes. Add 1 M sodium hydroxide, NaOH, alternately to each test tube one drop at a time. Record the color

changes observed. Retain these test tubes for step 5.

3. Repeat the procedure of step 2 with fresh solutions in clean test tubes, but add 1 M hydrochloric acid, HCl, drop by drop alternately to each test tube. Record the color changes observed. Retain these test tubes for step 4.

4. Add 1 M NaOH, drop by drop, to one of the tubes obtained in step 3 until a change is noted.

5. Add 1 M HCl, drop by drop, to one of the test tubes obtained in step 2 until a change is noted.

Calculations and results

1. (a) How does the chromate-dichromate equilibrium depend on hydrogen ions? Explain in terms of your data. (b) Balance the equation for the chromate-dichromate equilibrium by adding the proper number of $H^+(aq)$ ions and H_2O molecules to the appropriate sides of the equation. (c) Use Le Chatelier's principle to explain the color changes in steps 3 and 5.
2. (a) How does the dichromate-chromate equilibrium depend on hydroxide ions? Explain in terms of your data. (b) Balance the equation for the dichromate-chromate equilibrium by adding the proper number of $OH^-(aq)$ ions and H_2O molecules to the appropriate sides of the equation. (c) Use Le Chatelier's principle to explain the color changes in steps 2 and 4.

PART 2

The equilibrium between solid barium chromate, $BaCrO_4(s)$, and a saturated solution of its ions

1. Place 10 drops of 0.1 M K_2CrO_4 in a clean test tube. Add 2 drops of 1 M NaOH. Add 0.1 M barium nitrate, $Ba(NO_3)_2$, one drop at a time, until a change is noted. Record the result. Retain this test tube and solution for step 4.

2. Place 10 drops of 0.1 M $K_2Cr_2O_7$ in a clean test tube. Add 2 drops of 1 M HCl, then 10 drops of 0.1 M Ba(NO$_3$)$_2$. Record the result. Retain this test tube and solution for step 5.

3. Record your conclusions about the relative solubilities of BaCrO$_4$(s) and BaCr$_2$O$_7$(s) from your observations in steps 1 and 2.

4. To the solution saved from step 1, add 1 M HCl, drop by drop, until a change is noted. Record your observations.

5. To the solution saved from step 2, add 1 M NaOH, drop by drop, until a change is noted. Record your observations.

6. Suggest a way to reverse the changes and reactions you observed in step 4. Do the same for step 5. Try these experiments.

7. Place 10 drops of 0.1 M K$_2$Cr$_2$O$_7$ in a clean test tube and the same amount of 0.1 M K$_2$CrO$_4$ in another clean test tube. Add a few drops of 0.1 M Ba(NO$_3$)$_2$ to each. Record your observations.

Calculations and results

1. (a) Write the equation for the equilibrium reaction between solid BaCrO$_4$ and its ions. (b) Using the above equation, those you balanced in calculations 1b and 2b of Part 1, and Le Chatelier's principle, explain the results you obtained in steps 3, 4, and 5 of Part 2.

2. From your observations in step 7, what can you conclude about the relative equilibrium concentrations of CrO$_4$$^{--}$($aq$) ion in each of the solutions 0.1 M K$_2$Cr$_2$O$_7$ and 0.1 M K$_2$CrO$_4$ *before* the Ba(NO$_3$)$_2$ solution is added?

PART 3

Additional experiments on the chromate-dichromate equilibrium

1. Place 10 drops (about 1/2 ml) of K$_2$Cr$_2$O$_7$ solution in a clean test tube and 10 drops of K$_2$CrO$_4$ solution in another clean test tube. Add 4 to 5 drops of 1 M acetic acid (CH$_3$COOH) to each test tube. Record any changes in color.

2. Repeat step 1, using fresh solutions of K$_2$Cr$_2$O$_7$ and K$_2$CrO$_4$ each time. Test, in turn, 4 to 5 drops of 1 M solutions of each of the following: nitric acid, HNO$_3$; potassium hydroxide, KOH; ethyl alcohol, C$_2$H$_5$OH; lithium hydroxide, LiOH; and ammonia, NH$_3$. Record any changes in color.

Calculations and results

1. (a) Which substances caused the color to change from that of the Cr$_2$O$_7$$^{--}$ (aq) ion to that of the CrO$_4$$^{--}$($aq$) ion? (b) Which substances caused the color to change from that of the CrO$_4$$^{--}$($aq$) ion to that of the Cr$_2O_7$$^{--}$($aq$) ion?

2. What ions do the solutions you listed in calculation 1a have in common? Answer the same question for the solutions listed in calculation 1b.

3. Give an explanation for the results noted when (a) ethyl alcohol, C$_2$H$_5$OH, was added; (b) the solution of aqueous ammonia, NH$_3$(aq), was added.

4. On the basis of your answers to calculation 2, predict some additional substances that might have the same effect on the chromate-dichromate equilibrium as those categorized in calculations 1a and 1b.

Quantitative titration

Titration is the name given to the process for determining the volume of a solution needed to react with a given mass or volume of a sample. You will use this process to study quantitatively the reaction between an acid and a base. A common reaction in water solution is that of the hydrogen ion of an acid with the hydroxide ion of a base to form water. Phenolphthalein will be used as the indicator in this experiment since its color change occurs when the same number of moles of acid and base have been added. This point in the reaction is called the *end point*.

P R O C E D U R E

Using hydrochloric acid of known concentration, you will first standardize a sodium hydroxide solution—that is, determine its concentration expressed as moles per litre. Using the standard base, you will then titrate a known mass of an unknown solid acid and calculate the number of grams of this acid that will react with one mole of the base. After this experimental value has been determined, your teacher will tell you the formula of the acid. You will then write the equation for the reaction. From the equation, you will calculate the value for the number of grams of acid that will react with one mole of the base. You will then compare this value with the experimental value.

PART 1

Standardization of the solution of a base

1. Obtain two burets. See the section on the care of burets at the end of this experiment. Clean the burets and rinse one with 10 ml of the standard hydrochloric acid. Rinse the other with 10 ml of the sodium hydroxide solution you are *instructed to use*. If there are not enough burets, you will use pipets to measure the volume of acid (see Experiment 13 for an explanation of their use). After rinsing the burets, fill the first with

the standard acid and the second with the base. See Figure 50, on page 73.

2. Record the liquid level in each buret by reading the bottom of each meniscus to the nearest 0.1 ml. Let about 10 ml of hydrochloric acid flow into a clean 250-ml Erlenmeyer flask. Add about 15 ml of distilled water and 3 drops of phenolphthalein.

3. Hold the neck of the Erlenmeyer flask with one hand and manipulate the buret with the other. As you add the sodium hydroxide, gently swirl the flask so the solutions will become mixed. Continue adding sodium hydroxide until the first faint pink color develops. If the color disappears upon mixing the solution, add more sodium hydroxide, drop by drop, until a persistent pink color is obtained. If you go beyond this endpoint, you may add a few drops of acid, and then complete the titration with a few more drops of sodium hydroxide. (Take care not to go beyond the last calibration marks on the buret.) Record the liquid level at the bottom of the meniscus of each buret. Rinse the Erlenmeyer flask thoroughly before repeating the titration.

4. Refill the burets with the proper solutions and perform at least one more titration. Repeat until you obtain ratios of volume of acid to volume of base that agree to 1 percent or 2 percent.

PART 2

Titration of an unknown acid

1. Obtain a solid unknown acid from your teacher. Find the mass of the vial or test tube containing the sample to the nearest ±0.01 g. Remove a suitable amount (about 0.7 g, or as directed by your teacher) of the solid acid into a clean flask, as shown in Figure 49. Find the mass of the vial and contents again. Dissolve the sample in 50 ml of distilled water, and add 3 drops of phenolphthalein. If all the acid does not dissolve at this point, it will dissolve later during the titration when the acid will be converted to the more soluble sodium salt.

2. Refill the proper buret with some of the solution of base used previously, and record the initial reading. Add the base to the acid solution until the first persistent, faint pink color appears. Be careful not to overrun the endpoint. If you

pass the endpoint, add a little more of the solid acid and reweigh the vial. Be sure to include the mass of any solid acid added to the mass of your sample. Retitrate to the endpoint, and record the final buret reading.

3. Repeat the titration with a similar sample. Use the knowledge you gained in the first titration. That is, assuming you used 40 ml of base to titrate a certain mass of acid, and that you have almost the same mass of acid for the second trial, you can run 35 ml of base into the flask rapidly and complete the last part of the titration cautiously.

PART 3

Optional titration

If time permits, you may bring from home commercially available household acidic or basic substances to titrate with either your standard acid or base. Examples of items readily available are lemon juice, vinegar, household ammonia, and washing powders. Determinations that are possible are the percent acetic acid, CH_3COOH, in vinegar; the percent citric acid, $C_6H_8O_7$, in lemon juice; the percent ammonia, NH_3, in household ammonia. If you need help in deciding on sample size or the proper indicator, ask your teacher.

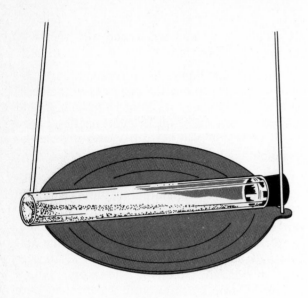

Figure 49 Finding the mass of a sample and transferring it to a flask.

Calculations and results

1. From the concentration given and the volume used, calculate the number of moles of hydrochloric acid involved in each titration of Part 1.
2. Use the equation for the reaction to calculate the number of moles of base that are used per mole of acid in Part 1.
3. From the relationship of calculation 2, determine the number of moles of base actually used.
4. Calculate the molar concentration of the base.
5. From the mass of the solid acid and the volumes involved in its titration in Part 2, calculate the mass of the solid unknown acid that will react with 1 mole of the base.
6. Use the formula of the acid (from your teacher) and the equation for the reaction to calculate the theoretical value for the mass of the acid that will react with 1 mole of the base.
7. Determine the percentage error, using the value determined in calculation 6 as the accepted value.

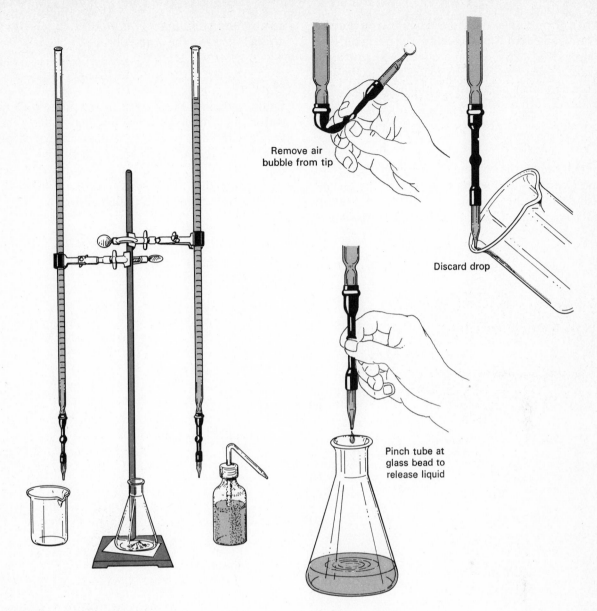

Remove air
bubble from tip

Discard drop

Pinch tube at
glass bead to
release liquid

Figure 50 Titration techniques.

8. (*Optional*) Calculate the percentage of acid or base in the household product used in Part 3.

Care of burets

CLEANING

Place a few millilitres of a detergent solution into a buret, then use a buret brush to clean the inside surface. Rinse well, first with tap water and then with distilled water. After draining the buret, note if there are any droplets still adhering to the sides of the tube. If there are, the glass is not thoroughly cleaned and should be rewashed. When glass is clean, water wets it evenly.

PREPARING FOR USE

After cleaning a buret, add 5 ml to 10 ml of the solution that is to be used in that buret. Let several millilitres of solution flow through the tip. Turn the buret to a horizontal position and with a rotary motion, slowly pour the rest of the solution out of the top. Make sure that the solution wets the inside completely. For a more complete rinsing, repeat the above.

Fill the buret to the top with the solution to be used. Permit air bubbles in the tip to escape by turning the tip upward, as shown in Figure 50. Let the solution flow from the tip until the bottom of the meniscus is at zero or below.

If a drop hangs on the tip before you start a titration, discard it by touching it to a beaker (see Figure 50). However, a drop formed *during* a titration must be caught by touching it to the side of the container being used and rinsing it into the container with distilled water.

READING THE VOLUME

When reading the volume on the buret, be sure to have your eye level with the bottom of the meniscus and read the volume carefully at the bottom of the curve (see Figure 36). In each titration use an absolute minimum of 10 ml of each solution to attain a precision of 1 percent.

AFTER USE

Drain and rinse the buret several times with tap water. As a final rinse, use distilled water. Glass reacts with basic solutions, so take special care in rinsing a buret that has had such solutions in it. A rinse with dilute acid after one water rinse will help assure that the base is removed. Follow this with the water rinses described above.

In this experiment, by using appropriate indicators, you will determine the $[H^+]$ of an unknown solution by comparing the color of the unknown solution with the color of the standard solutions. You will also determine the hydrogen ion concentration of a solution of a weak acid and calculate its equilibrium constant.

Acid-base indicators are dyes whose colors depend upon the hydrogen ion concentration, $[H^+]$, of a solution. There are numerous dyes that are suitable for this purpose, and each one changes color over a particular range of hydrogen ion concentration. You are already familiar with one dye, phenolphthalein, which is colorless when $[H^+] = 10^{-8}$ M or greater, and purple when $[H^+] = 10^{-10}$ M or less.

In this experiment you will use two indicators that have color changes in the acid range, methyl orange and orange IV, and two indicators for the basic range, indigo carmine and alizarin yellow R.

First, you will make up a series of standard acidic solutions with known concentration of $H^+(aq)$ by diluting a solution of a strong acid, 0.1 M HCl. Second, you will prepare a series of standard basic solutions by diluting a solution of a base, 0.1 M NaOH. These solutions will be your standards.

You will work in pairs during Part 1 of this experiment. Student A will prepare the standard acidic solutions and student B will prepare the standards for the basic range. Label the test tubes so that each of you can use the standards to determine the $[H^+]$ of an unknown solution in Part 2 and of acetic acid in Part 3.

PROCEDURE

PART 1

The preparation of standard solutions

(*Student A: The Acid Range: [H⁺] = 10⁻¹ M to 10⁻⁴ M*)

1. Obtain about 5 ml of 0.1 M HCl in a clean, dry 13 × 100-mm test tube. Label this test tube

"$[H^+] = 0.1$ M." Since hydrochloric acid is a strong acid, it can be assumed to be completely ionized in this dilute solution.

2. Prepare some 0.01 M HCl by diluting one volume of 0.1 M HCl with nine volumes of distilled water. Use a calibrated pipet or a 10-ml graduated cylinder. An appropriate volume to use would be 1.0 ml of 0.1 M HCl and 9.0 ml of distilled water. Thoroughly mix this solution and label it "$[H^+] = 0.01$ M, or 10^{-2} M."

3. In a similar manner prepare 10 ml of 0.001 M HCl by diluting some of the standard solution prepared in step 2. Mix it thoroughly and label it "$[H^+] = 0.001$ M, or 10^{-3} M."

4. Finally prepare 10 ml of 0.0001 M HCl by diluting some of the standard solution prepared in step 3. Mix it thoroughly and label it "$[H^+] = 0.0001$ M, or 10^{-4} M."

5. Pour about half of each standard solution into another clean test tube so that you will have two sets of standards. Label each new test tube with the $[H^+]$ of the solution it contains. For one set of standards, add 2 drops of orange IV solution to each of the 4 test tubes. For the other set, add 2 drops of methyl orange solution to each test tube.

6. Make a table for recording the colors observed in each of the solutions for the various $[H^+]$. *Retain these standards for Parts 2 and 3.*

(*Student B: The Basic Range: [OH⁻] = 10⁻¹ M to 10⁻⁴ M*)

Follow the directions of steps 1, 2, 3, and 4, except to prepare the solutions in the basic range, use 0.1 M NaOH instead of 0.1 M HCl.

Since sodium hydroxide is a strong electrolyte, a dilute solution of NaOH can be considered completely ionized. The hydroxide ion concentration of 0.1 M NaOH is 0.1 M, or 10^{-1} M.

Label the solutions prepared according to steps 2, 3, and 4 as "$[OH^-] = 10^{-2}$ M," "$[OH^-] = 10^{-3}$ M," and "$[OH^-] = 10^{-4}$ M," respectively.

7. Divide the solutions to obtain two sets of the four standards, as outlined in step 5. For one set, add 2 drops of the indigo carmine solution to each of the 4 test tubes. To the other set, add 2 drops of alizarin yellow R solution to each test tube.

8. Make a table for recording the colors observed in each of the solutions for the various [H$^+$]. *Retain these standards for use in Part 2.*

PART 2

The determination of the [H$^+$] of an unknown aqueous solution

(*To be done individually.*)

1. Obtain about 5 ml of an unknown solution from your teacher. Place it in a clean, dry test tube. Test a portion of it with litmus paper to determine whether the [H$^+$] is in the acidic or basic range. Remember that litmus is pink in acidic solutions and blue in basic solutions.

2. Place about 2 ml of the unknown solution into each of two small test tubes. If the solution is acidic, add 2 drops of orange IV solution to one test tube and 2 drops of methyl orange to the other test tube. If the solution is basic, use the indicators indigo carmine and alizarin yellow R.

3. Compare the colors with those of the standards prepared by either you or your partner. Record the hydrogen ion concentration of the unknown solution.

PART 3

The determination of the hydrogen ion concentration of a solution of a weak acid: Acetic acid, CH$_3$COOH

1. Obtain about 5 ml of a solution of acetic acid in a small, clean, dry test tube. Note and record the concentration. Some students will use a 0.1 *M* solution and others will use a 1.0 *M* solution. *Be sure you record the concentration of the acid you use.*

2. Place about 2 ml of the acetic acid solution assigned to you into each of two small, clean test tubes. Add 2 drops of orange IV solution to one test tube and 2 drops of methyl orange solution to the other.

3. Compare the colors with those of the standards containing the same indicators. Estimate and record the [H$^+$] of the acetic acid solution as accurately as you can.

Calculations and results

1. Calculate the equilibrium constant for acetic acid, CH$_3$COOH, a weak acid.

$$CH_3COOH \rightleftharpoons H^+(aq) + CH_3COO^-(aq)$$

Use the value for [H$^+$] determined in Part 3. You may assume that the concentration of the acetate ion, [CH$_3$COO$^-$], is equal to the [H$^+$] and that the concentration of acetic acid is essentially the concentration of the solution you used, either 0.1 *M* or 1.0 *M*.

2. Predict qualitatively the effect of each of the following experiments on the acetic acid equilibrium reaction: (a) Some sodium acetate, which produces the ions Na$^+$(aq) and CH$_3$COO$^-$(aq), is dissolved in the 0.1 *M* acetic acid solution. Would the [H$^+$] increase or decrease? Explain. (b) Some sodium hydroxide solution is added, drop by drop, to the 0.1 *M* CH$_3$COOH.

3. The [H$^+$] of a 1 *M* solution of benzoic acid is 8 × 10^{-3} *M*. What percent of the benzoic acid, C$_6$H$_5$COOH, is ionized in this aqueous solution?

4. Calculate the [H$^+$] of each of the solutions prepared by student B. Use the relation [H$^+$][OH$^-$] = 10^{-14}.

5. What is the *p*H of the solutions prepared by student B?

6. What is the *p*H of your unknown solution?

In Experiment 8 you observed the reaction in which zinc metal was oxidized to zinc(II) ions by lead ions. In the process, lead ions were reduced to lead metal. In this reaction, there was a transfer of electrons from $Zn(s)$ to $Zn^{++}(aq)$. The $Zn(s)$ is the reducing agent, or the substance that reduced the $Pb^{++}(aq)$ ion. The $Pb^{++}(aq)$ ion is the oxidizing agent, or the substance that oxidized the $Zn(s)$.

$$Zn(s) \rightarrow Zn^{++}(aq) + 2e^-$$
$$2e^- + Pb^{++}(aq) \rightarrow Pb(s)$$

$$Pb^{++}(aq) + Zn(s) \rightarrow Pb(s) + Zn^{++}(aq)$$

In Part 1 of this experiment you will observe some possible oxidation-reduction reactions involving several metals and metallic ions. The results can be used to estimate the ease of reduction of the metallic ions relative to each other.

In Part 2 you will make a similar comparison of the relative ease of reduction of the three halogen elements Cl_2, Br_2, and I_2. Specifically, you will determine which of these halogens is capable of removing electrons from which of the halide ions, $Cl^-(aq)$, $Br^-(aq)$, or $I^-(aq)$. From this information you will be able to arrange the halogen element-halide ion half-reactions in order of decreasing ease of reduction.

PROCEDURE

PART 1

Some possible oxidation-reduction reactions

1. Obtain small, clean strips of the metals zinc, copper, and lead. Also have available 0.1 M solutions of $Zn(NO_3)_2$, $Cu(NO_3)_2$, and $Pb(NO_3)_2$.

2. Record your observations of the reactions of *each metal in each solution.* For each combinations use 3 ml of solution in a 13 × 100 mm test tube and a small, freshly cleaned strip of metal.

PART 2

Test for spontaneous oxidation-reduction reactions

1. In separate test tubes, obtain about 3 ml of the three halogens in solution: in the first, chlorine in water, $Cl_2(aq)$; in the second, bromine in water, $Br_2(aq)$; and in the third, iodine in water containing a little ethanol (I_2 is only very slightly soluble in water).

2. Add 15 drops of trichlorotrifluoroethane, TTE, to each. Fit with a stopper and shake each test tube vigorously for a few seconds. Note the color of the TTE phase, which contains the dissolved halogen. (Make sure you know which *is* the TTE layer.)

3. Put about 3 ml of 0.1 M NaCl in a clean test tube, about 3 ml of 0.1 M KBr in a second test tube, and about 3 ml of 0.1 M KI in a third. Add 15 drops of TTE to each test tube. Fit with a stopper and shake each test tube for a few seconds. Note the color of the TTE layer.

4. Put about 3 ml of 0.1 M KBr in one test tube and about 3 ml of 0.1 M KI in another. To each test tube add 15 drops of TTE. Add 1 ml of a fresh solution of chlorine in water to each. Stopper and shake both test tubes for a few seconds. Note the color of the TTE phase and compare it with the preliminary tests in Part 2, steps 1 and 2.

5. Repeat the test outlined in step 4, except use 0.1 M NaCl and 0.1 M KI. Use 5 drops of bromine water in place of the chlorine water. After adding the bromine water, stopper the tubes and shake as directed above. Record your results.

6. Repeat the test outlined in step 4, except use 0.1 M NaCl and 0.1 M KBr, and use 5 drops of iodine water in place of the chlorine water. Add iodine water, stopper the tubes and shake as directed above. Record your results.

1. Which of the metallic ions tested was reduced by two metals? Which was reduced by only one of the metals? Which was reduced by none of the metals?

2. Arrange the metallic ion-metal half-reactions, $M^{++}(aq) + 2e^- \rightarrow M(s)$, in a column in order of decreasing ease of reduction. Other experiments show that the $Ag^+(aq)$ ion is reduced by $Cu(s)$. Use this information to add the half-reaction $Ag^+(aq) + e^- \rightarrow Ag(s)$ to your list in the appropriate place.

3. Write balanced, total reactions for the cases in which oxidation-reduction reactions between metals and metallic ions were observed. See the example for $Zn(s)$ and $Pb^{++}(aq)$ in the introductory section of this experiment.

4. Which of the halogens tested was reduced by two of the halide ions? Which halogen was reduced by only one halide ion? Which halogen was not reduced by any of the halide ions used?

5. Arrange the halogen element-halide ion half-reactions in a column in order of decreasing ease of reduction.

6. Write balanced, total reactions for the cases in which oxidation-reduction reactions occurred between halide ions and halogens.

7. Construct a series of all seven half-reactions discussed in this experiment. List them in order of decreasing ease of reduction, given the following information: $Ag^+(aq)$ is less easily reduced than $Br_2(aq)$ and more easily reduced than $I_2(aq)$; and $I_2(aq)$ is less easily reduced than $Ag^+(aq)$ and more easily reduced than $Cu^{++}(aq)$.

8. Use the list constructed in question 7 to answer the following: (a) Would it be feasible to store a solution of copper sulfate in a container made of metallic zinc? Explain. (b) Would it be feasible to store a solution of copper sulfate in a container made of metallic silver? Explain. (c) Would you expect jewelry made from an alloy of silver and copper to tarnish (oxidize) in a laboratory where fumes of bromine are present? Explain your reasoning.

Electrochemical cells

In Experiment 27 you studied the ease of reduction of some metal ions by other metals. This qualitative study let you deduce which of these metal–metal ion combinations produce a spontaneous reaction.

In this experiment you will construct various electrochemical cells. In these cells the electrons are transferred from one metal to the other by a wire rather than by contact of the metal with the metal ion. The oxidation half-reaction occurs at the anode in one half-cell, and reduction occurs at the cathode in the other half-cell. When the two half-cells are connected with a salt bridge—a length of dental cotton soaked in a solution of an electrolyte such as NH_4NO_3—a cell is produced whose voltage is a quantitative measure of the tendency of the chemical reaction to take place.

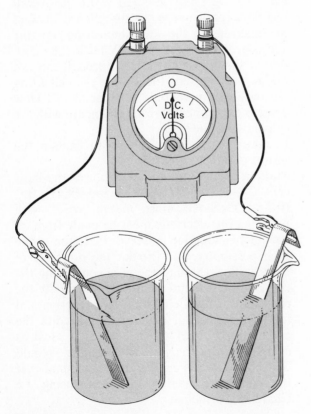

Figure 51 Assembling an electrochemical cell.

PROCEDURE

PART 1

A cell using the half-cells $Zn(s)-Zn^{++}$ (0.5 M) and $Cu(s)-CU^{++}$ (0.5 M)

1. Add 0.5 M copper nitrate, $Cu(NO_3)_2$, to a 150-ml beaker until it is about half full. Place a clean strip of copper in the solution, and connect the electrode to the positive terminal of the voltmeter.

2. Half fill another 150-ml beaker with 0.5 M zinc nitrate, $Zn(NO_3)_2$, solution. Place a clean strip of zinc in the solution, and connect it to the negative terminal of the voltmeter. See Figure 51.

3. Note the voltage reading with the half-cells at this point.

4. Bridge the dental cotton between the beakers and note the voltage reading. Remove the bridge and save both half-cells for use in other parts of the experiment.

PART 2

A cell using the half-cells $Pb(s)-Pb^{++}$ (0.5 M) and $Cu(s)-Cu^{++}$ (0.5 M)

1. In a clean beaker, prepare a half-cell using 0.5 M lead nitrate, $Pb(NO_3)_2$, solution and a lead electrode.

2. Using the same bridge, connect the new half-cell to the $Cu(s)–Cu^{++}$ (0.5 M) half-cell. Connect the lead electrode to the negative terminal of the voltmeter and record the voltage.

PART 3

A cell using the half-cells $Ag(s)-Ag^+$ (0.5 M) and $Cu(s)-Cu^{++}$ (0.5 M) (Optional)

1. In a clean beaker prepare a half-cell using 0.5 M $AgNO_3$ and a silver electrode. **Caution: silver nitrate stains hands and clothing.**

2. Set up the cell as in Part 2, substituting a beaker with 0.5 M AgNO$_3$ and a silver electrode for the Pb(s)–Pb^{++} (0.5 M) combination. Touch the wire from the Ag electrode lightly to the negative terminal of the voltmeter. Note the deflection of the needle. If there is no deflection, connect the Cu electrode to the *negative* terminal of the voltmeter. Now touch the wire from the Ag electrode to the positive terminal of the voltmeter, and, if deflection occurs, note the voltage.

PART 4

Effect of a change in concentration

1. Reconstruct the cell used in Part 1 with the following changes:

1. Place the copper electrode in an empty beaker.
2. Put the 0.5 M Zn^{++} solution in a porous cup as shown in Figure 52.

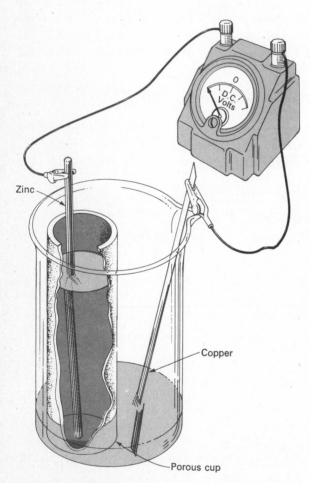

Figure 52 The operation of an electrochemical cell.

2. Connect the electrodes to the voltmeter as before, and then slowly add the 0.5 M Cu^{++} solution to the beaker until you get about the same voltage as obtained in Part 1. Use as little solution as possible. (Since the salt bridge and the porous cup differ slightly in resistance to charge flow, the readings will not be exactly the same.)

3. After recording the initial voltage, add a 2 M solution of sodium sulfide, Na$_2$S, to the beaker, stirring continually. Note the voltage reading and the appearance of the solution in the beaker. Continue adding the Na$_2$S solution little by little until no further change is noted in the voltage readings.

4. Clean up the cell and dispose of the solutions as directed by your teacher. *Do not contaminate the solutions in the half-cells as they will be used by students in other classes.*

Calculations and results

1. (a) Will a cell operate when arranged as in Figure 51? Explain. (b) What is the purpose of the salt bridge or porous cup?
2. Consider the cell in Part 1. (a) What are the spontaneous half-reactions taking place in the Zn(s)–Zn^{++} (0.5 M) half-cell and the Cu(s)–Cu^{++} (0.5 M) half-cell? (b) Write the overall reaction. (c) What is the direction of flow of the electrons in the wire connecting the zinc and copper electrodes? (d) What is the direction of flow of negative ions through the salt bridge? (e) Predict the E^0 for the cell using the reduction potentials in Appendix 5. How do your experimental results compare with the calculated value?
3. Use Le Chatelier's principle to explain the results obtained in Part 4.
4. Make a sketch of a cell which uses the half-cells Zn^{++} (0.5 M)–Zn(s) and Br$_2$(l)–Br$^-$ (0.5 M). Since most metals react with bromine, the electrode must be made from an inert yet conductive material. Platinum is one such possibility. (a) Predict the direction of electron flow through the wire connecting the zinc and inert metal electrodes. (b) Write the equation for each electrode half-reaction and for the overall cell reaction. (c) Predict the potential (voltage) of the cell. (d) Heat is evolved as zinc reacts with bromine. Would the voltage of this cell be greater or smaller if the cell were heated? Explain, using Le Chatelier's principle.

Corrosion of iron

Every year the corrosion of iron costs United States industry billions of dollars. What are some of the factors causing corrosion? What can be done to reduce this loss?

Corrosion is a general term applied to the process in which metals are converted to oxides or other compounds. This process causes gradual deterioration of the metals. Although the detailed chemistry of the corrosion of iron is not completely understood, it clearly involves oxidation.

In this experiment you will investigate some of the factors involved in corrosion and try to relate them through some generalizations.

PROCEDURE

PART 1
Reactions of iron with various aqueous reagents

1. Place a clean, bright nail in each of five test tubes. Slide each nail carefully down the side to avoid breaking the bottom of the test tube.

2. Partially fill each of the test tubes with one of the reagents in Table 10 so that the nail is just covered. Your teacher will tell you which one of the groups to use. All solutions are 0.1 M.

3. For each solution, determine whether it is acidic, basic, or neutral by using litmus or Hydrion paper. Allow the nails to stand overnight in the solutions and go on to Part 2.

4. After the solutions have stood overnight, observe and record any changes that have taken place. To each solution add 1 or 2 drops of 0.1 M

potassium hexacyanoferrate, $K_3Fe(CN)_6$, which contains the ions K^+ and $Fe(CN)_6^{---}$. Observe any changes. Compare your results with those of students using the other sets of reagents. Record their results along with yours.

5. Add 1 drop of 0.1 M potassium hexacyanoferrate solution to about 1 ml of iron(II) sulfate solution. Compare this result to that obtained when the potassium hexacyanoferrate was added to the various solutions containing nails. What conclusions can be made from the results in step 4?

PART 2
Reactions with two metals in contact

1. Prepare about 100 ml of agar mixture as follows: Heat about 100 ml of distilled water to a gentle boil. Remove the burner and stir in 1 g of powdered agar. Resume heating and stirring until the agar is dispersed evenly throughout the solution.

2. Add about 10 drops of 0.1 M potassium hexacyanoferrate and 10 drops of 1 percent phenolphthalein indicator to the agar mixture. Stir thoroughly.

3. While the agar mixture is cooling, prepare 4 clean, bright nails as shown in Figure 53. Place one nail on one side of a Petri dish or small beaker. Bend another nail sharply with a pair of pliers, and place it on the other side of the dish. Twist a clean piece of bare copper wire around a

Table 10 Groups of reagents

Group A	Group B	Group C
NaOH	KOH	Na$_3$PO$_4$
Na$_2$Cr$_2$O$_7$	Na$_2$CO$_3$	Na$_2$C$_2$O$_4$
NaCl	KNO$_3$	KSCN
HCl	HNO$_3$	H$_2$SO$_4$
water	water	water

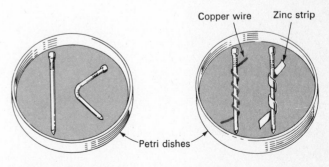

Figure 53 Studying the corrosion of iron.

third nail. Then remove the nail and tighten the wire coil so that when the nail is forced back through, it makes tight contact with the wire. Place this in a second dish.

Repeat the above procedure using a zinc strip on a fourth nail. If a strip of zinc is not available, a piece of mossy zinc may be attached by forcing the nail through the zinc piece in at least two places. Place this nail in the second Petri dish, as shown in Figure 53. Be sure the nails do not touch one another.

4. While the agar mixture is still fluid but has cooled to lukewarm, pour it carefully into the Petri dishes until the nails and attached metals are covered to a depth of about 0.5 cm.

5. Make observations during the time remaining in the class period. Place the dishes in your locker and observe them again after they have stood overnight.

Questions and regularities

1. List the reagents in Part 1 in which no indication of corrosion was observed.
2. List the reagents in Part 1 in which there was an indication of corrosion.
3. Are there any regularities? What is the evidence? How do you account for the regularity?

4. What did you observe regarding the reactions at the head, the pointed end, or the sharp bend of the nail that were different from the rest of the nail? Account for this in terms of the mechanical treatment of the nail during its manufacture.
5. Why is it that a nail can stand for many days on the shelf in a hardware store and not rust, but when it is placed in tap water, it rusts quickly?
6. Iron(II) ions react with potassium hexacyanoferrate to form a colored precipitate. Write the equation for the reaction.
7. Which color in Part 2 indicates the site of the oxidation reaction? Which color indicates the site of the reduction reaction? Account for the formation of each color.
8. Write the oxidation and reduction reactions for each case in which you observed a reaction in Part 2.
9. Consult the E^0 table in Appendix 5 and predict another metal that is more readily oxidized than iron and that will protect it from corrosion. Test your prediction by an experiment.
10. How does a coating of zinc on iron (galvanized iron) protect iron from corrosion?
11. Magnesium metal rods are sometimes placed in hot water heaters. Why?

In this experiment, you will use your knowledge of solubility and electrochemistry to predict whether a reaction will occur when solutions of various ions are mixed together. The solubility table in Appendix 6 permits you to predict which ions in aqueous solutions combine to produce a precipitate of a slightly soluble compound. The oxidation-reduction table in Appendix 5 compares the relative strengths of oxidizing and reducing agents and permits you to predict when certain ionic species in solution will undergo an oxidation-reduction reaction.

Remember that predictions based on E^0 values show only whether the reactants or the products are favored after *equilibrium* is reached. They do not predict the rate of the reaction. In cases where the reaction you predicted does not occur immediately, make observations again later in the period, or the next day, before you evaluate your predictions.

In Part 1 of this experiment you are to predict, *before* coming to the laboratory, whether an appreciable reaction will take place when each of the ten combinations of solutions of ions are mixed. If you predict that a reaction will take place, write a balanced equation for it in your laboratory notebook. Use ions where appropriate, and label precipitates with "(s)" and gases with "(g)."

Check your predictions by performing the experiments in the laboratory. Include those for which you predicted no reaction. Do not be biased by your predictions. Record what you actually observe.

In Part 2 you need not make preliminary predictions. These reactions are somewhat more complex. Record your observations as you perform the experiments, and later attempt to explain the results. Write balanced ionic equations for the reactions you can interpret correctly.

PROCEDURE

PART 1
Predicted reactions

For each trial use about 3-ml portions of each solution and mix thoroughly in a 13 × 100 mm test tube. All solutions are 0.1 M unless otherwise noted.

1. magnesium nitrate, $Mg(NO_3)_2$, and sodium hydroxide, NaOH

2. magnesium nitrate, $Mg(NO_3)_2$, and sodium sulfate, Na_2SO_4

3. saturated barium hydroxide, $Ba(OH)_2$, and sulfuric acid, H_2SO_4

4. potassium dichromate, $K_2Cr_2O_7$, and sodium sulfite, Na_2SO_3 (acidified with 1 drop of 6 M H_2SO_4)

5. potassium permanganate, $KMnO_4$, and 1.0 M hydrochloric acid, HCl

6. potassium iodide, KI, and iron(III) chloride, $FeCl_3$. Add about 1 ml of TTE to the mixture and shake the test tube. This makes it easier to detect the presence of any halogen, owing to its greater solubility in the TTE phase. Recall the solubility of iodine in TTE in Part 2 of Experiment 27.

7. potassium bromide, KBr, and iron(III) chloride, $FeCl_3$. Add 1 ml TTE and shake the test tube.

8. iron(II) sulfate, $FeSO_4$ (acidified with 3 drops of 6 M H_2SO_4), and 0.01 M potassium permanganate, $KMnO_4$

9. zinc sulfate, $ZnSO_4$, and ammonium carbonate, $(NH_4)_2CO_3$

10. saturated barium hydroxide, $Ba(OH)_2$, and zinc sulfate, $ZnSO_4$

PART 2

Unpredicted reactions

The following reactions are more complex than those in Part 1. You are not expected to make predictions. Mix the solutions, make careful observations, and later attempt to interpret the results. Write ionic equations for the reactions you can interpret.

Trials 1 through 7 are a series involving reactions of hydrogen peroxide and some ions of chromium in an acidic or basic solution.

Use 3 ml of each solution and mix thoroughly. All solutions are 0.1 M unless otherwise noted.

1. chromium sulfate, $Cr_2(SO_4)_3$ (acidified with 3 drops of 6 M H_2SO_4), and 3 percent hydrogen peroxide

2. chromium sulfate, $Cr_2(SO_4)_3$, to which 6 M NaOH is added drop by drop until the precipitate $Cr(OH)_3$ first formed just redissolves and the $Cr(OH)_4^-$ ion is produced, and 3 percent hydrogen peroxide

3. potassium dichromate, $K_2Cr_2O_7$ (acidified with 3 drops of 6 M H_2SO_4), and 3 percent hydrogen peroxide

4. potassium dichromate, $K_2Cr_2O_7$ (to which 6 M NaOH is added drop by drop until the solution turns yellow), and 3 percent hydrogen peroxide

Trials 5 through 7 are a series involving reactions of the lead ion with various anions. All solutions are 0.1 M unless otherwise noted.

5. lead nitrate, $Pb(NO_3)_2$, and 1.0 M sodium chloride, NaCl

Allow the precipitate to settle a few minutes and decant about 3 ml of the liquid from the residue for use in trial 6. Some of the precipitate can be present in the decanted liquid. The liquid does not have to be clear.

6. Add 3 ml of the decanted liquid from trial 5 to 3 ml of potassium iodide, KI.

Allow the precipitate to settle, and decant the liquid from the residue for use in trial 7. Some of the precipitate can be present in the decanted liquid. The liquid does not have to be clear.

7. Add 3 ml of the decanted liquid from trial 6 to 3 ml of sodium sulfide, Na_2S.

Electrolysis of aqueous potassium iodide

You will recall that when water undergoes electrolysis, the oxidation occurring at the anode produces oxygen gas while the reduction at the cathode produces hydrogen gas. Electrolysis of some aqueous salt solutions, however, may lead to the oxidation or reduction of the ions from the salt—if these ions are more easily oxidized or reduced than water itself.

In this experiment you will electrolyze an aqueous solution of potassium iodide and then identify the products that are formed at the electrodes.

PROCEDURE

1. Set up the electrolysis apparatus as shown in Figure 54.

2. Add enough 0.5 M potassium iodide solution to fill the U-tube about three-fourths full. Make the electrical connections and allow the electrolysis to proceed for about 15 minutes.

3. Note and record any observable products and color changes that occur at the electrode connected to the positive terminal of the battery (the anode). Make the same observations for changes occurring at the electrode connected to the negative terminal of the battery (the cathode).

4. When you complete the electrolysis, carefully remove the anode and note its odor. Using a medicine dropper, transfer about 2 ml of the dark brown liquid from the anode side into a small test tube. Add about 1 ml of trichlorotrifluoroethane, TTE. Stopper and shake the test tube for a few seconds. Allow the more dense TTE to settle, and note the color of the two liquid layers. What material is present in the solution around the positive electrode (anode)?

5. Using a medicine dropper, transfer about 2 ml of solution from the cathode side into another test tube. Add a few drops of phenolphthalein indicator to find the approximate hydrogen ion concentration of the solution. Add 1 ml of TTE and shake the tube. Then add a few ml of 0.1 M iron(III) chloride solution drop by drop (with shaking between drops), and note the results.

Questions and regularities

1. Write the equation for the half-reaction occurring at the anode.
2. As iodine is produced at the anode, it forms the brown, complex ion I_3^- with the iodide ion of the electrolyte solution. (a) Write the equation for the reaction, using reversible arrows to show that equilibrium is involved. (b) What effect did the addition of TTE in step 4 have on the equilibrium? Use your observations on the color of the two layers to explain the effect.

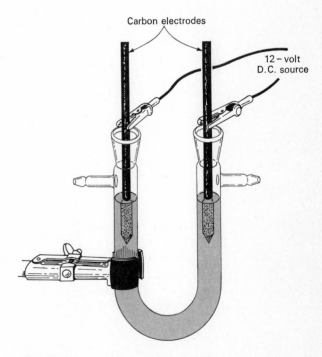

Figure 54 An electrolysis apparatus.

3. (a) Is the solution around the cathode acidic or basic? Write the equation for the half-reaction occurring at the cathode. (b) Write the equation for the reaction of 0.1 M $FeCl_3$ with the sample of solution taken from the cathode side.

4. When iodine, I_2, reacts with a basic solution, it undergoes a self-oxidation-reduction reaction to form iodide ions, I^-, and iodate ions, IO_3^-. Both of these ions are colorless in aqueous solution. Give a plausible explanation for the appearance of the sharp color boundary noted near the bottom of the U-tube. Explain in terms of your knowledge of the products at each electrode. Write the equation for the reaction involved.

Relationship between moles of copper and moles of electrons involved in electrolysis

While investigating electrolysis in 1830, Michael Faraday determined the relationship between the "amount of electricity" flowing through a circuit and the change in mass of the electrodes. Today we can interpret these results in terms of electrons instead of the "amount of electricity."

Figure 55 shows the details of the electrical circuit we shall use. The source of electrons is a battery or other suitable source of direct current so constructed that the electrons are forced to flow in one direction. The ammeter measures the rate of flow of electrons through the circuit in a given unit of time. In our measurements, we shall use a unit of electricity based on moles of electrons: 1 ampere is that amount of current flowing when 1.0×10^{-5} mole of electrons passes through any cross section of the conductor in 1 second. Since electric charge does not build up in any part of the circuit, the current must be the same in all sections of the circuit.

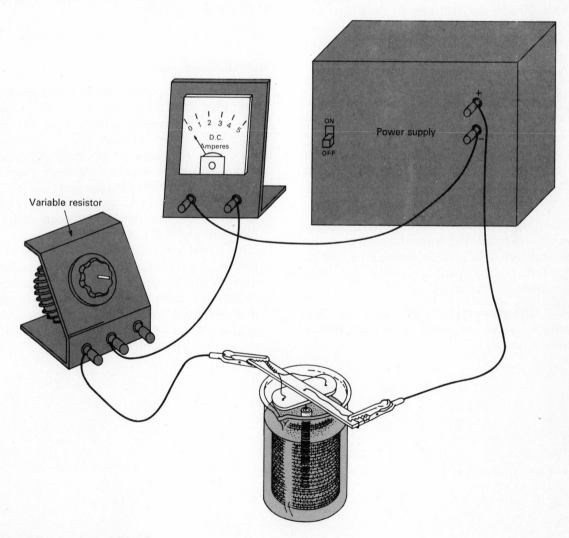

Figure 55 An electrolytic cell.

The source of direct current causes the electrons to be crowded onto one electrode and to be drained away from the other. The circuit is complete when at one electrode an ion or molecule in the electrolyte solution accepts electrons, while at the other electrode an ion or molecule loses electrons. Electrons are accepted at the negative electrode (called a *cathode*), and electrons are lost at the positive electrode (called an *anode*).

Using the materials and circuitry shown in Figure 55, determine the relationship between the number of moles of electrons flowing during the experiment and the number of moles of copper atoms gaining electrons.

PROCEDURE

1. Obtain a cylinder of copper screen to be used as the negative electrode and a sheet of copper wound into a spiral, or a heavy copper wire wound into a tight coil, to serve as the positive electrode. **Handle the electrodes by the connecting wires only.** Otherwise, your fingers may leave grease marks upon which the copper deposit will not adhere well.

2. Find the mass of the clean, dry negative electrode (screen cylinder) to the nearest 0.01 g.

3. Suspend the electrodes in a 400-ml beaker by attaching them to a wooden holder or clamping them with clothespins as your teacher directs. Be sure that the positive electrode is centered within the cylindrical negative electrode and that the electrodes do not touch each other.

4. Make all of the connections in the circuit as shown in Figure 55, but leave the switch on the power pack "off." Adjust the variable resistor so that its full resistance will be utilized. Ask your teacher to check your setup.

5. Add enough electrolyte solution containing the copper ions to just cover the copper screen (negative electrode).

6. Turn on the power supply and *quickly* adjust the current to 1.0 ampere by decreasing the resistance being used in the variable resistor. Record the time to the nearest second.

7. Let the current flow for 30 minutes. Watch the ammeter, and keep the current as close to 1.0 ampere as possible by adjusting the variable resistor.

8. Record the time to the nearest second as you turn off the power supply. Rinse the screen electrode by gently dipping it into a beaker containing cold water. Do not agitate the electrode so vigorously that the deposit is dislodged.

9. Rinse the electrode with acetone as above to remove the water droplets. Allow to dry by evaporation (about 2 or 3 minutes).

10. When thoroughly dry, find the mass of the electrode to the nearest 0.01 g on the same balance you used before.

Calculations and results

1. Calculate the number of moles of electrons that were used. Recall that 1.0×10^{-5} mole of electrons is involved when a current of 1 ampere flows for 1 second.
2. Calculate the number of moles of copper deposited on the negative electrode from the electrolyte containing copper ions.
3. Using the answers to calculations 1 and 2, calculate the relationship between moles of electrons and moles of copper deposited.
4. How would you expect the loss in mass at the positive copper electrode to compare with the gain in mass at the negative copper electrode?
5. What are some sources of error in your measurements and procedures? How many significant figures in the mole relationship can be justified by your data?

In the first part of this experiment you will investigate the reactivity of some examples of different classes of *hydrocarbons*—compounds containing carbon and hydrogen only. You will use

cyclohex*ane*
saturated, cyclic
C_6H_{12}

cyclohex*ene*
unsaturated, cyclic
C_6H_{10}

toluene
substituted aromatic
$C_6H_5CH_3$

xylene
substituted aromatic
$C_6H_4(CH_3)_2$

You will investigate the relative ease of oxidation of these compounds by a strong oxidizing agent, an alkaline solution of potassium permanganate. You will also compare their ability to add or substitute a bromine atom for a hydrogen atom when they are treated with a solution of bromine, Br_2, in trichlorotrifluoroethane.

In the second part of the experiment, you will investigate some of the reactions of *alcohols*—organic compounds that contain the functional group—OH. Alcohols are classified as *primary, secondary,* or *tertiary,* according to the number of groups that are bonded to the carbon atom to which the—OH group is attached. You will use the following primary alcohols:

$$CH_3OH$$
methanol

$$CH_3CH_2OH$$
ethanol

1-butanol
primary butyl alcohol

You will also use the following secondary and tertiary alcohols:

2-butanol
secondary butyl alcohol

2-methyl-2-propanol
tertiary butyl alcohol

Note that all three of the butyl alcohols have the same formula, C_4H_9OH. They are *structural isomers*—compounds with the same *empirical formula,* but with different *structural formulas.*

Note: **Safety goggles must be worn throughout this experiment.**

PROCEDURE

PART 1

Reactions of hydrocarbons

1. First you will study oxidation. Label a clean, dry, 13 × 100 mm test tube for each of the hydrocarbons to be tested: cyclohexane, cyclohexene, toluene, and xylene. Add about 10 drops of the appropriate hydrocarbon to each test tube. Prepare about 4 ml of 0.005 *M* alkaline potassium permanganate solution by adding 2 ml of 0.01 *M* KMnO₄ to 2 ml of 6 *M* NaOH. Add 20 drops (about 1 ml) of this solution to each of the test tubes containing the different hydrocarbons. Stopper each test tube and shake gently to obtain more complete contact between the two phases. Note any changes in the color of the aqueous

layer after about 1 minute. Shake the contents occasionally, and observe the tubes after 5 minutes.

2. Now you will observe addition and substitution of Br_2. Place about 10 drops of each hydrocarbon into four small test tubes, properly labeled. Add about 20 drops (about 1 ml) of bromine water, $Br_2(aq)$, drop by drop, to each of the test tubes. Stopper each tube and shake the contents occasionally as you add the bromine solution. Note any changes in color. If a change is noted, continue the addition of the bromine until the bromine color persists.

PART 2

Some reactions of alcohols

1. Observe the reaction of ethanol, C_2H_5OH, with neutral, acidic, and basic solutions of potassium permanganate. Place about 2 ml of 0.01 M $KMnO_4$ in each of three small test tubes. Add 2 ml of distilled water to one, 2 ml of 6 M H_2SO_4 to the second, and 2 ml of 6 M NaOH to the third. Label them neutral, acidic, and basic $KMnO_4$. Now add 2 drops of C_2H_5OH to each, shake the contents, and note any changes in the color of the permanganate solutions. Add another drop or two of ethanol and observe any further changes that may take place after 5 minutes. Note any differences in the rate of oxidation as well as in the reaction products. *Note:* The color of a solution containing the manganate ion, MnO_4^{--}, is green; manganese dioxide, MnO_2, is a brown precipitate; and a solution containing the manganese(II) ion, Mn^{++}, is very light pink, almost colorless.

2. Now you will observe the reaction of methanol, CH_3OH, with hot copper oxide (**This reaction is to be done in a fume hood.**) Wrap a penny with a few turns of heavy copper wire so that it can be suspended above about 10 ml of methanol in a small beaker. Place a glass stirring rod across the beaker, and hook the wire over it so that the penny is suspended about 1 cm above the surface of the methanol. Remove the penny and wire to a flame placed well away from the beaker and heat to a dull red heat. Quickly suspend the hot penny above the methanol in the beaker and note the interesting cyclical reaction that occurs.

Note the change in the appearance of the copper. Cautiously smell the vapors and compare them with those of methanol. The new substance formed is formaldehyde, HCHO, which you may recognize as the liquid used to preserve specimens in the biology laboratory.

3. Compare the behavior of three isomeric alcohols in the following reactions.

First, you will observe reaction with concentrated HCl. (*Note:* concentrated HCl is used to compare the ease with which the —OH group of the alcohol R—OH reacts with 12 M HCl to form H_2O and the alkyl chloride, R—Cl. The alkyl halide is only slightly soluble in the aqueous phase and its presence is shown by a cloudiness due to the suspension of R—Cl droplets in the water.)

Place about 1 ml of 1-butanol in a small test tube. Add about 5 ml of 12 M HCl. Stopper the test tube, shake the mixture *very carefully,* and after a minute look for the presence of the slightly soluble alkyl chloride.

Repeat this test with the other two isomeric alcohols.

Second, observe reaction with a neutral solution of 0.01 M $KMnO_4$. Place about 2 ml of 0.01 M $KMnO_4$ solution in a small test tube. Add an equal volume of 1-butanol. Add 1 ml of distilled water, stopper the tube, and shake the contents. Observe the color of the permanganate solution over a period of 5 minutes. Shake occasionally during this period.

Repeat this test with the other two isomeric alcohols.

Third, observe reaction with metallic sodium, *which your teacher will demonstrate.* Place about 1 ml of 1-butanol in a small, *dry* test tube. Add a very small piece of freshly cut metallic sodium. Note any reaction that occurs. (**Caution: sodium is a very reactive and potentially dangerous metal. Keep it away from water or acids.**)

Repeat this test with the other two isomeric alcohols.

Questions and regularities

1. Examine models of the various hydrocarbons you tested. Which contain double bonds? Which of the models are planar, and which are nonplanar? Is there an alternate structure for cyclohexane?
2. (a) Which of the hydrocarbons were readily oxidized by the alkaline solution of $KMnO_4$? (b) Which hydrocarbon was reactive with the bromine solution? (c) What is the relationship between the reactivity noted in (a) and (b) and the structure of the hydrocarbons?
3. Write the balanced equation for the reaction in which methanol was oxidized by the hot copper oxide.

4. What differences were noted when C_2H_5OH reduced the neutral, acidic, and basic solutions of $KMnO_4$? Assuming that in each case C_2H_5OH was oxidized to acetic acid, CH_3COOH, write balanced equations for each reaction. Be sure to use the reduction half-reaction that involves the reduction product of manganese you observed.

5. In the reactions involving the three isomeric alcohols with the formula C_4H_9OH, what did each of the following tests show about the functional group —OH and its position in the alcohol in (a) the test with concentrated hydrochloric acid; (b) the test with neutral potassium permanganate; and (c) the test with metallic sodium?

6. Write a balanced equation for each case in question 5 in a, b, and c where a reaction occurred.

7. (*Optional*) There is a fourth alcohol with the formula C_4H_9OH. Draw a structural formula for it and name it. How do you predict that it would react with each of the following: (a) 12 *M* HCl, (b) neutral 0.01 *M* $KMnO_4$, and (c) metallic sodium?

One of the most useful of the benzene derivatives is aspirin, which is acetylsalicylic acid. Aspirin is synthesized by the reaction of salicylic acid and acetic anhydride:

salicylic acid   acetic anhydride

acetylsalicylic acid   acetic acid

In this experiment you will prepare and purify aspirin and test the product. **Caution: safety goggles must be worn throughout this experiment.**

PROCEDURE

PART 1

Preparation of aspirin

1. Obtain a sample of about 4 g of salicylic acid and determine its mass to the nearest 0.01 g. Transfer it to a 25 × 200 mm Pyrex test tube and add exactly 8 ml of acetic anhydride. **Acetic anhydride is a powerful lachrymator (a substance that irritates the eyes) so this process must be done in the fume hood.**

2. Stir the salicylic acid–anhydride mixture with a stirring rod until all the solid has dissolved. Add, with continued stirring, 4 drops of 18 M H$_2$SO$_4$. Place the test tube containing the mixture

in a 600-ml beaker of boiling water, and allow the reaction to proceed for 15 minutes.

3. To separate the aspirin from the reaction mixture, pour the mixture into a 150-ml beaker containing 20 g of crushed ice and 20 ml of cold water. Rinse the test tube with 10 ml of ice water,

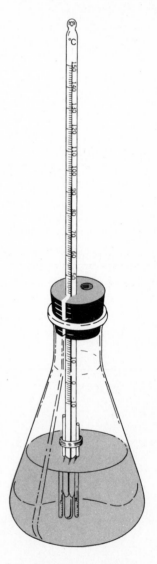

Figure 56 A melting point apparatus with capillary tubes.

and add the rinse water to the rest of the mixture.

4. Place the beaker containing the reaction mixture into an ice bath, and stir until crystallization appears to be complete, which is about 5 to 10 minutes.

5. Filter the crystals, using a vacuum filter if available. Wash the crystals with three 5-ml portions of ice water, and allow to dry. Determine the mass of dry aspirin obtained. **Caution: the aspirin you have prepared contains contaminants and is not to be taken internally.**

PART 2

Testing the purity of aspirin

1. Using capillary tubes and melting point apparatus shown in Figure 56, determine the melting point of your aspirin and of commercial aspirin as follows:

Obtain two capillary melting-point tubes (1.0 to 1.5 mm in diameter and 6 to 12 cm long). Make one tube shorter than the other by cutting off a centimetre or so. Seal one end of each tube by placing it in a burner flame. Place commercial aspirin in the shorter tube to identify it.

Push the open end of the shorter tube into some dry, powdered commercial aspirin. Tap the closed end gently on the table so the solid packs down in the tube. Continue to do this until the depth of solid is about 1 cm. Similarly, fill the longer tube with some of the aspirin you have prepared.

Attach the tubes to a thermometer (labeled $-10\ °C$ to $+150\ °C$) with a small rubber circle cut from the end of a piece of rubber tubing, as shown in Figure 56. The liquid in the flask is vegetable oil.

Clamp the melting-point apparatus in place, and heat it gradually with a low burner flame.

Move the flame occasionally to achieve more uniform heating of the oil bath. Heat slowly and watch the capillary tubes closely as the temperature approaches 120 °C At the sign of first melting of each solid, record the temperature. **Caution: do not exceed the 150 °C limit of the thermometer.**

2. Stir a small sample of your aspirin into a millilitre or two of cold 0.5 M sodium bicarbonate ($NaHCO_3$) solution. Observe the solubility. Add 0.5 M hydrochloric acid solution, drop by drop, until a change is observed. Record your observations.

3. Place a few crystals of your aspirin and of commercial aspirin on a piece of moist blue litmus paper. Record your observations.

4. Place a few crystals of salicylic acid in a clean, dry test tube. Add 1 ml of methanol and 1 drop of 0.1 M ferric chloride, $FeCl_3$, solution. Observe the color. Repeat, using the aspirin you prepared and commercial aspirin. What differences are noted?

Calculations and results

1. Calculate the percent yield of aspirin obtained.
2. (a) Use the results of your tests on salicylic acid, commercial aspirin, and your preparation of aspirin to suggest a reason why your aspirin and commercial aspirin may have different melting points. (b) Commercial aspirin contains 5 grains of aspirin (0.324 g) in a tablet that weighs approximately 0.35 g. Suggest another reason for any melting-point differences that you noted.
3. Aspirin passes through the stomach unchanged, but is absorbed in the intestines. Suggest a reason for this.

Organic acids may be represented by the structural formula

$$R-\overset{\overset{\displaystyle O}{\|}}{C}-OH$$

in which R stands for an alkyl group such as —CH$_3$, —C$_2$H$_5$, or —C$_3$H$_7$. The carboxyl group,

$$-\overset{\overset{\displaystyle O}{\|}}{C}-OH$$

is the functional group that is characteristic of all organic acids. The preparation of various acid derivatives involves substitution for the OH portion of this group.

$$R-\overset{\overset{\displaystyle}{C}}{\underset{\underset{\displaystyle O}{\|}}{}}-Cl \qquad R-\overset{\overset{\displaystyle}{C}}{\underset{\underset{\displaystyle O}{\|}}{}}-NH_2$$

an acid chloride   an acid amide

$$R-\overset{\overset{\displaystyle}{C}}{\underset{\underset{\displaystyle O}{\|}}{}}-OR' \qquad R-\overset{\overset{\displaystyle}{C}}{\underset{\underset{\displaystyle O}{\|}}{}}-O^--NH_4^+$$

an ester   an ammonium salt

In this experiment you will prepare an ester.

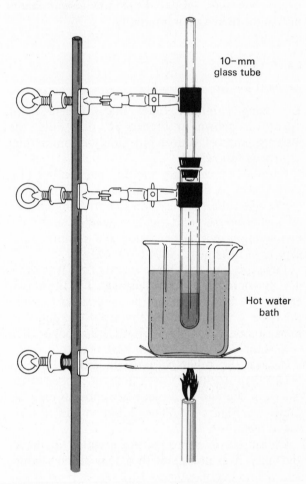

Figure 57   Test tube with reflux condenser.

PROCEDURE

PART 1

Preparation of ethyl acetate, C$_2$H$_5$OH + CH$_3$COOH → CH$_3$COOC$_2$H$_5$ + H$_2$O

Caution: safety goggles must be worn throughout this experiment.

1.   Use a 25 × 200 mm test tube fitted with a one-hole cork wrapped in aluminum foil. Insert through the cork a 60 cm to 70 cm length of 10

mm glass tubing to serve as a reflux condenser* (see Figure 57). The tubing must be open at both ends, and one end should just barely pass through the cork.

2.   Place 5 ml of ethanol, 6 ml of glacial acetic acid, 8 to 10 drops of 18 M H$_2$SO$_4$, and a boiling

*Warming is needed to make this reaction proceed at a reasonable rate. Since the components are quite volatile, a reflux condenser is needed to allow the gases (which would otherwise escape) a chance to cool, condense back to a liquid, and return to the reaction vessel.

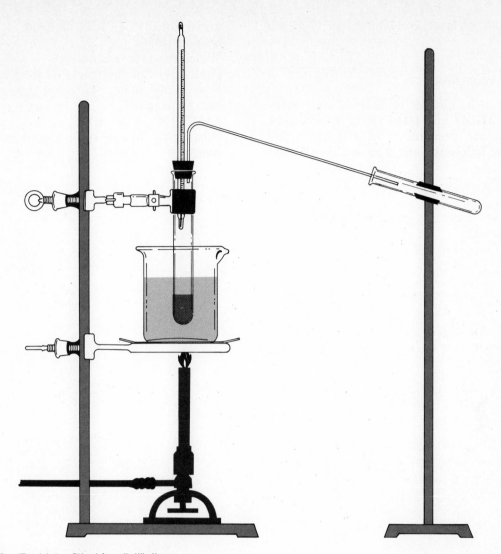

Figure 58 Test tube fitted for distillation.

chip into the test tube. (The boiling chip minimizes bumping while the solution is boiling.)

3. (Caution: do not heat the reaction mixture directly with a flame since the organic liquids and their vapors are flammable.) Clamp the test tube in an upright position, then immerse it part way in a 250-ml beaker about half filled with water. Attach the stopper and condenser tube. Heat the water until the reaction mixture is gently boiling. Continue heating for about 15 minutes. Allow to cool. Note the characteristic odor of the ester in the test tube.

PART 2

Separation of the ester (*optional*)

1. Attach the test tube to a distillation condenser and heat in a bath of boiling water until no more distillate comes over (see Figure

58). Record the temperature at which distillation starts and the temperature at which it stops. (*Note:* if standard condensers are not available, a 30-cm piece of 10-mm glass tubing can serve as an air condenser.) Collect the distillate in an 18 × 150 mm test tube. What remains behind in the reaction vessel?

2. Add to the distillate, a small amount at a time, about 2 ml of a saturated solution of sodium carbonate. While ethyl acetate is only slightly soluble, ethanol is extremely soluble in saturated sodium carbonate solution. This process separates the ethyl acetate from any unreacted ethyl alcohol. If necessary, add more sodium carbonate solution until no further reaction is visible. Which of the two layers is the water layer?

3. Separate the two layers by decantation or use a separatory funnel if available. Discard the aqueous-solution layer. Note the properties of the ester.

Calculations and results

1. Calculate the number of moles of each reactant, C_2H_5OH and CH_3COOH, which were used in the preparation of $CH_3COOC_2H_5$ from the following data: 1 ml of C_2H_5OH has a mass of 0.79 g; 1 ml of CH_3COOH has a mass of 1.05 g.

2. Which reactant is in excess?

3. If all of one of the reactants were consumed, how many moles of ethyl acetate could be produced? How many grams of $CH_3COOC_2H_5$ is this?

4. What is the role of sulfuric acid in the reaction?

Polymerization involves the chemical combination of a number of identical or similar molecules to form a complex molecule of high molecular weight. The small units may be combined by *condensation polymerization* or *addition polymerization*.

Condensation polymers are produced by reactions during which some simple molecule, such as water, is eliminated between functional groups, such as alcoholic —OH or acidic —COOH groups. In order to form long-chain molecules, two or more of each of these groups must be present in each of the reacting units.

Addition polymers are formed by the reaction of the monomeric units without the elimination of atoms. The monomer is usually an unsaturated organic compound such as ethylene, $H_2C{=}CH_2$, which in the presence of an initiator will undergo an addition reaction to form a long-chain molecule such as polyethylene.

In this experiment directions are given for the preparation of three polymers of the condensation type: a Glyptal resin, an amine-aldehyde polymer, and nylon.

PROCEDURE

PART 1

Preparation of a glyptal resin

(Caution: this reaction must be done in a fume hood.)

The condensation of polyhydroxyl alcohols and polybasic acids or anhydrides leads to polyesters known as alkyd resins. These are used in making modern paints and enamels. A common member of this type is Glyptal resin, formed from both glycerol and *ortho*phthalic acid:

glycerol   *ortho*phthalic acid

1. Place 2 g of glycerol and 3 g of powdered phthalic anhydride into a 50-ml beaker or a small tin can. Mix with a glass stirring rod. Cover with a watch glass and heat gently over an electric hot plate. A low burner flame may be used but care should be taken since the resin is flammable. Keep heating until large bubbles form and the mixture puffs up. Allow the resin formed to cool.

2. Remove the resin from the container and grind it in a mortar. Try to dissolve some of it in a solvent suggested by your teacher. **Do not heat over an open flame.** When you have obtained a solution of the resin, pour some of it out onto a piece of wood or metal to dry. Note the nature of the residue. Suggest a practical use for this type of resin.

PART 2

Preparation of an amine-aldehyde-type polymer

In 1909, Leo Baekeland (1863–1944) first demonstrated the possibilities of forming plastics with formaldehyde, HCHO, and substituted aromatics such as phenol,

in the presence of acid or alkaline catalysts. Such polymers are called Bakelite plastics. The first stages in the condensation reaction between phenol and formaldehyde are as follows:

In this preparation, we shall use an aromatic amine called aniline, instead of phenol. Its reaction with formaldehyde is analogous to the phenol-formaldehyde condensation.

Measure 10 ml of 40 percent formaldehyde solution, called Formalin, into one test tube, and 10 ml of a saturated aqueous solution of aniline hydrochloride into another test tube. Pour the solutions into a 50-ml beaker or a small tin can *simultaneously*, in order to mix them. Note whether the reaction is exothermic or endothermic. Examine the product and record its properties.

PART 3

Preparation of nylon, a polymeric amide

Nylon, a polymer familiar to everyone because of its wide use in fabrics, is a condensation polymer made by the removal of water molecules from adipic acid,

$$HOOC—CH_2—CH_2—CH_2—CH_2—COOH$$

and 1,6-diaminohexane,

$$H_2N—CH_2—CH_2—CH_2—CH_2—CH_2—CH_2—NH_2$$

to form the polymer

In this experiment, we shall use the chloride of adipic acid, adipyl chloride,

$$ClOC—CH_2—CH_2—CH_2—CH_2—COCl$$

which combines with 1,6-diaminohexane by the removal of HCl molecules. The two reactants will be dissolved in immiscible solvents, so that the reaction takes place only at the interface. In this way, the polymer can be obtained in strands.

1. Make a hook out of a 10 to 15 cm piece of copper wire and have it in readiness to remove the nylon film as it is formed.

2. Obtain 3 ml of 0.5 *M* 1,6-diaminohexane in 0.5 *M* sodium hydroxide (NaOH) solution, and place it in a 50-ml beaker.

3. Hold the beaker containing the 1,6-diaminohexane at a slant, and carefully add 3 ml of a 0.25 *M* solution of adipyl chloride in hexane to it. The two solutions are not soluble in each other, so a distinct layering should take place.

4. Use the hooked copper wire to withdraw the film that forms at the boundary of the two liquids. Continue to withdraw the film as it forms at the boundary until the strand breaks.

5. Place the nylon strand on a watch glass and wash generously with water. Conclude with an alcohol rinse.

Questions and regularities

1. Write equations for reactions involved in each preparation you performed, using structural formulas for the monomers and polymers involved.
2. The nylon produced by the E.I. duPont de Nemours Company, Nylon 6-10, is made by condensing sebacic acid,

with 1,6-diaminohexane. Show how these polyfunctional molecules can condense and form a long-chain polymer.

The preparation of soap from fat and lye has been, historically, a household task. Only in the last century has the making of soap become a commercial undertaking. Our ancestors made soap by boiling animal fats with the lye obtained from leaching wood ashes. In this experiment, we will make soap by the same process, called *saponification,* but we will use modern ingredients.

In the process of making soap, an animal fat, which is a triglyceride, is hydrolyzed by the action of a strong base, such as sodium hydroxide, and heat. The resulting products are soap and glycerol:

$$R-\overset{\overset{O}{\|}}{C}-O-CH_2$$
$$R'-\overset{\overset{O}{\|}}{C}-O-CH \quad + 3Na^+(aq) + 3\,OH^-(aq) \rightarrow$$
$$R''-\overset{\overset{O}{\|}}{C}-O-CH_2$$

a fat / sodium hydroxide

$$[R-\overset{\overset{O}{\|}}{C}-O]^-Na^+ \quad CH_2OH$$
$$[R'-\overset{\overset{O}{\|}}{C}-O]^-Na^+ \quad + \quad CHOH$$
$$[R''-\overset{\overset{O}{\|}}{C}-O]^-Na^+ \quad CH_2OH$$

soap / glycerol

Caution: safety goggles must be worn throughout this experiment.

PROCEDURE

1. Obtain 15 ml of 6 *M* NaOH and 10 ml of vegetable oil, and place them in a 100-ml beaker.

2. Continue boiling the mixture over the lowest flame that will sustain the boiling process. Stir the mixture constantly to avoid spattering. If spattering occurs, remove the flame and continue stirring the mixture. Replace the flame and continue heating after the spattering stops.

3. Continue boiling and stirring for about 20 minutes, or until it appears that all of the water has been evaporated. Test a few drops of the reaction mixture by adding them to a small amount of water. If no droplets of fat are observed, saponification is complete. If fat droplets are seen, add another 5 ml of 6 *M* NaOH and continue the heating process as before.

4. As the crude soap cools, a waxy solid should form. Add to it 15 ml of distilled water and 50 ml of hot, saturated sodium chloride solution. Stir the mixture, breaking up lumps with your stirring rod. Decant the wash solution by pouring it through a wire screen, which will trap small soap particles.

5. Repeat the washing process twice. After the final washing, press the soap between two sheets of paper toweling to expel as much water as possible.

6. Dissolve a small portion of your soap in 5 ml of warm distilled water in a test tube. Add a few drops of phenolphthalein solution, and record the result. Repeat the test, using a few flakes of commercially prepared soap flakes.

7. Make another solution of a small portion of your soap in distilled water, and add three drops of 0.1 *M* calcium chloride, $CaCl_2$, solution to it. Record the results. Repeat the test, using a few flakes of commercially prepared soap flakes. Repeat the test once more, using a few drops of dishwashing detergent in place of soap. Record your observations in each case.

8. Obtain 10 ml of distilled water in a test tube and add 1 ml of vegetable oil to it. Shake vigorously. Record your observations for five minutes. Now add a small portion of your soap to the test tube, shake vigorously again, and observe for five minutes. Repeat the procedure, using small portions of commercially prepared soap flakes and of dishwashing detergent.

Questions and regularities

1. What was the purpose of the salt solution added to the reaction mixture after saponification was complete?
2. What was the purpose of adding phenolphthalein to your soap solution and to a solution of commercially prepared soap? Explain any differences in results.
3. How did the addition of 0.1 M CaCl$_2$ solution affect the soap and detergent solutions in step 7? Explain any differences noted.
4. How did the addition of your soap, commercial soap, and dishwashing detergent affect the mixing of oil and water? Explain any differences noted.

Separation of some transition metal ions with an anion exchange resin

Ion exchange resins are high-molecular weight polymers that contain a framework of covalently bonded carbon and hydrogen atoms. The resins have centers of high positive or negative charge attached to the framework. A typical structure for a portion of a resin polymer is

About one ring in ten is cross-linked into two other chains of the polymer to give it a three-dimensional structure. The groups designated by an —X determine the resin type. If they are —COOH or —SO$_3$H groups, cations will be exchanged for the hydrogens. This is the type that is used in water softeners in which objectionable ions such as Ca^{++} and Mg^{++} are exchanged for H$^+$.

If the —X groups are substituted ammonium groups such as —N(CH$_3$)$_3$$^+Cl^-$, anions will be exchanged for the chloride ions. In this experiment you will use an anion-exchange resin of this type because some of the metal ions used will be converted to complex chloride ions such as FeCl$_6$$^{---}$ and CoCl$_4$$^-$. For example, when a salt containing the hydrated iron (III) ion is dissolved in 9 M HCl, a complex ion is formed:

$$Fe(H_2O)_6^{+++} + 6Cl^- \rightleftharpoons FeCl_6^{---} + 6H_2O$$

The complex anions will be exchanged for the chloride ions of the resin. If the concentration of the chloride ion is then decreased, by using 5 M HCl and finally 1 M HCl, the chloride complexes will successively shift their equilibria to form the hydrated metal cations that are no longer

retained by the resin and can be washed through (eluted from) the column. The chloride complex that is the least stable will be eluted even at the higher concentration of the chloride ion (9 M HCl), while the most stable complex will not be eluted until the chloride ion concentration has been reduced to that of 1 M HCl.

The ions of three closely related transition metals—iron, cobalt, and nickel—were selected because each has a characteristic color in solutions containing chloride ions. The ions can thus be readily distinguished by color as they are washed from the resin. The test solution you will use contains salts of iron, cobalt, and nickel dissolved in 12 M HCl.

After the ions have been separated on the anion exchange column, you will test the eluted samples to determine the efficiency of the separations. **Caution: safety goggles must be worn throughout this experiment.**

PROCEDURE

1. Obtain an ion exchange column and set it up as shown in Figure 59. Attach a piece of white paper with plastic tape so you can distinguish the characteristic colors of the anions as they come off the column. The solution on the column is 2 M HCl. Leave this on the column until you are ready to add another solution. *Do not allow the column to run dry,* since this may lead to uneven flow (channeling) later and decrease the efficiency of the separation. *Either add the next solution or close the screw clamp whenever the level of the liquid in the tube drops to the glasswool plug at the top of the column.*

2. Obtain about 50 ml of 9 M HCl solution. From this prepare 45 ml of 1 M HCl solution by diluting 5 ml 9 M HCl with 40 ml of distilled water. Prepare 30 ml of 5 M HCl by mixing 15 ml 9 M HCl with 15 ml 1 M HCl. Place each of these solutions in clean, labeled beakers for use when needed. Obtain about 2 ml of the test

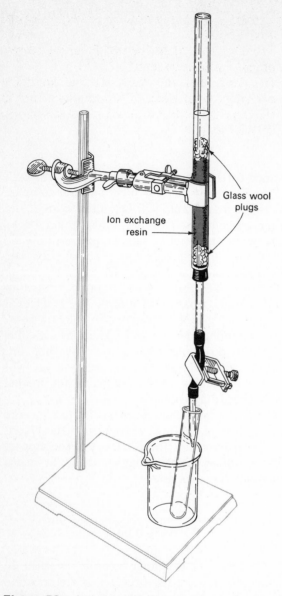

Figure 59   An ion-exchange column.

solution containing the three ions to be separated.

3.   Open the screw clamp to allow the 2 *M* HCl solution already on the column to drop to the level of the top glasswool plug. Add 9 *M* HCl to refill to the top of the tube. Adjust the screw clamp so the flow will be about 2.5 ml per minute.

4.   When the 9 *M* HCl has dropped to the top of the glasswool plug, close the clamp and *add the 2 ml of the colored test solution.* Open the clamp to obtain the same rate of flow as before.

5.   When the level again drops to the glasswool plug, add 5 ml of 9 *M* HCl. Collect 5 ml of eluate

(the solution that passes through the column). Add another 5-ml portion of 9 *M* HCl and collect 5 ml of eluate in a separate test tube. Repeat this procedure with another 5 ml of 9 *M* HCl. Label the three test tubes "e-1," "e-2," and "e-3." Note the color of the eluate in each test tube.

6.   Repeat step 5, but use four 5-ml portions of 5 *M* HCl solution in place of the 9 *M* HCl. Collect the eluate, about 5 ml in each of four test tubes labeled "f-1," "f-2," "f-3," and "f-4."

7.   Repeat step 5 using four or five 5-ml portions of 1 *M* HCl solution. Collect the eluate, about 5 ml in each test tube labeled "g-1," "g-2," and so on.

8.   After the last 5-ml portion of 1 *M* HCl solution drops to the glasswool plug at the top of the column, add 10 ml of distilled water to rinse the resin. Dilute 4 ml of 9 *M* HCl with 14 ml of water to make some 2 *M* HCl solution. Add this to the column so it will be ready for use again by another student. Close the clamp when the acid level is about 2 cm above the top of the glasswool plug.

9.   Identify the different colored solutions by comparing them with hydrochloric acid solutions of iron, cobalt, and nickel chlorides, which your teacher will have available.

10.   Test a drop of each eluted sample separately with each of the reagents below to determine the efficiency of the separation. Place the drops on a glass plate that is on a piece of white paper.

1. Add a drop of 0.1 *M* KSCN solution. A blood-red coloration due to formation of $Fe(SCN)^{++}$ ion indicates the presence of Fe^{+++} ion.

2. Place a fresh drop of each eluate on the glass plate. Make each basic by adding a few drops of 15 *M* NH_3 solution. **Caution: the solution will become hot during neutralization.** Use litmus to check when basic. Then, add a drop of dimethyl glyoxime reagent. A brilliant red precipitate indicates the presence of nickel.

3. Place a fresh drop of each eluate on the glass plate. Add a drop of 10 percent solution of NH_4SCN in acetone to each drop being tested. The appearance of a blue color, due to the formation of $Co(SCN)_4^{--}$ ions, indicates the presence of CO^{++} ions.

Record all observations neatly, in tabular form when appropriate.

Questions and regularities

1. One of the metallic ions was eluted with 9 M HCl. It would also have been eluted with the 5 M or 1 M HCl solutions. Which one was it? Give a reason for this ease of elution in terms of the stability of its complex chloride anions.
2. The color of some of the ions on the column was different from the color of the final eluate.

Explain this in terms of the properties of the complex ions.
3. What are the conditions that favor the release of ions from the column?
4. Recalling that the resin used is an anion exchange type, which of the metallic ions in this experiment forms the most stable complex chloride anion?

Preparation of a complex salt: Tetramminecopper (II) sulfate monohydrate

Many salts crystallize out of aqueous solution as hydrates—for example, $CuSO_4 \cdot 5H_2O$, $FeSO_4 \cdot 7H_2O$, and $Al_2(SO_4)_3 \cdot 9H_2O$. The building blocks in the crystals are hydrated cations and anions, such as $Cu(H_2O)_4^{++}$ and $SO_4(H_2O)^{--}$ in the case of $CuSO_4 \cdot 5H_2O$.

Many of the transition metals form stable complex ions in which the metal ion is bound to molecules or ions other than water—for example, $Co(NH_3)_6^{+++}$ or $Fe(CN)_6^{---}$. Salts containing such complex ions as these are called *coordination compounds* or *complex salts*—for example, hexamminecobalt(III) chloride, $Co(NH_3)_6Cl_3$, and potassium hexacyanoferrate(III), $K_3Fe(CN)_6$. The building blocks in these crystalline solids are shown in Figure 60. **Caution: safety goggles must be worn throughout this experiment.**

PROCEDURE

1. Place 8 ml of 15 *M* ammonia water diluted with 5 ml of distilled water in a small evaporating dish.

2. Obtain a 0.02 mole sample of $CuSO_4 \cdot 5H_2O$ (249.5 g/mole). Use a mortar and pestle to pulverize the copper(II) sulfate crystals, if necessary. Add the powdered crystals to the ammonia solution, and stir until all the copper(II) sulfate pentahydrate is dissolved.

3. Pour 8 ml of ethyl alcohol slowly down the side of the evaporating dish so as to cover the solution with alcohol. Do not stir or agitate the mixture. Cover with a watch glass and let stand overnight.

4. After the mixture has been allowed to stand overnight, stir slowly and gently to insure complete precipitation. Allow the crystals to settle. Decant and discard the supernatant liquid. Transfer the crystals to a filter by rinsing with 3 ml to 5 ml portions of a mixture of equal volumes of 15 *M* $NH_3(aq)$ and ethyl alcohol.

5. Finally, wash the crystals on the funnel with 5 ml of ethyl alcohol. Attach the hose from an aspirator to the funnel stem to pull off the liquid from the crystals. Apply the suction gently to

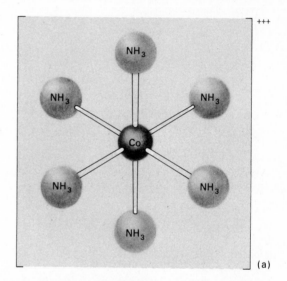

(a)

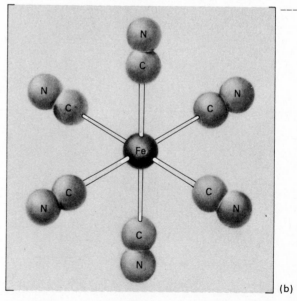

(b)

Figure 60 The structures of two complex ions: (a) $Co(NH_3)_6^{+++}$, (b) $Fe(Cn)_6^{---}$

avoid tearing the filter paper. Repeat the washing and drying operation.

6. Remove the filter paper and spread it out on a paper towel.

7. Determine the mass of the dry crystals. Save them for use in the next experiment.

Calculations and results

1. Did you obtain 0.02 mole of the complex salt? Calculate the percent yield obtained.
2. Based on the formula of the salt, $Cu(NH_3)_4SO_4 \cdot H_2O$, and assuming 100 percent yield, how many moles of NH_3 were used?

Double salts are formed when two salts crystallize out together in simple molecular proportions. They have their own crystal form, which need not be the same as that of either component salt. The alums are double salts with the general formula $M^+ M^{+++} (SO_4^{--})_2 \cdot 12H_2O$, of which potassium alum, $KAl(SO_4)_2 \cdot 12H_2O$, is an example. Another class has the formula $M^{++} (M^+)_2 (SO_4^{--})_2 \cdot 6H_2O$, of which iron(II) ammonium sulfate, $Fe(NH_4)_2(SO_4)_2 \cdot 6H_2O$, is an example. Double salts in solution exhibit, the properties of each of the ions (usually hydrated) present in their component salts.

After preparation of the double salt in this experiment, you will compare some of the properties of a single salt, $CuSO_4$, with those of the double salt and the complex salt prepared in the last experiment.

PROCEDURE

PART 1

Preparation of a double salt:
Copper(II) ammonium sulfate,
$CuSO_4 \cdot (NH_4)_2SO_4 \cdot 6H_2O$

1. Obtain a 0.02 mole sample of copper(II) sulfate pentahydrate, $CuSO_4 \cdot 5H_2O$ (249.5 g/mole), and pulverize the crystals in a mortar and pestle. Also obtain 0.02 mole of ammonium sulfate, $(NH_4)_2SO_4$ (132 g/mole), and mix with the pulverized $CuSO_4 \cdot 5H_2O$ crystals in 10 ml of distilled water in a 100-ml beaker. Heat gently until the salts are dissolved.

2. Allow the solution to cool slowly to room temperature until crystals form. Larger crystals may be obtained by allowing the solution to stand overnight.

3. Cool the mixture further in a cold-water bath. Decant the solution off the crystals.

4. Dry the crystals on a filter paper, using a paper towel as a blotter. Examine them carefully, and describe them in your lab notebook. These crystals belong to the monoclinic system.

5. Determine the mass of the dry crystals.

PART 2

Comparison of some of the properties of a single salt, a double salt, and a complex salt

1. Place a small amount (about 1 ml) of *anhydrous* copper(II) sulfate crystals into a small, dry test tube. Note the change in color that takes place when 2 ml to 3 ml of water are added. Now add 6 M ammonia solution, a few drops at a time, until 5 ml have been added. Record your observations.

2. Dissolve a small amount of the double salt you prepared in Part 1 in about 5 ml of water in a large test tube. Make a similar solution using the complex salt from Experiment 39. Compare the colors of the solutions. Dilute each solution with about 20 ml of water, and record any changes in color.

3. Place small quantities of each of the dry salts you prepared in separate, small test tubes. Heat each gently and note any color changes. Identify the gas given off from each sample.

Calculations and results

1. Note the number of moles of reactants used and moles of products formed. Calculate the percent yield you obtained in Part 1.
2. Why was a yield of 0.02 mole expected for both the double salt you prepared here and the complex salt prepared in the last experiment?
3. In Part 2, step 1, account for the successive color changes that you noted in terms of the structure of the ion containing copper.
4. From your observations in Part 2, step 2: (a) What are the ionic species present when the double salt copper(II) ammonium sulfate dissolves in water? (b) What are the ionic species present when the complex salt tetramminecopper(II) sulfate is dissolved in a small amount of water? Give a reasonable explanation for the changes that took place as more water was added.
5. Account for the changes noted when each salt was heated.

The transition metals can form compounds containing the elements in a variety of oxidation states. In the next two experiments you will study some of the oxidation-reduction chemistry of chromium as you prepare some common compounds of this element. In Table 11 note the color and formulas for the ionic species of chromium with various oxidation numbers which are present in the acidic and basic solutions. Use this table to follow the reactions as you prepare potassium dichromate, $K_2Cr_2O_7$, from chromium(III) acetate, $Cr(CH_3COO)_3 \cdot H_2O$.

Hydrogen peroxide is a suitable oxidizing agent in a basic solution. Since H_2O_2 is a weak acid, the HO_2^- ion or the peroxide ion, O_2^{--}, are ionic species formed in a basic solution. See Table 12.

The E^0 values for the half-reactions in basic solution are

$$CrO_4^{--} + 4H_2O + 3e^- \rightarrow 4OH^- + Cr(OH)_4^-*$$

$$E^0 = -0.13 \text{ volt}$$

$$HO_2^- + H_2O + 2e^- \rightarrow 3OH^-$$
$$E^0 = +0.88 \text{ volt}$$

Before you proceed with the preparation, balance the equations for the reactions involved so you can calculate the number of moles of reactants required for each of the steps in the preparation. Record these in your notebook before coming to the laboratory.

Step 1 will be the conversion of $Cr(H_2O)_6^{+++}$ to $Cr(H_2O)_2(OH)_4^-$ with an excess of strong base. Step 2 will be the oxidation of $Cr(H_2O)_2(OH)_4^-$ to CrO_4^{--} by peroxide ion in a basic solution. Step 3 will be the conversion of CrO_4^{--} to $Cr_2O_7^{--}$ by acidification with H_2SO_4. **Caution: safety goggles must be worn throughout this experiment.**

PROCEDURE

1. Obtain a 0.01 mole sample of chromium(III) acetate, $Cr(CH_3COO)_3 \cdot H2O$ (247.2 g/mole).

*$Cr(OH)_4^-$ is a simplified formula for $Cr(H_2O)_2 \cdot (OH)_4^-$ ion without the water of hydration.

Table 11

Oxidation number of chromium	Ionic species present	
	Acidic solution	Basic solution
+6	$Cr_2O_7^{--}$ (orange)	CrO_4^{--} (yellow)
+3	$Cr(H_2O)_6^{+++}$ (gray green*)	$Cr(H_2O)_2(OH)_4^-$ (green)

*By reflected light, this may appear violet.

Dissolve it in about 20 ml of distilled water in a small beaker. Warm slightly to hasten dissolving.

2. Pour 25 ml of 6 M KOH solution into a 250-ml Erlenmeyer flask. Add the chromium(III) acetate solution slowly to the flask. Swirl the flask to mix the solutions and to make sure that any chromium(III) hydroxide formed will dissolve in the excess base present.

3. Refer to the equation you balanced for step 2, and note the number of moles of hydrogen peroxide required to oxidize the 0.01 mole of chromium(III) ion. Calculate the volume of commercial hydrogen peroxide, 3 percent by weight, required to obtain this number of moles. Add an excess of about three times the calculated volume of hydrogen peroxide solution, add 1 or 2 boiling chips, and heat the flask to boiling. If the solution does not become yellow in color after boiling for a minute or two, add about 10 ml more hydrogen peroxide solution and bring to a boil again. Repeat if necessary but avoid too large an excess of H_2O_2.

4. After the solution turns yellow, boil it very gently until its volume has been reduced to about 30 ml. Any excess hydrogen peroxide should be decomposed during the boiling.

Table 12

Oxidation number of oxygen	Molecular or ionic species present	
	Acidic solution	Basic solution
0	O_2	O_2
−1	H_2O_2	O_2^{--} or HO_2^-
−2	H_2O or H_3O^+	OH^-

5. Allow the solution to cool for a few minutes. Acidify by adding glacial acetic acid, 18 M CH_3COOH, drop by drop, until the solution becomes orange in color. The color of the dichromate ion, $Cr_2O_7^{--}$, in solution is orange. Add 1 ml of 18 M CH_3COOH in excess.

6. Heat the solution to boiling and reduce it to a volume of about 25 ml. Cool the solution using an ice bath to crystallize the $K_2Cr_2O_7$.

7. Filter the solid and wash with two 5-ml portions of ethyl alcohol. Transfer the crystals to a watch glass to dry. Find the mass of the crystals when dry. Compare the quantity obtained with the theoretical amount expected, as calculated from the equations.

Calculations and results

1. Write the equations for the reactions involved in each of the steps used in the preparation of $K_2Cr_2O_7$. Show your calculations for the amount of H_2O_2 required and for the expected yield of $K_2Cr_2O_7$.
2. What ionic species were present in the final acidic solution before it was cooled? What equilibria are established?
3. Considering the solubility data in Table 13, would you expect your sample of $K_2Cr_2O_7$ to be relatively pure? Why?

Table 13

Temperature (°C)	Solubility in g/100 g water	
	KCH$_3$COO	K$_2$Cr$_2$O$_7$
0	217	5
20	256	12
40	323	26
60	350	43
80	380	61
100	—	80

4. Compare the E^0 value of the half-reaction for the oxidation of Cr(III) to Cr(VI) in a basic solution with that for the oxidation in an acidic solution. See the introductory section of this experiment for the former value and Appendix 5 for the latter value. Which oxidation will give a higher concentration of products at equilibrium?
5. Note the half-reaction for the reduction of H_2O_2, for which the E^0 value is +0.68 volt (Appendix 5). Can you now suggest a reason for decomposing the excess H_2O_2 in step 4 before the solution was acidified to convert CrO_4^{--} to $Cr_2O_7^{--}$?
6. Is the conversion of chromate ion to dichromate ion an oxidation reaction? Explain.

In the previous experiment, you prepared potassium dichromate from chromium(III) acetate by carrying out an oxidation process in a basic solution. In this experiment, you will reverse the process and reduce potassium dichromate with sulfur dioxide in an acidic solution to produce a chromium(III) salt called chrome alum. Study the chart listing various oxidation numbers for chromium given in Experiment 41 and note the changes in color and ionic species that will be involved. Recall also from Experiment 40 that chrome alum, $KCr(SO_4)_2 \cdot 12H_2O$, is a double salt resulting from the crystallization of the ionic species $Cr(H_2O)_6^{+++}$, K^+, and SO_4^{--} within the same crystal lattice. Additional water is held in the crystal.

Refer to Appendix 5 for the E^0 values of the half-reaction involving the reduction of Cr(VI) to Cr(III) and the half-reaction involving the oxidation of SO_2 to SO_4^{--}, both in acid solution. Before coming to the laboratory, balance the equation for this oxidation-reduction reaction and record it in your laboratory notebook.

Caution: safety goggles must be worn throughout this experiment.

PROCEDURE

1. Obtain a 0.05-mole sample of $K_2Cr_2O_7$ (294.2 g/mole), and add it to 60 ml of 3 M H_2SO_4, in a 125-ml or 250-ml Erlenmeyer flask. Warm to dissolve the $K_2Cr_2O_7$. Set aside to cool to room temperature.

2. Set up the sulfur dioxide generator as shown in Figure 61. Clamp the flask on an iron ring over a wire screen so that a burner may be used to heat the flask if necessary.

How many moles of SO_2 are required to reduce 0.05 mole of $K_2Cr_2O_7$? See the equation you balanced previously. How many moles of $Na_2S_2O_5$ should be used to produce this SO_2 by reaction with 6 M H_2SO_4? Convert the number of moles to grams of $Na_2S_2O_5$ and use about double this amount in the generator.

3. Add about 50 ml of tap water to the solid $Na_2S_2O_5$ in the generator. Attach a 10-cm piece of glass tubing to the hose leading from the generator and place it in the 125-ml Erlenmeyer flask.

4. Cool the $K_2Cr_2O_7$ solution to about 25 °C before starting to generate the SO_2. **Caution: use**

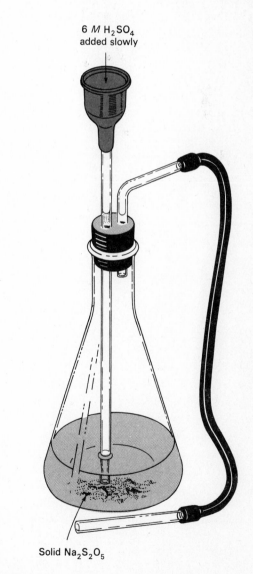

6 M H_2SO_4 added slowly

Solid $Na_2S_2O_5$

Figure 61 A sulfur dioxide generator.

an ice bath when necessary to maintain the $K_2Cr_2O_7$ solution below 40 °C during the reduction of the dichromate. This is necessary to prevent complicated side reactions. Use a fume hood if available.

5. Add 10-ml portions of 6 *M* H_2SO_4 very slowly to the generator as needed to produce a steady flow of SO_2 gas. Warm the generator with a small flame from time to time as necessary.

6. Allow the reaction to continue until the solution turns from orange to a dark blue-green color. Stir or swirl the solution periodically, watching the temperature carefully. To check the color of the solution, place a drop on a filter paper and note the circle of color produced as the solution diffuses. The reduction is complete when no orange color is noted before the spot dries. (Estimated time for reaction is about 30 minutes.)

7. Pour the solution into an evaporating dish. Cover loosely and allow it to stand until crystals of chrome alum have formed. If the crystallization is allowed to proceed slowly, over a period of several days, larger crystals will be formed. Filter and allow to dry.

8. Find the mass of the dry crystals and calculate the percent yield you obtained.

Calculations and results

1. Show calculations of the amounts of reactants required and the theroetical yield expected.
2. Under what conditions could you grow large crystals of chrome alum?
3. Examine one of the larger crystals you prepared. Note any outstanding features of its geometric symmetry and prepare a sketch showing these.

The presence of NO$_2$ in air is the result of the combining of atmospheric oxygen and nitrogen at the high temperatures found in internal combustion engines and the fires used to generate heat for power plants and other industrial processes. The reaction

$$43.2 \text{ kcal} + N_2(g) + O_2(g) = 2NO(g)$$

produces nitric oxide, which then further combines with oxygen in the presence of sunlight to form NO$_2(g)$:

$$2NO(g) + O_2(g) = 2NO_2(g)$$

Nitrogen dioxide, NO$_2(g)$, is a brown, irritating, toxic gas which is visible as a brown smog layer in polluted air. It further reacts with water vapor to produce nitrous and nitric acids, which contribute to the acid rain problems of the world.

In this experiment, the NO$_2$ content of local air samples will be analyzed to measure the air pollution problem existent in various communities.

PROCEDURE

PART 1

Developing a testing procedure

1. Obtain a 250-ml graduated cylinder, a 500-ml or 1-litre bottle, a bicycle pump, an eyedropper, a 50-cm length of rubber tubing, and a pan for water. Pour water into the pan until it is about two-thirds full.

2. Fill the bottle to the top with water, place your hand over the mouth of the bottle, invert it, and place it in the water in the pan.

3. Attach the eyedropper to one end of the rubber tubing and the bicycle pump to the other end. Pull the plunger of the pump out as far as possible. Insert the eyedropper end of the rubber

tubing into the mouth of the inverted bottle. Slowly push in the plunger of the pump until all of the air in the pump has been discharged into the bottle.

4. Remove the rubber tubing and eyedropper from the mouth of the bottle, place your hand over the mouth of the bottle, and return it to the upright position.

5. Fill the graduated cylinder with water to the 250-ml mark, and measure the amount of water necessary to refill the bottle. This volume of water is equal to the volume of air discharged by one stroke of the bicycle pump.

6. Repeat the calibration of the bicycle pump two additional times, and calculate the average volume of air delivered by one stroke of the pump.

7. Calculate the number of pump strokes necessary to obtain a 10,000 cm^3 sample of air. Use the relationship

$$\text{number of strokes} = \frac{10,000 \text{ cm}^3}{\text{number of cm}^3/\text{stroke}}$$

PART 2

Building a sampling device

1. Obtain a 50-cm^3 Erlenmeyer flask, a two-holed rubber stopper to fit, and a 6–8 cm piece of glass tubing fire-polished at both ends. Using lubricant on the glass and a towel around your hands for protection (see page 17), gently insert the glass tubing through one hole of the stopper and the eyedropper through the other. The glass tubing should barely go through the stopper, but the eyedropper must extend nearly to the bottom of the Erlenmeyer flask when the stopper is inserted tightly in it.

2. When the pump is attached to the sampler as shown in Figure 62, the sampling device is complete.

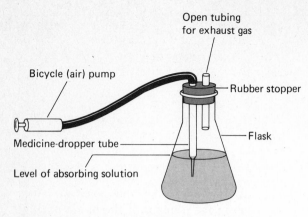

Open tubing
for exhaust gas

Bicycle (air) pump

Rubber stopper

Medicine-dropper tube

Flask

Level of absorbing solution

Figure 62 Sampling device for the absorption of NO_2.

PART 3

Obtaining an air sample

1. Place 25 cm³ of NO_2 absorbing solution in the sampling device and seal the Erlenmeyer flask with a solid rubber stopper. It is essential that the absorbing solution remains sealed until you are ready to obtain your air sample.

2. With the help of your teacher, choose a sampling site in your community and take the sealed Erlenmeyer flask with absorbing solution in it and the rest of the sampling device to that location.

3. At the sampling site, reassemble the sampling device and *slowly* pump air through the sampling solution until 10,000 cm³ have passed through the solution. Use the number of pump strokes calculated in Part 1, number 7. Be sure that no more than 250 cm³ of air pass through the solution per minute in order that all of the NO_2 is absorbed by the solution. It will take about 40 minutes to collect the sample properly.

4. When sampling is complete, remove the bicycle pump assembly from the Erlenmeyer flask and restopper the flask tightly with the solid rubber stopper before taking it back to the laboratory for analysis.

PART 4

Preparation of standard NO_2 solutions for comparison

1. Obtain five clean, dry 50-cm³ graduated cylinders. Label them as follows:

1. 0 mg NO_2
2. 0.006 mg NO_2
3. 0.012 mg NO_2
4. 0.018 mg NO_2
5. 0.024 mg NO_2

2. Using a 1-ml pipette and bulb, add the following amounts of standard $NaNO_2$ reagent to each:

1. none
2. 0.5 ml
3. 1.0 ml
4. 1.5 ml
5. 2.0 cm³

3. Add NO_2 absorbing solution to each of the graduated cylinders containing standard solutions until the total volume is 25 cm³.

4. To each of the graduated cylinders containing standard solutions add 1 cm³ hydrogen peroxide solution, 10 cm³ of sulfanilimide solution, and 2 cm³ of N–NED reagent. Mix thoroughly, using a clean stirring rod for each solution.

5. Label five clean, dry 13 × 150 mm test tubes with the NO_2 concentrations of the standard solutions and pour a portion of each standard into the corresponding test tube. Place the test tubes in a rack, in order, for color comparison.

PART 5

Sample comparison

1. Pour the contents of the Erlenmeyer flask in which you collected your air sample into a 50-cm³ graduated cylinder. Add more NO_2 absorbing solution, if necessary, until the total volume is 25 cm³.

2. Add, as you did to the standard solutions, 1 cm³ of hydrogen peroxide solution, 10 cm³ of sulfanilimide solution, and 2 cm³ of N-NED reagent.

3. Mix thoroughly, using a clean stirring rod, and place a portion of the solution in a clean, dry 13 × 150 mm test tube for comparison with the standard solutions. Allow ten minutes for color development.

4. After the color in the sample solution has developed for ten minutes, compare the color in the sample solution to the colors of the standard solutions. Find which of the standard solutions matches your sample most closely, and estimate the concentration of NO_2 in your sample.

Calculations and results

1. Calculate the concentration of NO_2 in your sample in micrograms of NO_2 per cubic metre

of air. Use the equation

$$\frac{\mu g \ NO_2}{m^3}$$

$$= \left\{ \begin{array}{l} \text{concentration of your sample} \\ \text{in mg } NO_2/10,000 \ cm^3 \text{ of air} \end{array} \right\}$$

$$\times \frac{1,000 \ \mu g}{1 \ mg} \times \frac{10^6 cm^3}{1 \ m^3}$$

2. Use unit analysis to show that the above equation converts $mg/10,000 \ cm^3$ to $\mu g/m^3$.
3. Report the location of your sampling site.

4. Obtain data from your classmates of the NO_2 concentrations found at different locations. Determine the locations in your community which have the highest and lowest NO_2 concentrations.
5. The EPA maximum for NO_2 concentration is $100 \ \mu g/m^3$. Did any of the samples obtained by you or your classmates exceed this "allowable value"?
6. Can you suggest any reasons why some of the samples obtained by you and your classmates are higher than others? Are there ways by which the NO_2 concentrations in the air in your community could be lowered?

S-1

Combustion of a candle

In your description of a candle, some of your recorded observations in Experiment 1 probably were "the candle decreases in length as it burns" and "the candle material is consumed." What is happening to the candle and what is causing it to happen? These are questions with a ready answer. We all know the candle is burning. But what does the word *burning* really mean? Let us try some experiments to find out.

PROCEDURE

PART 1

Using cobalt chloride test paper

1. Invert a large (1000-ml) beaker or jar over a burning candle, and leave it there until the candle is extinguished. (See Figure 63.) Test the thin liquid film on the inside of the beaker with a strip of cobalt chloride test paper. Record your observation.

2. Moisten a second piece of cobalt chloride test paper with a drop of tap water. Suggest one possible product of the combustion reaction.

PART 2

Time of combustion

1. Determine the length of time (seconds) a candle continues to burn when a quart jar or litre beaker is placed over it, as shown in Figure 64.

2. Relight the candle and repeat Part 2, step 1, but use a jar with only half the volume.

As often happens in science, the attempt to answer one question raises other questions. What causes the candle flame to be extinguished when confined for a short time? Here are two possible answers:

1. The burning process *produces* a gaseous material that somehow "quenches" the flame.

2. The burning process *consumes* a gaseous material present in air. When this component of air is gone, the burning ceases.

PART 3

Addition of air

1. Using a blowpipe, add air to a candle flame to produce a jet. (See Figure 65.)

2. Place a 250-ml Erlenmeyer flask over a burning candle, as in Part 2, step 1. After the candle flame is extinguished, quickly place the flask upright on the table. Obtain a second, clean, 250-ml Erlenmeyer flask to be used as a control. Add about 25 ml of limewater solution to each of the flasks. Swirl the solution in each flask simultaneously until a change occurs in one of the flasks.

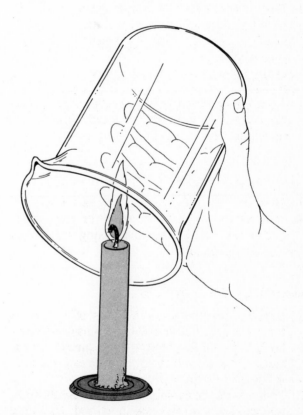

Figure 63   Testing for a product of combustion.

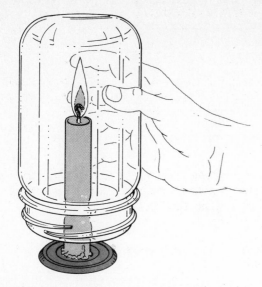

Figure 64   Combustion inside a container.

3. Using a glass tube or a straw, blow your breath into a third flask containing some lime-water solution.

Questions and regularities for part 1

1. What conclusions can be drawn from this experiment?
2. Does the evidence you have gathered eliminate the possibility that something other than water caused the observed changes? Explain your answer.
3. If the liquid film is water, where does it come from?
4. Would you expect water to be produced if an electric heater were used in place of the candle under the beaker? Explain your answer.

Questions and regularities for part 2

1. How does the time required to extinguish the candle flame using the quart jar or liter beaker compare to the time required using the pint jar or 500-ml beaker?

Questions and regularities for part 3

1. Explain how these experiments offer a basis for preference between the two answers postulated in Part 2 for the following question: what causes the candle flame to be extinguished when confined for a short time?
2. Name some possible products of combustion for candle material as indicated by these experiments.

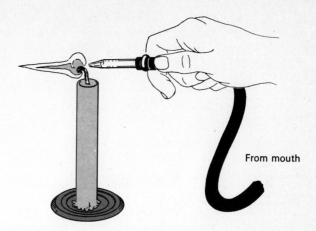

Figure 65   Blowing air into the flame.

OPTIONAL HOME EXPERIMENTS

Refer to Experiment S-2 for suggested home experiments to study further the properties of a burning candle.

S-2
Further investigations of a burning candle

As you investigated the burning candle, many unanswered questions may have come to mind. The purpose of this experiment is to help you to find clues that will enable you to postulate answers to some of the unanswered questions. As you perform the experiments outlined below, keep thinking about possible answers to the following questions:

1. Why is the flame blue at the base, dark in the center, and yellow elsewhere?
2. What is the purpose of the wick in a candle?
3. Why is it possible to extinguish a candle flame by blowing on it?
4. Why is the flame shaped as it is?

PROCEDURE

1. Using a clothespin for a clamp, hold a piece of glass tubing about 8 cm in length and 8 mm in diameter in the flame of a burning candle so that one end of the tubing is well within the inner dark part of the flame. After holding the tubing steadily in this position for a few seconds, hold a lighted match to its outside end. (See Figure 66.) Record your observations.

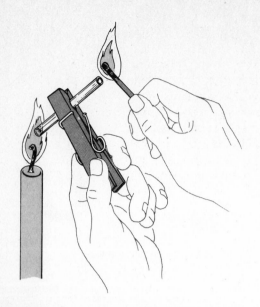

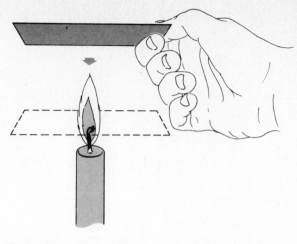

Figure 68 Zones in the flame.

Figure 66 Investigating the dark zone of the flame.

2. Hold the same piece of glass tubing in the upper bright part of the flame, and again hold a lighted match to its outside end. Record your observations.

3. Light a candle and allow it to burn for about half a minute. With a lighted match in hand, quickly blow out the candle and hold the match about an inch from the wick in the column of "smoke" emanating from it. (See Figure 67.) Record your observations.

4. Move a horizontally held piece of white cardboard quickly down over the flame of a burning candle to the position shown in Figure 68. Hold the cardboard in this position just long enough for the flame to scorch through to the upper side of the cardboard but not long enough to cause it to burst into flame. Note the pattern of the scorched area.

5. Try lighting some candle wax without a wick. Try lighting wick material, such as a piece of string, without candle material. Try several different materials as wick materials by sticking them into the side of your candle (as shown in Figure 69): a toothpick, a paper matchstick, a piece of yarn, braided picture wire, a piece of copper wire, a piece of string. Try your best to make each one function properly. What are some of the properties necessary for wick materials?

6. Scrape some soot from the piece of glass tubing used earlier into the liquid in the bowl of a burning candle. Observe the motion of the particles in the liquid. (See Figure 70.)

7. Snuff out the candle flame by wetting your thumb and forefinger and quickly pinching the burning wick. Relight the candle and try blowing out the flame by using different breath velocities.

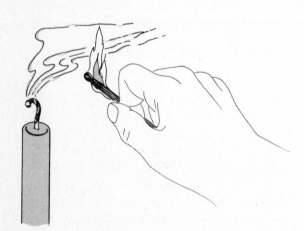

Figure 67 Investigating the vapors.

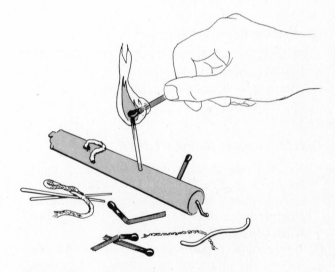

Figure 69 The nature of wicks.

© 1982 Prentice-Hall, Inc.

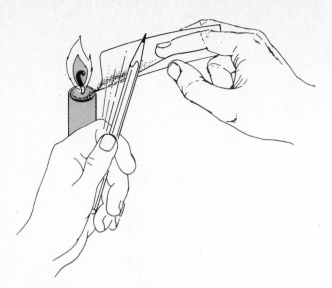

Figure 70 Investigating the liquid in the bowl of a candle.

8. Slide a horizontally held piece of slotted aluminum foil around the wick just below the base of the flame and above the melted wax, as shown in Figure 71. Leave the aluminum in place for about 30 seconds. Account for the observed results.

9. Using a medicine dropper, place 1 or 2 drops of water on the molten wax in the bowl of the lighted candle. What happens?

Questions and regularities

1. Will a candle of larger diameter produce a larger flame? How can you construct a candle so that it will produce a larger flame? Test your hypothesis by experiment.

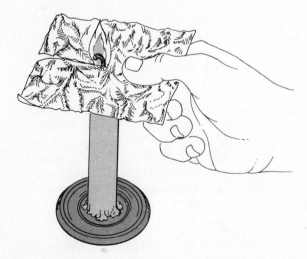

Figure 71 Inserting an aluminum foil below the flame.

2. List as many of the necessary properties of a good wick material as you can.
3. Write a paragraph describing *what you think* is taking place within the candle flame. Justify your arguments with experimental evidence. Propose answers to as many of the introductory questions as you can.
4. How is the solid wax, which is composed of carbon and hydrogen transformed into the products of combustion?

S-3

Behavior of solid copper in an aqueous solution of silver nitrate

In this experiment, you will determine the relationship between the number of moles of copper and the number of moles of silver involved in a chemical reaction. You will find the mass of a sample of solid silver nitrate and prepare a water solution of it. You will also find the mass of a piece of copper wire, place it in the solution, and observe its behavior. By finding the mass of the copper wire at the close of the experiment, you will be able to investigate quantitatively any changes that occur.

In keeping with chemical practice, we shall refer to the chemical substances by using appropriate symbols. Copper is an element; it contains only one kind of atom. The symbol for copper is Cu. Silver nitrate is a compound and the formula identifies it by using the symbol Ag^+ for the silver part and the symbols NO_3^- for the nitrate part. The group of atoms, NO_3^-—consisting of one nitrogen atom and three oxygen atoms, plus an electron—is often found in chemical compounds. It has the name nitrate ion.

PROCEDURE

1. Obtain a piece of heavy copper wire. Straighten out the wire with your hands as well as possible. Starting at one end, wrap a piece of fine copper wire around the heavy wire to within 4 or 5 cm of the other end. Start by putting a tight loop around the end, then a loose spiral for about 4 cm, another tight loop, then a loose spiral, and so on. (See Figure 72.)

2. Find the mass of the wire assembly and of a piece of weighing paper, each to the nearest 0.01 g.

Figure 72 Copper wire assembly.

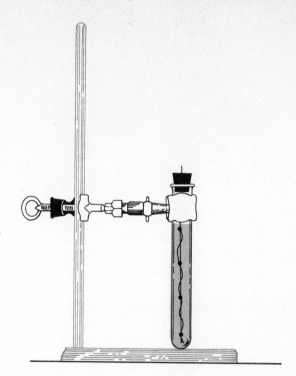

Figure 73 Copper wire assembly in silver nitrate solution.

3. With the weighing paper on the pan of the balance, its mass recorded, and the masses still in place on the balance arm, add exactly 3.00 grams of mass to the arm of the balance. Then open the vial of silver nitrate (AgNO₃) and tap out crystals until exactly 3.00 g have been added to the weighing paper.

4. Put about 10 ml of distilled water into a clean, dry 50- or 100-ml beaker. Add the solid silver nitrate (AgNO₃) to the water and swirl gently until all the solid has dissolved. (**Caution: silver nitrate, solid or solution, reacts with skin and turns it black. Be careful to avoid spillage on your skin or clothing.**)

5. Pour the silver nitrate solution into an 18 × 150 mm test tube that is held by a utility clamp attached to a ring stand. Rinse out the beaker with two 5-ml portions of distilled water. Add the rinses to the solution in the test tube. Mix with a stirring rod. Rinse off the stirring rod with a small quantity of distilled water. Add this rinse to the test tube.

6. Put the wire assembly into the test tube. Make sure it is centered at the bottom. Put a one-hole no. 2 rubber stopper over the wire and fit it loosely into the top of the test tube. (See Figure 73.)

7. For several minutes observe any changes that take place. Let the assembly stand for at least 30 minutes.

8. Meanwhile, determine the mass of a piece of filter paper to the nearest 0.01 g. After folding

the paper, fit it into a funnel and moisten it with some distilled water from a wash bottle.

9. At the end of the 30 minutes, observe any changes that have taken place in the test tube. Record *all* your observations.

10. Remove the rubber stopper, shake the crystals off the wire into the test tube, and remove the wire from the test tube. Use your wash bottle to rinse onto the filter paper any crystals that tend to adhere to the wire. (See Figure 74.) Set the wire aside and weigh it when dry.

11. Pour the contents of the test tube into the filter. Collect the blue solution. Put a fresh beaker under the funnel. Now use your wash bottle to rinse out any particles of silver that may have been left behind in the test tube. Wash the silver thoroughly with distilled water.

12. Clean, dry, label, and determine the mass of the beaker you used in step 4. Set the filter paper cone with the silver into the beaker and put it where it can be dried. Your teacher will suggest a suitable place and method. If the sample is dried overnight with heat lamps or in a drying oven, it should be dry when you return to the laboratory the next day.

13. Allow the beaker containing the filter paper and silver to cool before determining its mass.

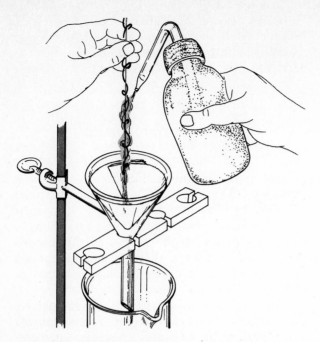

Figure 74 Rinsing crystals from the copper wire.

Record the mass, along with the uncertainty. Return the silver to your teacher for reclaiming.

Your data table should include the following:

1. Numbers that permit you to calculate the mass of the $AgNO_3$ used: the mass of the weighing paper and $AgNO_3$, and the mass of the weighing paper alone.
2. Numbers that permit you to calculate the mass of copper metal used: the mass of the copper wire assembly before and after the reaction.
3. Numbers that permit you to calculate the mass of silver produced: the mass of the empty beaker, the mass of the filter paper, and the mass of the beaker with the filter paper and silver in it.

Calculations and results

1. Calculate the change in mass of the copper wire during the experiment.
2. Calculate the mass of silver obtained in the experiment.
3. Calculate the number of moles of copper that reacted. Recall that the mass of a substance divided by the mass per mole equals the number of moles. Express the uncertainty in your answer as directed by your teacher.
4. Calculate the number of moles of silver. Express the uncertainty in your answer as directed by your teacher.
5. Determine the ratio moles Ag/moles Cu. Express your answer as a decimal. Express the uncertainty in your answer as directed.
6. Calculate (a) the mass of $AgNO_3$ used in the experiment, and (b) the number of moles of $AgNO_3$ used in the experiment.
7. Determine the ratio moles Ag/moles $AgNO_3$. Express your answer as a decimal. Express the uncertainty in your answer as directed.
8. Using the results of calculations 5 and 7, write whole-number coefficients in the following statement:

$$\left[\frac{1\,\text{mole}}{\text{of Cu}(solid)}\right] + \left[\frac{\text{mole(s) of}}{AgNO_3(solution)}\right] \rightarrow$$

$$\left[\frac{\text{mole(s) of}}{Ag(solid)}\right] + \left[\frac{\text{mole(s) of}}{Cu(NO_3)_2(solution)}\right]$$

9. Collect the results obtained by other members of your class. Make a graph of these results. Plot the ratio of moles Ag/moles Cu along the horizontal axis and the number of groups obtaining a particular ratio along the vertical axis.
10. Considering only the middle two-thirds of the data plotted, estimate the range of the values obtained. How does this compare with the uncertainty you considered justifiable from your measurements?
11. How many individual atoms of copper metal were involved in *your* experiment?
12. How many individual atoms of silver metal were produced in *your* experiment?

Questions

1. What causes the color in the solution after the reaction is completed?
2. What is the nature of the particles remaining in the water solution?

FOR FURTHER STUDY

(To be undertaken as an extracurricular experiment. Consult your teacher before proceeding.)

Divide the blue solution obtained in step 11 into equal portions, and conduct the following investigation:

1. Carefully evaporate the solution to dryness. Describe the product.
2. Place a piece of zinc or another metal in the other portion of the blue solution. Describe what you see.

S-4

Half-life of radioactive elements

Nuclear processes can be far more spectacular than chemical processes. Strangely, they can also be far more subtle in their effects than chemical reactions. People now recognize both the power of nuclear chemistry and the responsibility required in its study and use. Many nations have laws and governmental commissions, such as the United States Atomic Energy Commission, charged specifically with promoting and regulating the study and use of nuclear processes.

In Experiments S-4 and S-5, you will investigate a few nuclear reactions, using special apparatus—the Minigenerator—developed by research scientists at Union Carbide Corporation.* Experiments S-4 and S-5 are slightly modified versions of those suggested by Union Carbide. The Minigenerator is a convenient, safe generator of short-lived radioisotopes. Its use will be described along with that of radiation detection equipment.

Precautions for handling radioactive materials

The handling of radioactive materials is safe *provided* that simple laboratory safety precautions are carefully observed. Let us review these precautions here:

1. **Using cosmetics, eating, and drinking are prohibited in the laboratory.**
2. **Under no circumstances should radioactive materials be removed from the laboratory.**
3. Rubber gloves should *always* be worn when working with any radioactive liquid.
4. Any cut or wound that occurs while you are working with radioactive materials must be reported *immediately* to the teacher.
5. *All* radioactive wastes should be stored in special containers. **Do not pour liquids in the sink or put solid wastes in regular waste jars. Use special containers.**
6. Learn to use the radiation detection safety equipment. Your teacher will demonstrate.

7. Before leaving the laboratory, always wash your hands thoroughly and check to be sure that you have no radioactivity on you.
8. If you have any questions on safety, ask your teacher.

INTRODUCTION TO EXPERIMENT S-4

Several types of radioactive decay have been recognized. The text mentions loss of α particles ($_2^4\text{HE}^{++}$), and loss of β particles ($_{-1}^0 e^-$). Another process is loss of gamma radiation ($h\nu$), where $h\nu$ represents rays of high energy. In this experiment, nuclear change through loss of gamma radiation will be considered, using isotopes of indium and barium.

An important characteristic of any radioactive decay process is that *the amount of time required for 50 percent* (or any other convenient percentage) *of the sample to decompose is characteristic of that isotope*. It is determined by the percentage decomposing per minute *and is independent of the size of the sample chosen. The time required for 50 percent* of a given sample to undergo radioactive decay is the *half-life of the isotope*. The half-life of an isotope is characteristic of that particular isotope. In this experiment, you will determine the half-lives of In-113*m* and Ba-137*m* by determining the time required for the radiation emitted by a sample of each to fall to 50 percent of its original intensity.

Indium-113 (In-113*m*) is formed from tin-113 (Sn-113) through capture of an electron by the nucleus. The equation for the reaction is

$$_{50}^{113}\text{Sn} + {}_{-1}^0 e^- \longrightarrow {}_{49}^{113}\text{In-}m$$

The indium-113*m* obtained as a product is an unstable and highly energetic form of indium-113. This is indicated by the *m*, which represents *metastable*. The isotope releases its excess energy as gamma rays. Normal stable indium-113 is the final product.* The process can be described by the equation

$$\text{In-113}m \longrightarrow \text{In-113} + h\nu$$

Barium-137*m* is a metastable isomer of stable barium-137. It is formed by the emission of a

---

*Henry W. Kramer and Wayne J. Gemmill, "Minigenerator Experiments in Nucleonics," 1968, Union Carbide Corporation. Sterling Forest Research Center, Tuxedo, New York 10987. The term Minigenerator is a trademark of the Union Carbide Corporation.

*Usually gamma rays are given off immediately when a nuclear reaction occurs. The formation of a metastable (In-113*m* or Ba-137*m*) nuclear isomer is a more unusual situation, but is a convenient process for study.

beta particle from the nucleus of cesium-137. The equation for the reaction is

$$^{137}_{55}\text{Cs} - {}^{0}_{-1}e^{-} \rightarrow {}^{137}_{56}\text{Ba-}m$$

The isomer exists in this radioactive state until the nucleus achieves stability by emitting a gamma ray. This process can be described by the equation

$$\text{Ba-137}m \rightarrow \text{Ba-137} + h\nu$$

During any period of time a *certain fraction* of the unstable nuclei (In-113m or Ba-137m) will undergo gamma ray loss. By measuring the activity of gamma-ray emission of In-113m and of Ba-137m, the half-life of each will be determined.

PROCEDURE

PART 1

The half-life of indium-113m

1. Turn on the radiation detector and allow it to warm up for five minutes.

2. Measure the number of counts of background activity for one minute. This is the normal level of radiation present in the laboratory. This value must be subtracted from all subsequent activity readings. It is the reading given by your detector when no sample is placed in it.

3. Rinse the $^{113}\text{Sn}/^{113}\text{In-}m$ Minigenerator with about 3 ml of the liquid provided. This procedure is done as follows:
1. Use the plastic bottle supplied with the Minigenerator. Fill it to the line with approximately 5 ml of 0.04 M hydrochloric acid-saline solution.
2. Remove the cap from the spout of the plastic bottle and place the tip of the bottle firmly into the larger opening of the Minigenerator. The tip will "snap" into place, securing the Minigenerator to the bottle.
3. Gently squeeze the plastic bottle to force the rinsing solution through the generator at a rate of 2 to 3 drops per second. Collect the emerging liquid in a small beaker or test tube. As with any other radioactive source in liquid form, care should be taken not to spill the solution. If a spill should occur, it should be wiped up immediately. Notify your teacher.

4. Place the liquid obtained next to the radiation detector.

5. Record two 1-minute readings of the activity of the solution of indium-113m. The average of these readings, corrected for background, becomes A_0 at the time = 0.

6. Measure the activity of the liquid in counts per minute each half-hour for at least three hours. Your teacher may arrange for students in other classes to take later readings if necessary. It is advisable to measure the background activity before each reading on the solution. Record the time of each measurement.

Calculations and results for part 1

1. Subtract the background activity from each activity reading of the sample.
2. Plot your readings of *corrected activity* (in counts per minute) versus *time* on graph paper. Draw the best smooth curve as described by the points.
3. Find two convenient points on the graph in which the initial occurring count rate is exactly twice the later count rate. Draw perpendicular lines from these points to the time axis. The distance along the time axis between these lines represents the half-life of $^{113}\text{In-}m$ (that is, the time required for the activity of a radioactive sample to decrease to half of its original value).
4. Repeat calculation 3 for at least two other sets of count rates.
5. Compute the percent error in your experiment by comparing the average of the values you obtained with the accepted value for the half-life of indium-113m. Your teacher will give you this value.
6. What will be the effect on the half-life of indium-113m when it is: (a) heated to a temperature twice as high on the Kelvin scale? (b) chemically combined with chlorine to form InCl_3? (c) placed in a vacuum of 0.001 atm?

PART 2

The half-life of barium-137m

1. Turn on the radiation detector and allow it to warm up for five minutes.

2. Measure the number of counts of the background activity for one minute. This is the normal level of radiation present in the laboratory, and must be subtracted from all subsequent activity readings.

3. Rinse the $^{137}\text{Cs}/^{137}\text{Ba-}m$ Minigenerator with about 3 ml of the proper solution. This is done as follows:

1. Use the plastic bottle supplied with the Mini-generator. Fill it to the line with approximately 5 ml of 0.05 M hydrochloric acid-saline solution.

2. Remove the cap from the spout of the plastic bottle and place the tip of the bottle firmly into the larger opening of the Minigenerator. The tip will "snap" into place, securing the Minigenerator to the bottle.

3. Gently squeeze the plastic bottle to force the rinsing solution through the generator at a rate of 2 to 3 drops per second. Collect the emerging liquid in a small beaker or test tube. As with any other radioactive source in liquid form, care should be taken not to spill the solution. If a spill should occur, it should be wiped up immediately. Notify your teacher.

4. Place the liquid from the Minigenerator next to the radiation detector.

5. Measure the number of counts emitted by the sample in a one-minute interval, and record that activity. Wait one minute, then proceed, recording one-minute activity readings every other minute for a total of six recordings.

Calculations and results for part 2

1. Subtract the background activity reading from each activity reading for the barium sample.
2. Plot your readings of *corrected activity* (in counts per minute) versus *time* on graph paper. The points should be placed halfway through the first, third, fifth minutes, and so forth. Draw the best smooth curve as described by the points.
3. Select any two convenient points on the graph in which the initial count rate is exactly twice the later count rate. Draw perpendicular lines from these points to the time axis. The distance on the time axis between the lines represents the half-life of ^{137}Ba-m (that is, the time required for the activity of a radioactive sample to decrease to half of its original value).
4. Repeat calculation 3 for at least two other sets of count rates.
5. Compute your percent error by comparing the average of the values you obtained with the accepted value for the half-life of barium 137m.
6. If a reading of 20,000 counts per minute was made on a sample of barium-137m, what should that count be 468 seconds later?

7. When you graphed the activity versus time, you were told to plot each point halfway through the time interval. Why was this done?

S-5

Determination of the shielding thickness of lead

As gamma rays pass through matter they interact with the atoms of the matter. Some of the gamma rays lose all their energy in the collisions. Others give up only part of their energy in a collision and are scattered out of the original beam of gamma rays. The combination of these interactions results in a decrease in intensity of the gamma-ray beam from that which would be observed if the shielding material were not present.

In this experiment, we will determine the thickness of lead sheet that will reduce the intensity of a beam of gamma rays to one-half its original value.

PROCEDURE

1. Turn on the radiation detector and allow it to warm up for five minutes.

2. Measure the number of counts of background activity for one minute. This is the normal level of radiation present in the laboratory. It must be subtracted from all subsequent activity readings.

3. Place the Minigenerator about 2 cm from the detector and record several one-minute activity readings. The average value, corrected for background, is I_0, the original intensity of gamma rays.

4. Measure the thickness of the lead sheets by measuring ten sheets in a stack and dividing that thickness by 10. This gives the average thickness of one sheet.

5. Now record readings as successive sheets are placed between the Minigenerator and detector until the count rate is reduced to less than one-half of the original count rate. Repeat if time permits.

Calculations and results

1. Subtract the background activity from each activity reading of the Minigenerator.

2. Plot your readings of *corrected activity* (in counts per minute) against *thickness* (measured in millimetres). Draw the best smooth curve as described by the points.

3. From this graph, select two points such that the earlier intensity reading is just twice the latter. The distance along the x-axis between these two points represents the thickness of material that reduces the gamma-ray intensity by half—that is, the half-value thickness.

4. Repeat calculation 3 for two different sets of count rates. Compute the average half-value thickness.

5. If 2 inches of lead shielding reduces the radiation from an atomic reactor to one-half its unshielded value, what thickness of lead is necessary to reduce the intensity to 1/64 the unshielded value?

S-6

Some properties of cis-trans isomers

Maleic acid and fumaric acid have the same molecular formula: $C_4H_4O_4$. Each contains two carboxyl,—COOH, groups and each exhibits the properties of an unsaturated organic compound, which indicates the presence of a double bond,

$$\diagup \!\!\! C = C \diagdown$$

Yet each possesses its own distinctive properties, such as melting point, solubility, density, and stability. Chemists attribute these differences to the geometry, or arrangement in space, of the atoms in the molecule. Observe the space-filling and the ball-and-stick molecular models of the two acids illustrated in Figure 75. Note that in the *trans*-form the carboxyl groups are on opposite sides of the molecule; in the *cis*-form, they are on the same side. The fact that the two forms can be isolated indicates that rotation of the molecule at the double bond does not occur readily.

In this experiment, you will convert some maleic acid to fumaric acid by heating it in an aqueous solution containing some hydrochloric acid. The hydrochloric acid is not used up by the reaction but serves merely as a source of H^+, which is the catalyst. You will be able to determine the completeness of the conversion by separating the fumaric acid and comparing its mass with that of the maleic acid initially used. You will also compare some of the properties of the

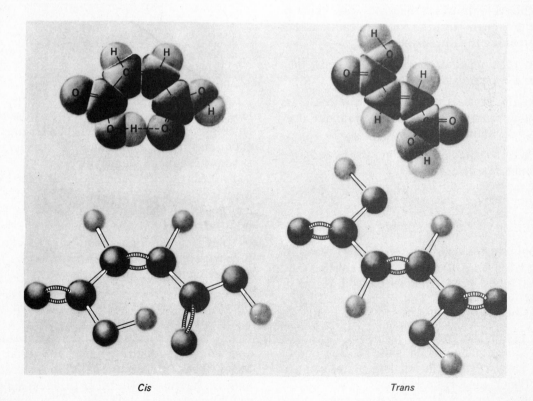

Cis   Trans

Figure 75   Molecular models of two isomeric organic acids.

acids and attempt to explain any differences in terms of their structures. This should enable you to develop some arguments about which acid, maleic or fumaric, is the *trans-* form and which is the *cis-* form.

PROCEDURE

PART 1

Conversion of maleic acid to fumaric acid

1. Obtain a 6.0 g sample of maleic acid and place it in a clean, dry 100-ml beaker. Add 10 ml of distilled water, and warm slightly to dissolve the acid.

2. Add 15 ml of 12 *M* HCl and cover the beaker with a watch glass. Place the beaker inside a 250-ml beaker that is about one-third full of water. Heat this water bath to boiling for about 5 minutes or until a solid material forms in the smaller beaker.

3. Cool the solution to room temperature by placing the smaller beaker in a cold-water bath.

4. Pour the mixture into a filter. Wash any remaining solid into the filter by rinsing the beaker with small amounts of cold water from a wash bottle. Allow the crystals to drain. If an aspirator is available, attach its hose to the stem of the funnel to draw out the wash water remaining in the funnel. Turn the water on cautiously to avoid breaking the filter paper.

5. Find the mass of a watch glass, and then transfer the crystals to the glass.

6. Dry the crystals by placing the watch glass over an appropriately sized beaker about one-third full of boiling water.

7. When the sample is dry, find its mass. Label the sample *Fumaric Acid*.

PART 2

Comparison of the two isomers

1. Compare the solubility of the two acids by placing 1.0 ± 0.1 g of each into separate 18 × 150 mm test tubes, properly labeled. Add 10 ml of distilled water to each and make a qualitative comparison of solubility.

2. Compare the melting points of the acids using the setup shown in Figure 76. See Figure 19, on page 17, for the method of inserting a thermometer into a rubber stopper.

   1. Obtain two capillary melting point tubes (1.0 mm–1.5 mm in diameter and 6 cm–12 cm in

Figure 76 A melting point apparatus.

length). Make one tube shorter than the other by cutting off a centimetre or so. Seal one end of each tube in a burner flame. Place maleic acid in the shorter tube to identify it.

   2. Push the open end of the shorter capillary tube into some *dry* maleic acid. Tap the closed end gently on the table so the solid packs down into the tube. Continue to do this until the depth of solid is 1 cm–2 cm. Similarly, fill the longer tube with a sample of *dry* fumaric acid.

   3. Attach the tubes to a −10 °C–150 °C thermometer with a small rubber circle cut from the end of a piece of rubber tubing. The liquid in the flask is vegetable oil.

   4. Clamp the melting-point apparatus in place and heat it gradually with a low burner flame. Move the flame occasionally to achieve more uniform heating of the oil bath. Heat slowly and watch the capillary tubes closely as the temperature approaches 120 °C. At the sign of first

melting of either solid, record the temperature. **(Caution: do not exceed the 150 °C limit of the thermometer.)** The melting point of the other sample is 287 °C.

3. Compare the chemical properties of the two isomers as follows:

1. Prepare a solution of maleic acid by adding approximately 0.1 g to about 20 ml of distilled water. Divide the solution among three small test tubes. Estimate the hydrogen ion concentration by testing one portion with a few drops of orange IV. To another portion add a 3-cm strip of magnesium ribbon. Record the results. To another portion add a small amount (size of a pea) of sodium carbonate. Record the results.

2. Repeat the above tests, using fumaric acid. Record the results and compare them with those obtained with maleic acid.

3. (*To be assigned to selected students or demonstrated by the teacher.*) Titrate a 1.00 ± 0.01 g sample of each acid with a standard base solution using phenolphthalein as the indicator. Refer to Experiment 50 for directions about carrying out the titrations.

Questions and regularities

1. Assuming that equilibrium concentrations were achieved in Part 1, which acid would you classify as the more stable with respect to the transformation of one into the other?
2. What does each of the following experiments contribute to your knowledge of the structure of each isomer: (a) the reactions with magnesium and with sodium carbonate; (b) the titration data—that is, the number of moles of base required to titrate each acid; (c) the reactions of solutions of each acid with an indicator; (d) the melting-point determination?
3. Maleic acid can lose a molecule of water from each molecule of acid when its two carboxyl groups react to form an anhydride. Which structural isomer, *cis-* or *trans-*, do you predict it is? Fumaric acid cannot do this. Explain.

S-7

A study of reaction rates: Decomposition of hypochlorite ion

In this experiment we shall continue our study of the factors that influence the rate of a reaction. We shall investigate the rate of decomposition of aqueous sodium hypochlorite, $NaOCl(aq)$. We shall use a commercially available bleaching solution that contains about 5 percent by weight sodium hypochlorite as a source of the hypochlorite ion, OCl^-. This ion decomposes according to the following equation:

$$2\,OCl^-(aq) \rightarrow O_2(g) + 2Cl^-(aq)$$

Since the rate of this reaction is extremely slow under normal conditions, we shall use a solid catalyst, an oxide of cobalt, to catalyze each of the reactions studied. The catalyst will be prepared right in the reaction vessel by allowing a few millilitres of a 0.17 *M* solution of cobalt nitrate, $Co(NO_3)_2$, to react with some of the bleaching solution. The reaction for the formation of the solid catalyst is thought to be

$$2Co^{++}(aq) + OCl^-(aq) + 2H_2O \rightarrow$$
$$Co_2O_3(s) + 4H^+(aq) + Cl^-(aq)$$

Decomposition starts as soon as the catalyst forms. The rate of the hypochlorite decomposition will be followed by measuring at definite time intervals the volume of water displaced by the oxygen formed. The effect of temperature will be studied by determining the rate at room temperature and at approximately 10 degrees Celsius above and below room temperature. The effect of concentration on the rate will be determined by diluting the bleaching solution.

Your teacher will designate which part or parts of the experiment are to be done by you and your partner. One of the partners should prepare a data table for recording the time, every 30 seconds, and the volume of water displaced by the oxygen. Before you write up the experiment, you should exchange data with other partners so you will be able to plot the results of Parts 1, 2, 3, and 4.

PROCEDURE

Set up the apparatus as shown in Figure 77. If the bent glass tubing is not available, see pages 16–18, which describe how to cut, bend, and fire polish glass tubing. Also note the proper technique illustrated for inserting glass tubing through rubber stoppers. Your teacher may prefer to furnish you with pre-assembled stoppers and glass tubing. Use 125-ml Erlenmeyer flasks.

The apparatus will require less attention if the second flask is clamped to a ring stand.

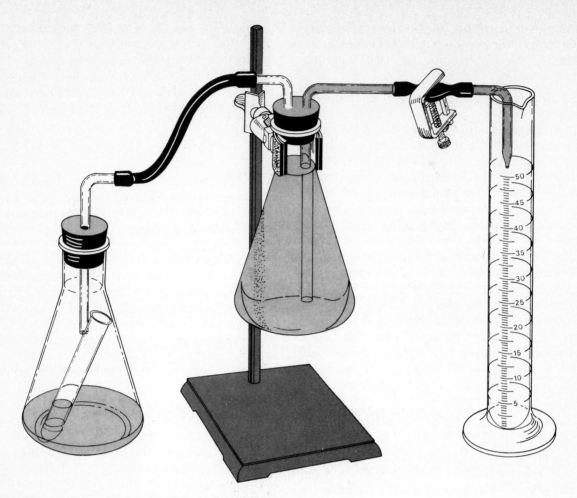

Figure 77 Apparatus for measuring the rate of decomposition.

PART 1

Decomposition rate at room temperature

1. Measure carefully 15.0 ml of the sodium hypochlorite solution into a graduated cylinder. Determine its temperature and then pour it into the first Erlenmeyer flask. Place 3 ml of the cobalt nitrate solution into a 13 × 100 mm test tube and insert it carefully into the same Erlenmeyer flask, as shown in Figure 77.

2. Fill the second Erlenmeyer flask full of water and replace the stopper.

3. Open the pinch clamp and fill the delivery tube leading to the 50-ml graduated cylinder by blowing into the rubber tubing attached to the short glass elbow inserted in the second Erlenmeyer flask. Close the pinch clamp while the tube is full of water.

4. Make all connections and check that the rubber stoppers fit tightly in the flasks. Remove the pinch clamp. If your apparatus is airtight,

only a few drops of water will drip into the graduated cylinder.

5. Note the time as you quickly tip the reaction flask slightly to pour the cobalt nitrate solution out of the test tube into the sodium hypochlorite solution.

6. Hold the erect flask at its neck and move it constantly with a *gentle* swinging motion to dislodge the gas bubbles from the solid catalyst in a uniform manner. This motion *must* be gentle and uniform in all trials.

7. Record the volume of water in the graduated cylinder every 30 seconds until about 50 ml have been collected.

PART 2

Decomposition rate above room temperature

Rinse out the reaction flask and repeat the procedure as directed above, but have the temperature of the solutions in the reaction flask at about 10 degrees Celsius above room temperature by warming in a lukewarm water bath.

PART 3
Decomposition rate below room temperature

Repeat the procedure with the solutions in the reaction flask at about 10 degrees Celsius below room temperature. Cool the flask and solutions in a cold-water bath.

PART 4
Decomposition rate using a twofold dilution of the bleaching solution

Repeat the procedure at room temperature as in Part 1, but add 18 ml of water to the sodium hypochlorite solution in the flask in order to effect a twofold dilution in the final volume.

PART 5
Decomposition at other dilutions as directed by your teacher

PART 6
Optional extensions of this experiment to be assigned to selected students

1. Investigate another solid oxide as a possible catalyst by using 3 ml of 0.17 M iron(III) nitrate solution in place of the 0.17 M cobalt nitrate solution.

2. Investigate a combination of solid oxide catalysts by using a 1-to-1 mixture of solutions of $Co(NO_3)_2$ and $Fe(NO_3)_3$, and precipitating mixed oxides as possible catalysts.

Calculations and results

1. After exchanging data with other students, plot the data from Parts 1, 2, 3, and 4 on the same graph paper. Plot the volume of oxygen produced along the vertical axis and time along the horizontal axis. Label each curve.
2. Make as quantitative a statement as possible concerning the relation between the temperature and the rate of the reaction.
3. If you had carried out the decomposition at 60 °C, what would you predict the appearance of the curve to be?
4. Compare the observed rates for diluted and nondiluted NaOCl solutions.
5. Predict where the rate curve would be if the concentration of sodium hypochlorite in the

bleaching solution were 10 percent instead of the 5 percent present in the commercial bleach.
6. (*Optional*) Did the solid oxide formed when you used $Fe(NO_3)_3$ solution serve as a catalyst? What was the effect that you noted for a mixture of oxides?

S-8
Developing a scheme of qualitative analysis

In your experiments so far you have studied the chemical behavior of many substances. But in every case those substances that were in solution were kept in separate bottles. What happens if there are several substances in the same solution? In this experiment you will develop the type of reasoning that is used in *qualitative analysis,* a branch of chemistry that deals with the *separation* and *identification* of substances present in mixtures.

To develop a scheme of analysis, it is necessary to determine how solutions of pure substances react with each other and then to study the differences in behavior so that each substance can be distinguished from all others. Consider the following hypothetical case, in which reagents marked X, Y, and Z were allowed to react with samples of each of the unknown solutions 1, 2, 3, and 4. The observations are shown in Table 14. The $+$ means a distinctive reaction was observed, and the $-$ means no evidence of reaction was noted. The color of precipitates or changes in color of solutions are also noted. If you were given an unknown that you were told was either solution 1, 2, 3, or 4, what method would you outline to identify the unknown by its reactions with reagents X, Y, and Z? How many tests would be involved? If an unknown gives a $-$ test with X and a $+$ test with Y, does this identify it? Suppose another unknown gives a $+$ test with X. Is this sufficient to identify it?

In this experiment you are to discover how four solutions, labeled 1, 2, 3, and 4, react when each is added to three reagents labeled A, B, and C. You should observe in which reactions a precipitate is formed, and note color changes and other evidences of reaction. The solutions and reagents are deliberately *not* labeled (other than by letter and number) so that you can focus your attention on the *reasoning* that must be used to develop a scheme of analysis.

Table 14

Solutions	Reagents		
	X	Y	Z
1	−	+ (yellow)	+ (yellow)
2	+ (white)	−	+ (white)
3	−	−	+ (blue)
4	−	+ (white)	−

Organize a table similar to Table 14. After you have recorded the results in tabular form, study them carefully and develop a scheme for discriminating among the four solutions.

PROCEDURE

1. Obtain a square of thin plastic sheet. Place a drop of one of the solutions on the plastic. Add a drop of one of the reagent solutions to it. Make tests on each of the solutions 1, 2, 3, and 4 with reagents A, B, and C for all possible combinations. Record your results as a + or −, and note any distinctive characteristics for every + test.

2. Study the table carefully and note the differences in behavior. Obtain an unknown solution from your teacher and test it to determine whether it is solution 1, 2, 3, or 4. Report your results. Include a summary of the evidence that supports your conclusion.

3. If time permits, obtain another unknown solution that contains a mixture of *two* of the solutions. You may assume that the solutions 1, 2, 3, and 4 do not react with each other. Make tests and report your conclusion along with the supporting evidence.

S-9

Qualitative analysis of Ag^+, Hg_2^{++}, and Pb^{++}

Only three of the common metal ions, Ag^+, Hg_2^{++}, and Pb^{++}, form chlorides of low solubility. Because of this, the addition of chloride ion to a solution and the resulting formation of chloride precipitates will separate these ions from other cations. Differences in the reactions of these three chlorides can then be used to separate them from each other.

In the first part of this experiment, you will become familiar with a few reactions used to identify the silver, mercury(I), and lead ions in solution. From these observations you will be able to devise a method by which you can analyze an unknown solution and determine the presence or absence of each ion. Make a record of your observations for each test.

PROCEDURE

1. Start heating a 100-ml beaker half filled with water to serve as a hot-water bath in step 2. In small test tubes prepare separate samples of each precipitate—$AgCl$, Hg_2Cl_2, and $PbCl_2$—by adding 10 drops of 6 *M* HCl to 1 ml of each of the test solutions—$AgNO_3$, $Hg_2(NO_3)_2$, and $Pb(NO_3)_2$. You may need to cool the test tube containing the Pb^{++} ions to obtain a precipitate.

2. Allow the chloride precipitates to settle in each tube or use a centrifuge if available. Decant or draw off the liquid with a medicine dropper. Discard the solution. Add about 2 ml of distilled water to each precipitate and place the test tubes containing the mixtures in the boiling-water bath. With frequent shaking, heat the tubes for a few minutes. Which of the chlorides is most soluble in hot water?

3. With a medicine dropper remove about 5 drops of the solution containing the most soluble chloride. Transfer the drops to a clean test tube and add 5 drops of 0.1 *M* K_2CrO_4 solution.

4. Remove the three test tubes from the hot-water bath and cool them in cold water. Shake the tubes occasionally to stir the precipitates. Allow each precipitate to settle and decant the solution from each. Discard the liquid but keep the precipitates for additional tests.

5. Add about 3 ml of 6 *M* $NH_3(aq)$ to each of the precipitates. Shake the test tubes. Add about 3 ml of 6 *M* HNO_3 to the test tubes in which the precipitate dissolved.

6. Examine your results and use them to develop a scheme by which you can identify the presence of one, two, or all three of these cations in an unknown solution. Answer the two questions in Questions and regularities before going on to step 7.

7. Obtain an unknown from your teacher and analyze it for the presence of one or more of the cations used in this experiment. Report your results *along with supporting evidence.*

Questions and regularities

1. Write equations for all reactions occurring in this experiment.
2. Construct a flow chart summarizing the steps you would use to analyze an unknown solution containing all three cations—Ag^+, Hg_2^{++}, and Pb^{++}.

S-10
Qualitative analysis: Negative ions

In Experiment S-8 you considered the principles involved in developing a scheme of qualitative analysis with a group of unlabeled solutions. In this experiment you will observe and record some characteristic chemical reactions of several negatively charged ions—SO_4^{--}, CO_3^{--}, Cl^-, and I^-—with selected reagents. From a study of these observations, you will be able to develop a method for identifying each of these ions in the presence of the other ions.

Your work will be typical of the work done by those chemists who develop more elaborate schemes that can be used to identify dozens of cations and anions in a given sample. Organize a data table in which you can record your observations for the results obtained by adding each of the reagents to each of the solutions of anions to be studied (Table 15).

PROCEDURE

1. Use the testing technique developed in Experiments 14 and S-8. Place drops of both solution and reagent together on a thin plastic sheet or spot plate. Do not contaminate the dropper from the reagent bottle by allowing it to come into contact with the drop of solution already on the plastic sheet.

2. Test 3 to 4 drops of each solution separately with 1 to 2 drops of the 0.1 M $Ba(NO_3)_2$ reagent. After recording the results, add 2 to 3 drops of 1.0 M HNO_3 to each spot that contains a precipitate. Record any changes that you observe.

3. Test 3 to 4 drops of each solution separately with 1 to 2 drops of the 0.1 M $AgNO_3$ reagent. Record the results observed. To each spot that contains a precipitate, add 2 to 3 drops of 1.0 M HNO_3 and record any changes that you observe.

4. Prepare new samples of the silver precipitates that formed in step c. Add 2 to 3 drops of 6 M aqueous ammonia, $NH_3(aq)$, to the precipitates and record any changes that you observe.

5. Test 3 to 4 drops of each solution separately with 1 to 2 drops of 1.0 M HNO_3 and record the results.

6. Examine the pattern of reactions shown by your table of observations. Develop a scheme by which you can identify one or a combination of two of the anions in a single solution. Organize your scheme in such a way that another student can follow it. You may wish to try it out by making up your own "trial unknowns" containing various combinations of the anions.

7. Obtain an unknown from your teacher and analyze it for the four anions. Report your results. Include supporting evidence for your conclusions.

Questions and regularities

1. Write net ionic equations for the precipitation reactions that occurred when solutions of the anions were mixed with the solution containing Ba^{++} ions.
2. Do the same for the precipitation reactions that occurred in step 3 with the Ag^+ ions.
3. Write equations for the reactions that occurred when the precipitates were acidified with 1.0 M HNO_3.
4. Write equations for the reactions that occurred when the silver precipitates reacted

Table 15

Solutions	Anions	Reagents	Cations
0.1 M sodium sulfate, Na_2SO_4	SO_4^{--}	0.1 M barium nitrate, $Ba(NO_3)_2$	Ba^{++}
0.5 M sodium carbonate, Na_2CO_3	CO_3^{--}	0.1 M silver nitrate, $AgNO_3$	Ag^+
0.1 M sodium chloride, $NaCl$	Cl^-	1.0 M nitric acid, HNO_3	H^+
0.1 M sodium iodide, NaI	I^-		

with aqueous ammonia to form the complex ion $Ag(NH_3)_2^+$.

S-11

Qualitative analysis of some second-column compounds: Using relative solubilities

In this experiment, you will study the effect of adding reagents containing selected negative ions (anions) to solutions containing the positive ions (cations) of the metals of the second column. The chemical behavior of the elements in the second column of the periodic table is similar enough that a solution containing a mixture of their ions is difficult to separate. Many of the compounds they form are only slightly soluble, but it is possible to find differences in solubility that will permit you to separate the ions of these metals.

Before coming to the laboratory, you will *predict* which combinations are expected to form compounds of low solubility, using Table 16-7 on page 439 and Table 16-8 on page 449 of your textbook. After doing the experiment you will compare your predictions with the results obtained and attempt to explain any differences between them. You should then be able to make a qualitative analysis of an unknown solution containing one of the cations of the second column of the periodic table.

Organize a table in which you can record the *predictions* of the results that you will obtain when each solution containing a cation of the second column is tested with each of the reagents listed.

The solutions are

1. 0.1 M $Mg(NO_3)_2$, a source of Mg^{++}
2. 0.1 M $Ca(NO_3)_2$, a source of Ca^{++}
3. 0.1 M $Sr(NO_3)_2$, a source of Sr^{++}
4. 0.1 M $Ba(NO_3)_2$, a source of Ba^{++}

The reagents are

1. 0.5 M Na_2CO_3, a source of CO_2^{--}
2. 0.5 M K_2CrO_4, a source of CrO_4^{--}
3. 0.1 M $NaOH$, a source of OH^-
4. 0.5 M Na_2SO_4, a source of SO_4^{--}

List the cations in a vertical column at the left side of your prediction table. List the anions across the top of the table.

Using the information on page 434 and pages 448 to 452 of your text, predict which combinations of ions are expected to have low solubility.

In order to make predictions for the reactions with CrO_4^{--}, use the information on the relative solubilities given in Table 16-9 on page 451. Which cation is least soluble and which is most soluble in the presence of chromate ion? Show this part of your prediction by writing *most ppt* and *least ppt* in the appropriate spaces of your prediction table.

Now make a second table on your data page, identical to the first, in which you will record your *observations* of these reactions when you perform them in the laboratory. Leave room for recording the *degree* of solubility. Few substances are totally soluble or totally insoluble, and you will want to watch for and record differences in amounts of precipitates.

PROCEDURE

PART 1

Testing the solubilities of the cations

1. Use clean 13 × 100 mm test tubes. Test about 1 ml of each of the solutions of metal nitrates with about 1 ml of each of the reagents. Estimate these amounts in the manner your teacher suggests.

2. Record your observations completely in your data table. Make one observation immediately after mixing the two solutions and a second observation after 7 to 10 minutes.

3. In those test tubes in which precipitates were obtained with CrO_4^{--} ion, make careful observations of the relative amounts of the precipitates obtained. Dilute each of these solutions by adding distilled water until the test tubes are nearly full. Mix well. Does this procedure suggest a way of distinguishing between these cations?

4. Repeat your study of the reactions between Mg^{++}, Ca^{++}, Sr^{++}, Ba^{++} ions and OH^- ion, but use 0.5 M $NaOH$ as the source of the OH^- ions. Record the results and note any differences from the results obtained using 0.1 M $NaOH$.

5. Study all the data carefully and compare the results obtained with the predictions that you made. Note any differences.

PART 2

Qualitative analysis

Obtain an unknown solution from your teacher. It will contain only *one* of the cations of the second column. Test the solution to determine which of the cations it contains. Record all observations on the data page.

Calculations and results

1. Which of the cations did your unknown contain? Give the reasoning that supports your conclusion.
2. From your observations of the relative amounts of precipitated $MgCO_3$, $CaCO_3$, $SrCO_3$, and $BaCO_3$, which carbonate would you expect to have the largest K_{sp} value?
3. (a) Which metal chromate is the least soluble? (b) How could this difference in solubility be used to separate Ba^{++} from Sr^{++} in a solution that was 0.1 M in each of these ions?
4. (a) Account for the difference noted when 0.5 M NaOH was used in place of the 0.1 M NaOH. (b) Calculate the trial K_{sp} value for $Ca(OH)_2$ (1) when using 0.5 M NaOH and (2) when using 0.1 M NaOH. Remember that the original concentrations of Ca^{++} and OH^- are cut in half when equal volumes of the two solutions are mixed. (c) From your observations and the trial K_{sp} values calculated, estimate the K_{sp} value for Ca $(OH)_2$.
5. The solubility product constants for the sulfates of the cations of the second column are listed in Table 16-9, on page 451 of the text. If a 0.0020 M solution of Na_2SO_4 were added separately to an equal volume of a 0.0020 M solution of each of the cations of the second column, in which case(s) would a precipitate form?

1

Measurement

The International System of Units (SI): The scientific standard for measurement

The *metric system* of measurement is a decimal system with each component a multiple or subdivision of ten. It is used for everyday business in almost every country in the world except the United States. For scientific work, the metric system is used in all countries of the world.

In 1960, the General Conference of Weights and Measures (CGPM) established the International System of Units, or SI, as a revision and extension of the metric system. For each kind of measurement, a base unit or one derived from the base unit is defined. The base and derived units used in this course are given in Table 16. Multiples and subdivisions of a unit are named by attaching a prefix to that unit. The SI prefixes are listed in Table 17. Not all are used in this course.

A decimal system with which you are familiar is the United States monetary system. Let us see how the SI prefixes are or could be used in that system. The base unit of monetary measure is the *dollar*. Using some of the prefixes from Table 17 results in the values shown in Table 18.

Exercise 1

1. Give another name for the following monetary values: (a) decipenny, (b) milligrand, (c) kilodime, (d) centidime, (e) decidime, (f) kilopenny, (g) megabuck, (h) hectodollar.
2. How much money is represented by each of the following: (a) 25 decipennies, (b) 73 centidollars, (c) 95 centidimes, (d) 0.37 kilodollars, (e) 1610 millidollars, (f) 3.68 decidimes, (g) 0.042 megadimes, (h) 254 hectopennies.
3. (a) Name five common pieces of money (coin or bill) that are *not* multiples or submultiples of the dollar. Then convert the following amounts to the given multiples or submultiples of a dollar: (b) $75 to da$, (c) 56¢ to c$, (d) $1,027 to k$, (e) $2,080,000 to M$, (f) $3.54 to d$, (g) $967 to h$.

Now let us apply these principles to the kinds of measurements you will make in the laboratory.

Table 16

Quantity	Name of unit	Symbol
length	metre	m
mass	kilogram	kg
time	second	s
electric current	ampere	A
thermodynamic temperature	kelvin	K
amount of substance	mole	mol
area	square metre	m^2
volume	cubic metre	m^3
density	kilogram per cubic metre	$kg\, m^{-3}$
concentration	mole per cubic metre	$mol\, m^{-3}$
molar mass	kilogram per mole	$kg\, mol^{-1}$
molar volume	cubic metre per mole	$m^3\, mol^{-1}$

Table 17

Prefix	Symbol	Fractional part or multiple of unit	Prefix	Symbol	Fractional part or multiple of unit
tera-	T	10^{12}	deci-	d	10^{-1}
giga-	G	10^9	centi-	c	10^{-2}
mega-	M	10^6	milli-	m	10^{-3}
kilo-	k	10^3	micro-	μ	10^{-6}
hecto-	h	10^2	nano-	n	10^{-9}
deka-	da	10^1	pico-	p	10^{-12}
			femto-	f	10^{-15}
			atto-	a	10^{-18}

Table 18

Prefix	Metric name	Monetary name	Equivalents
milli-	*milli*dollar	mill	1 mill = $0.001 and 1,000 mills = $1.00
centi-	*centi*dollar	cent	1 cent = $0.01 and 100 cents = $1.00
deci-	*deci*dollar	dime	1 dime = $0.10 and 10 dimes = $1.00
kilo-	*kilo*dollar	grand (kilobuck)	1 grand = $1,000

LENGTH

The base unit of length in SI is the *metre,* a distance slightly longer than a yard. Table 19 should help you establish the relationships between the various units of length.

Exercise 2

1. Change (a) 13 mm to centimetres and metres, (b) 760 mm to centimetres and metres, (c) 4.1 m to centimetres and millimetres, and (d) 0.083 km to metres and millimetres.
2. A rectangular block of metal is measured and found to have the following dimensions: length = 12.1 cm, width = 9.8 cm, and depth = 6.4 cm. (a) Add two times the length and two times the width to obtain the perimeter of the largest face. Express your answer to the nearest 0.1 cm. (b) Find the area of the largest face.

MASS

The base unit of mass in the SI is the *kilogram.* However, from an experimental standpoint, the *gram* (1 g = 0.001 kg) is a more practical unit, and it is the one you will use most often in this course. (One way to get a feeling for the smallness of the gram unit is to remember that a five-cent piece has a mass of about 5 grams.) Table 20 should help you to establish the relationships between the various units of mass.

Exercise 3

1. Change (a) 454 g to kilograms, (b) 3.2 kg to grams and milligrams, and (c) 0.0056 centigrams to kilograms.
2. Weigh several different volumes of water (between 10 ml and 250 ml) at room temperature. Plot the masses on the vertical axis and the corresponding volumes on the horizontal axis of a graph. What can you deduce for the mass of 1 ml of water at room temperature?
3. Weigh 100 ml of water at different temperatures between 15 °C and 80 °C (heat the water to the temperature of interest, *then* measure the 100-ml volume). On a graph plot the mass on the vertical scale and the temperature of the water on the horizontal scale. Are you justified in assuming that 1 ml of water has a constant mass within these temperature limits?

VOLUME

Volume may be expressed in terms of any of the units of length cubed. Therefore, the base unit of volume in the SI is the *cubic metre,* m^3. However, the smaller submultiples, particularly cm^3 and dm^3, are more convenient sizes in the laboratory.

In measuring the volume of liquids, the *litre* unit is used. This latter term is used as a special name for the cubic decimetre, dm^3. A still smaller unit, the millilitre, is approximately equal to $1 cm^3$ (1 ml = 1.000 028 cm^3). For the precision

Table 19

Unit	Symbol	Metric equivalents	English equivalents
kilometre	km	1 km = 1,000 m 0.001 km = 1 m	1 mile = 1.6 km
metre	m	—	1 m = 39.37 in
decimetre	dm	1 dm = 0.1 m 10 dm = 1 m	
centimetre	cm	1 cm = 0.01 m 100 cm = 1 m 10 cm = 1 dm	1 in = 2.54 cm
millimetre	mm	1 mm = 0.001 m 1,000 mm = 1 m 10 mm = 1 cm	

Table 20

Unit	Symbol	Metric equivalents	English equivalents
kilogram	kg	—	2.2 lb = 1 kg
gram	g	1 g = 0.001 kg 1,000 g = 1 kg	1 oz = 28 g
decigram	dg	1 dg = 10^{-4} kg 10^4 dg = 1 kg	1 lb = 454 g
centigram	cg	1 cg = 10^{-5} kg 10^5 cg = 1 kg 100 cg = 1 g	
milligram	mg	1 mg = 10^{-6} kg 10^6 mg = 1 kg 1,000 mg = 1 g	

Table 21

Unit	Symbol	Metric equivalents	English equivalents
cubic metre	m³	—	1 m³ = 1.3 yd³
cubic decimetre (litre)	dm³ (l)	1 dm³ = 0.001 m³ 1,000 dm³ = 1 m³	1 litre = 1.06 qt
cubic centimetre (millilitre)	cm³ (ml)	1 cm³ = 10⁻⁶ m³ 10⁶ cm³ = 1 m³	

of the work that we shall do in the laboratory, we can consider the two units to be of equal size. Table 21 will help you establish the relationships between various units of volume.

Exercise 4

1. Change (a) 1500 ml to litres, (b) 250 ml to litres, (c) 1.3 litres to millilitres, and (d) 67.3 cubic metres to cubic decimetres.
2. Find the volume of the metal block for which dimensions were given in the exercises on length.

DENSITY

The density of an object is a *derived* quantity. It is not measured directly, but is derived from other direct measurements. Density, *D*, is the mass per unit volume of an object. In the English system, density has the units of pounds per cubic inch or pounds per cubic foot. In SI, density is expressed as kilograms per cubic metre or kilograms per cubic decimetre (for gases). In common usage, density is expressed in grams per cubic centimetre.

Exercise 5

1. Calculate the density of the metal block if the mass is 2.100 kg. Use the volume calculated in Exercise 4, question 2.

$$D = \frac{\text{mass}}{\text{volume}}$$

2. What is the density of water according to the information obtained in Exercise 3, question 2?

Expressing numbers: When does the number end?

As you do calculations for your laboratory work, you often will be faced with the question of how many digits to use in the answer. For example, in calculating the heat of fusion of a substance (calories per gram) you might be dividing 98.00 calories (cal) by 1.23 grams. The answer is 79.674 79 . . . with no end in sight. In fact, if you were to continue dividing, you would never finish because the answer is a five-digit repeating decimal.

In the absence of other information concerning the precision of our measurements, it is necessary, then, to follow a general rule governing the number of digits in an answer. The rule states that *when multiplying or dividing any set of numbers, the product or quotient will contain the same number of* significant figures *as the least precise component.* This is not an exact rule, since rare examples can be found that do not follow the rule, but it is an easy rule to follow and it works most of the time.

In the example above, 98.00 has four significant figures, 1.23 has three. Therefore, according to the rule, the answer should have three significant figures and be written as 79.7.

Obviously, our rule will be useful as long as we understand how many significant figures any given number contains. Before discussing that problem, it should be emphasized that using significant figures to express the precision of a number only gives an *approximate* idea of that precision. If data are available for making a calculation of the actual uncertainty of a value, they should be used. See pages 136–139 for a discussion of uncertainty in numbers.

SIGNIFICANT FIGURES

In making a measurement, *record all integers that are certain and one more in which there is some uncertainty.* You will then have recorded all the numbers that have meaning—all the significant figures. Note that the above statement says nothing about the location of the decimal point. Ther is *no* relationship between the number of significant figures and the decimal point. Each of the numbers 3,609, 0.036 09, and 0.000 000 000 003 609 has four significant figures.

There is only one numeral that might require a decision to be made when counting the number of significant figures. That numeral is *zero.* Unfortunately, we let 0 do two jobs—mark the decimal place and count—and sometimes in a given situation it is not clear whether it is doing one or the other or both jobs. For example, suppose that the population of a small town is reported as 25,000 people. Does this mean exactly 25,000? Probably not. An exact count of the residents might be

24,471, 25,303, or any number that rounds off to 25,000. Both 24,471 and 25,303 have five significant figures. With the number 25,000, it is impossible to tell the exact population. Suppose the actual population is *exactly* 25,000 people. How can this number be expressed to indicate that the zeros *are* significant?

The doubt concerning the significance of the last zero is caused by letting the zero do two jobs. One easy solution to this problem is to make a new rule that says *all* numerals can have only one job. That job is to count. This new rule now makes it necessary to develop a new method for locating the decimal point. One such method uses exponential notation.

EXPONENTIAL NOTATION

When a number is written in exponential notation, there is never any doubt about the number of significant figures. In addition, this shorthand method of writing numbers can be extremely useful in expressing very large or very small numbers.

The exponential form of a number consists of two parts. The first part is written as a number between one and ten and includes all significant figures. The second part locates the decimal point. In locating the decimal point, use is made of the fact that multiplying any number by ten moves the decimal point one place to the right. For example, $3.6 \times 10 = 36$. Similarly, dividing any number by ten moves the decimal point one place to the left. For example, $3.6/10 = 0.36$. Thus, by multiplying or dividing a number by ten the proper number of times, we can move the decimal point anywhere we want.

The shorthand part of the method concerns the way we indicate *how many tens* to multiply or divide by. If we want to move the decimal five places to the right, we could indicate this by multiplying by ten five times: $10 \times 10 \times 10 \times 10 \times 10$. A shorter way of indicating this is to write 10^5, where the 5 is called the exponent, or power of 10. Some examples of this usage of exponents are

$$1 = 10^0 \quad 10 = 1 \times 10 = 10^1$$
$$100 = 10 \times 10 = 10^2$$
$$1,000 = 10 \times 10 \times 10 = 10^3$$

Suppose we wish to write the number that represents the number of molecules in a mole. Using the normal notation for writing numbers, that number is 602,300,000,000,000,000,000,000.

To write this number using exponential notation, we have to know the number of significant figures expressed in normal notation. There are four significant figures. Now, in expressing our value as a number between one and ten, we write 6.023. But this is not the number we wish to express. We must move the decimal point 23 places to the right in order to have the same number that we wrote above. To move the decimal point 23 places to the right, we multiply by ten 23 times, or 10^{23}. Thus, the exponential notation for 602,300,000,-000,000,000,000,000 is 6.023×10^{23}.

In a similar manner, very small numbers can be simplified. In this case, we should be aware of the mathematical symbolism in which a *negative exponent* means *one divided by ten raised to that exponent*. For example,

$$0.1 = 1/10^1 = 10^{-1}$$
$$0.01 = 1/100 = 1/10^2 = 10^{-2}$$
$$0.001 = 1/1000 = 1/10^3 = 10^{-3}$$

Suppose we wish to write out the number representing the mass of an electron: 0.000 000 000 000 000 000 000 000 000 911 g. Note that this time there is no doubt as to how many significant figures there are, since all numerals past the last zero are significant. Zeros that occur between the decimal point and the first non-zero numeral are never significant. The first part of our new notation is 9.11. Again, by placing the decimal point after the 9 we are no longer writing the same value as the longer number. We need to divide 9.11 by ten 28 times to represent the same value. We can express this division by means of our new exponential notation as $9.11 \times 1/10^{28}$ or 9.11×10^{-28} g.

One of the benefits of learning to use exponential notation is to eliminate confusion about which zeros are significant. Any zero that disappears when the number is changed to exponential notation is *not* significant. Try a few of the exercises at the end of this section to check your understanding of exponential notation.

ROUNDING OFF NUMBERS

Now we can express a number in exponential notation and always be sure of the number of significant figures it contains. We have a rule for determining how many significant figures should be left in a product or quotient. But we still have the problem of how to round off an answer to the proper number of digits.

There are several conventions used to cover this problem. In this course we shall adopt the following rules.

1. Determine the decimal place to which the number is to be rounded. Consider all numbers to the right of that decimal place the remainder.
2. If the remainder is less than 500, drop the remainder; greater than 500, drop the remainder and *add one* to the decimal place that is being rounded; exactly equal to 500, drop the remainder and *add one* if the decimal place in question is *odd,* or leave the decimal place in question *unchanged* if it is *even.*

For example, to round the following numbers to four digits, 2.657*42* becomes 2.657, 981.6*501* becomes 981.7, 0.005 863 *50* becomes 0.005 864, and 0.859 4*50 0* becomes 0.8594.

SUMMARY

When multiplying or dividing any set of numbers, the product or quotient will contain the same number of significant figures as the least precise component.

Examples:

$$\frac{(0.047)(160.0)}{(93.05)} = 0.081$$

$$(654.94)(0.007) = 5$$

Every number consists of the *product* of (1) a *number* between one and ten that contains the proper number of significant figures, and (2) *a power of ten.*

Examples:

22,400 (three significant figures) $= 2.24 \times 10^4$

$$0.0056 = 5.6 \times 10^{-3}$$

Exercise 6

Determine the number of significant figures in each of the following: (a) 100.1, (b) 200.10, (c) 301.200, (d) 0.00546, (e) 0.0100, (f) 0.000103, (g) 0.00140620, (h) 1.2×10^{-2}, (i) 1.460×10^{-3}, (j) 1.000×10^5.

Exercise 7

1. Using three significant figures for each, express the following in exponential notation.

(a) 300, (b) 85,000, (c) 186,251, (d) 16,100,000, (e) 0.005 13, (f) 0.000 009 40, (g) 0.000 183, (h) 0.0155, (i) 0.008 05, (j) 80.10.
2. Change each of the following back to its non-exponential form: (a) 7.64×10^{-6}, (b) 1.00×10^{-3}, (c) 5.05×10^4, (d) 3.8×10^{-2}, (e) 2.19×10^9, (f) 9.44×10^5, (g) 1.77×10^1, (h) 4.628×10^{-4}, (i) 6.54×10^{-7}.

Exercise 8

Do the following multiplication and division problems. Express each to the correct number of significant figures: (a) 543/26, (b) 1.50×10^2/ 1.1, (c) 0.500/2.5, (d) 4.3×136, (e) $(2 \times 10^1)(76.9)$, (f) (0.200)(0.100), (g) (0.2) (0.100), (h) 0.500/0.100.

Uncertainty in numbers:
Precision in measurement

There is some degree of uncertainty in every measurement. This uncertainty is not due to blundering or improper procedures in making observations, but is simply due to limitations of the measuring device and the experimenter's ability to use the device. We shall distinguish between two factors contributing to uncertainty: limitations of *accuracy,* and limitations of *precision.* In order to draw this distinction more clearly, we shall discuss precision now and accuracy later on.

Precision refers to the *variation in results* obtained when an experiment is repeatedly performed with the same equipment and the same procedure. Thus, for precise work the experimenter must be able to obtain consistently the same results with the same instruments each time he or she performs a given experiment.

Although each instrument has its own *actual uncertainty,* we do talk about the *typical* or *average uncertainty* value of an instrument. Table 22 shows some of the typical uncertainty values for the type of apparatus generally used in this course.

But how close do these typical uncertainty values come to reality? What should be the uncertainty that *you* use with a *particular instrument?* The answers to these questions must be obtained by experiment. With some of the instruments—the balances, for example—you will be able to make a measurement close to the typical uncertainty after very little practice. For other instruments, such as the thermometer, it may take quite a lot of practice to be able to make a measurement with the uncertainty that is listed.

Table 22 Uncertainties associated with common instruments

Instrument	Typical uncertainty
triple-beam (centigram) balance	±0.01 g
platform balance	±0.5 g
50-ml graduated cylinder	±0.2 ml
10-ml graduated cylinder	±0.1 ml
−10 °C–110 °C thermometer	±0.2°C
50-ml gas measuring tube	±0.02 ml

There are many factors that determine the uncertainty of a measurement. How closely you can read the instrument is only one of them. You should not assume that the limit of your ability to estimate a measurement is necessarily the uncertainty that you will use. For example, on the centigram balance the smallest division represents 0.01 g. These divisions are spaced far enough apart that you can easily estimate to the nearest half-division (representing 0.005 g) or even possibly to the nearest fifth-division (representing 0.002 g). But the uncertainty of this instrument—the variation to be expected from repeated weighings—is 0.01 g or possibly even 0.02 g, depending on the balance. In other words, the variation in values from repeated measurements determines the uncertainty, not necessarily the size of the markings. (See the exercises on page 11 for determination of your uncertainty on the centigram balance.)

EXPRESSING UNCERTAINTY IN A SINGLE MEASUREMENT

In recording data it is important to estimate and record the uncertainty. For example, if you weigh a piece of copper wire on a triple-beam balance, you might record the mass of copper wire as 2.89 ± 0.01 g. The significance of ±0.01 g is that a repetition of the measurements is expected to yield 2.88, 2.89, or 2.90. If many repetitions of the measurement are made, the central value, 2.89, is expected to occur more often than the more extreme values, 2.88 and 2.90.

Another way to express the uncertainty is to indicate its magnitude as a percentage of the measured quantity. For the example given above, the percentage uncertainty is

$$\frac{0.01 \text{ g}}{2.89 \text{ g}} \times 100 = 0.3\%$$

So the mass of copper wire can be recorded as 2.89 g ± 0.3%.

A third way of indicating the uncertainty is by the number of figures recorded. This is known as the method of significant figures (review pages 134–136). Although it is often convenient, it does not give as much information as the two preceding methods. In spite of its limitations, the method of significant figures is satisfactory for most purposes in this course.

In this method all digits that are certain and one additional uncertain figure are given. In the preceding copper wire example, we would just record 2.89 g, indicating 3 significant figures. Note that the amount by which the last digit is uncertain is not specified when using just the number 2.89. The numbers 2.89 ± 0.02 g, 2.89 ± 0.03 g, or 2.89 ± 0.04 g would also be written as 2.89.

THE ACCUMULATION OF ERRORS IN CALCULATED RESULTS

So far, we have discussed how to record a single measurement and the uncertainty connected with that measurement. Since each measurement has an uncertainty, the combination of several measurements in a calculation must have an uncertainty. When quantities are added or subtracted, the maximum uncertainty in the result is the sum of the uncertainty for each of the component measurements.

Example 1: In Experiment 7, you weighed a sample of potassium chromate, $K_2CrO_4(s)$, with an uncertainty of ±0.02 g. Later you added this mass to the mass of lead nitrate, $Pb(NO_3)_2(s)$, also known with an uncertainty of ±0.02 g:

Mass of $K_2CrO_4(s)$	0.97 ± 0.02 g
Mass of $Pb(NO_3)_2(s)$	1.66 ± 0.02 g
Sum	2.63 ± 0.04 g

Note that the uncertainty in the derived result is ±0.04 g. Let us check this by using the values that will give the greatest and least values:

(0.97 + 0.02)	0.99 g	(0.97 − 0.02)	0.95 g
(1.66 + 0.02)	1.68 g	(1.66 − 0.02)	1.64 g
Sum	2.67 g		2.59 g

These numbers are in agreement with the notation 2.63 ± 0.04 g.

Example 2: In Experiment 8, you obtained the mass of lead acetate, $Pb(CH_3COO)_2 \cdot 3H_2O$, by subtracting two weighings such as these:

Mass of weighing paper +
Pb(CH₃COO)₂ · 3H₂O .... 3.06 ± 0.01 g

$$\text{Mass of weighing paper} \quad \underline{1.06 \pm 0.01 \text{ g}}$$

Mass of Pb(CH₃COO)₂ · 3H₂O .... 2.00 ± 0.02 g

Note that the uncertainty in the derived result is ±0.02 g, or the sum of the individual uncertainties. Again, we can check this by using the values that will give the greatest and least differences:

$$
\begin{array}{ll}
(3.06 + 0.01) & 3.07 \text{ g} \\
(1.06 - 0.01) & \underline{1.05 \text{ g}} \\
\text{Difference} & 2.02 \text{ g} \\
\\
(3.06 - 0.01) & 3.05 \text{ g} \\
(1.06 + 0.01) & \underline{1.07 \text{ g}} \\
\text{Difference} & 1.98 \text{ g}
\end{array}
$$

These values are in agreement with the notation 2.00 ± 0.02 g.

Exercise 9

Calculate the maximum uncertainty in each of the following:

1. $40.2 \pm 0.2 \text{ °C}$
    $\underline{-\ 10.2 \pm 0.2 \text{ °C}}$

3. $1{,}500 \pm 10 \text{ cm}$
    $1{,}500 \pm 10 \text{ cm}$
    $480 \pm \ \ 1 \text{ cm}$
    $\underline{+\ \ \ 940 \pm \ \ 6 \text{ cm}}$

2. $103.24 \pm 0.01 \text{ g}$
    $\underline{-\ \ 98.13 \pm 0.01 \text{ g}}$

4. $5.48 \pm 0.02 \text{ g}$
    $\underline{+\ 1.76 \pm 0.01 \text{ g}}$

In multiplication and division, the derived uncertainty is not simply the sum of the uncertainties in the factors. It is the sum of the *percentage* uncertainties in the factors.

Example 3: As in Experiment 9, calculate the heat, ΔH, absorbed by 306 ± 2 g of water when its temperature changes by 20.0 ± 0.4 °C. Since it takes 1 cal to raise the temperature of 1 g of water 1 °C, it takes 306 cal to heat 306 g of water 1 °C and 306×20 cal to heat 306 g of water 20 °C. Let us find the uncertainty in the calculated product by considering the maximum and the minimum value we could obtain.

Maximum:

$$(306 + 2 \text{ g})(20.0 + 0.4 \text{°C})\left(\frac{1 \text{ cal}}{\text{g°C}}\right) = 6{,}283.2 \text{ cal}$$

Minimum:

$$(306 - 2 \text{ g})(20.0 - 0.4 \text{°C})\left(\frac{1 \text{ cal}}{\text{g°C}}\right) = 5{,}958.4 \text{ cal}$$

The average of these two products is 6,120.8 cal, which we can also approximate by multiplying (306 g) × (20.0°C) × (1 cal/g°C). The maximum and minimum values are 162.4 cal above and below the average value. We express these results as 6,120.8 ± 162.4 cal. The uncertainty first appears in our answer in the hundreds decimal place. Therefore, both the answer and the uncertainty are rounded off to that place, and the final answer should be written

$$\Delta H = 6{,}100 \pm 200 \text{ cal}$$

You will note that under normal circumstances the maximum value is as far above the average value as the minimum is below it. Thus, it is unnecessary to determine both values in a calculation. Calculate just the average value and either the maximum or the minimum.

Example 4: A shorter method for determining the uncertainty of a product or quotient is to use the percentage uncertainty of each measurement. Using the data in example 3, we find

$$\% \text{ uncertainty in } 306 = \frac{2}{306} \times 100 = 0.7\%$$

$$\% \text{ uncertainty in } 20.0 = \frac{0.4}{20.0} \times 100 = 2.0\%$$

(Note that the value 1 cal/g °C is a defined quantity and as such is an exact value without uncertainty.) Thus, our original calculation

$$(306 \pm 2 \text{ g}) \times (20.0 \pm 0.4 \text{ °C}) \times \left(\frac{1 \text{ cal}}{\text{g °C}}\right)$$

can be expressed in the form

$$(306 \text{ g} \pm 0.7\%) \times (20.0 \text{ °C} \pm 2.0\%) \times \left(\frac{1 \text{ cal}}{\text{g °C}}\right)$$

Now we can add the uncertainties directly to obtain the answer 6,120 cal ± 2.7 percent. The actual value of the uncertainty in the answer is usually of more use than the percentage uncertainty.

$$2.7\% \text{ of } 6{,}120 \text{ cal} = 160 \text{ cal}$$

Upon rounding off, we obtain the same result as before: 6,100 ± 200 cal.

Exercise 10

1. Find the area of a rectangle measured as 10.0 ± 0.1 cm by 2.5 ± 0.1 cm, and calculate the uncertainty by each method (maximum-minimum method and summing of percentage uncertainty). Make a drawing of the rectangle, shading in the area of uncertainty. Calculate the area of the shaded part, and compare this to the calculated uncertainty.

2. Find the heat absorbed if 200 ± 5 g of water are heated 5.0 ± 0.2 °C. Calculate the uncertainty by both methods.

3. Find the heat of combustion (cal/g) for a substance if 9600 ± 200 calories are liberated when 1.13 ± 0.02 g burn. Calculate uncertainty by either method.

4. Calculate the heat of solidification of a substance if 210 ± 70 cal of heat are liberated as 10.3 ± 0.2 g solidify. Calculate the uncertainty by either method.

Accuracy in numbers:
The counterpart of precision

In our discussion of uncertainty in measurement, we emphasized that precision and accuracy are not the same thing and that there is some degree of uncertainty in every measurement. These statements probably left you with some questions. For example, if accuracy and precision are not the same, how do they differ?

As we have defined it, precision expresses the variation in results obtained from repeated determinations of the same quantity. In contrast, *accuracy* expresses *how close a measurement comes to the true or accepted value.* A measurement may give the same results time after time, varying only by the stated precision, yet it may not be at all close to the true value. For example, an incorrectly calibrated thermometer may give very consistent results, but it will not determine the correct temperature.

This raises a second and even more important question: if every measurement has *some* uncertainty, how do you know the *true value?* The answer is that true values are *not* known except when they are defined as such. In most cases an accepted value must be used. By *accepted value*

we mean *that value which is considered to be the best approximation to the true value.*

When different experimental methods are used for determining the same quantity, the variation in the results indicates their accuracy, and the accepted value can be determined from such results. The many attempts to determine c, the velocity of light in a vacuum, illustrate this point. The year 1676 apparently marked the first demonstration that light does travel with a finite velocity. From that time until 1849, various methods were used to determine this velocity. The experimental approach in each case was to find the length of time it took light to travel a very long distance, such as from Jupiter to Earth. A value of 214,200 km/sec represented the best value obtained until 1849. However, this value was known to be in error because the value for the radius of Earth's orbit (used in the calculations) was not itself known accurately. To avoid this problem, all methods since 1849 have used a light path of a mile or less. Much work between 1935 and 1941, using several methods, yielded values in close agreement with each other: between 299,771 and 299,776 km/sec. However good the agreement, it was shown that there were systematic errors in each of the experiments. The present accepted value is $299,793.0 \pm 0.3$ km/sec. Experimentation continues even today.

There are several methods used for indicating the accuracy of a measurement. If the true or accepted value is known,

$$\% \text{ difference} = \frac{(\text{accepted value} - \text{experimental value})}{\text{accepted value}} \times 100$$

If the true or accepted value is not known, there is *no* way to establish the accuracy of a measurement with certainty. Our faith in the accuracy of a measured quantity is increased if the same number can be obtained by several different experimental techniques with different kinds of experimental error. For this reason, scientists always try to determine important quantities, such as the speed of light, by a number of different methods. If all methods agree, the accuracy is assumed to be high.

Approximation of answers

Suppose you were doing a simple division problem—1693/3.30—or a more complex problem—(67.30)(1640.1)/0.08101. In the first example, you can quickly estimate in your head that the answer is between 500 and 600. In the second example, the estimate is more difficult to determine. In these two cases, finding the approximate answer helps check that the decimal place is located properly in the precise answer. It also is an important step in calculating the final answer. We shall use these two examples to show how approximations are made.

APPROXIMATION BY MENTAL ARITHMETIC

For simple calculations the actual work can be done in your head. *Round off each of the numbers involved to one (or two) significant figures, noting whether your estimate is going to be on the high or low side of the more precise answer.*

For the first problem above—1693/3.30—estimate that 1693 is almost 1700 and that 3.30 is a little more than 3. 1700 divided by 3 is between 500 and 600. Since you used 3 as a divisor instead of 3.3, your estimate will be on the high side of the actual answer. Your final approximation should be that the answer is between 500 and 600, and closer to 500 than 600. (The answer is 513.)

Study the next few examples, and then try the exercises that follow.

Examples: *Approximations:*

1. $(27.1)(0.41)$ $(30)(0.4) = 12$
2. $79.1/6.75$ $80/7 = 11{-}12$

Exercise 11

1. $(1.740)(1.342) =$
2. $(1601.2)(0.008\ 400\ 0) =$
3. $(4.85)(0.313) =$
4. $(1018)(54.30) =$
5. $14.8/756 =$
6. $6361/0.030\ 30 =$
7. $711/288 =$
8. $0.0930/44.2 =$

APPROXIMATION BY EXPONENTIAL NOTATION

For more complicated problems the same general rule applies, but a more definite manner of writing the approximation is used.

1. *Express all numbers in exponential form,* rounded off to one significant figure.
2. Collect all the numerical factors together and mentally carry out the multiplication or division.
3. Add or subtract the exponential factors as indicated.

In our second example—(67.30)(1640.1)/0.081 01—express 67.30 as (7×10^1); 1640.1 as (2×10^3); and 0.081 01 as (8×10^{-2}). The approximate calculation is then

$$\frac{(7 \times 10^1)(2 \times 10^3)}{(8 \times 10^{-2})}$$

or

$$\left(\frac{7 \times 2}{8}\right)\left(\frac{10^1 \times 10^3}{10^{-2}}\right)$$

For the numerical factor, mentally calculate that $(7 \times 2)/8$ is about 2; and for the exponential factor, $(10^1 \times 10^3)/10^{-2} = 10^6$. Thus, very quickly we have an estimate of about 2×10^6 or 2 million.

Note that the approximation of 2000 for 1640.1 is on the high side by quite a bit, while the other approximations are fairly close. This information enables you to decide that the answer should be *less* than two million. The slide rule answer of 1.102×10^6 is in agreement with this idea.

Study the following examples carefully before going on to the exercises. Use a calculator or longhand to get the precise value after finding the approximate answer.

Examples:

1. $\dfrac{(4.6)(65)}{8.1}$

2. $\dfrac{(423)(6.48)(0.006\ 53)}{(61.7)(0.256)}$

Approximations:

1. $\dfrac{(5 \times 10^0)(7 \times 10^1)}{(8 \times 10^0)} =$

$$\left(\frac{5 \times 7}{8}\right)\left(\frac{10^0 \times 10^1}{10^0}\right) = 5 \times 10^1 \text{ or } 50$$

2. $\dfrac{(4 \times 10^2)(6 \times 10^0)(7 \times 10^{-3})}{(6 \times 10^1)(3 \times 10^{-1})} =$

$$\left(\frac{4 \times 6 \times 7}{6 \times 3}\right)\left(\frac{10^2 \times 10^0 \times 10^{-3}}{10^1 \times 10^{-1}}\right) =$$

$$9 \times 10^{-1} \text{ or } 0.9$$

Exercise 12

1. $\dfrac{(9.01)(472)}{607} =$

2. $\dfrac{(0.0081)(47,000)}{(73)(0.000\ 56)} =$

3. $\dfrac{(58.93)(0.2157)}{0.000\ 040\ 01} =$

4. $\dfrac{(71)(25)(85)}{(92)(15)} =$

5. $\dfrac{(1.602)(1788)}{0.041\ 80} =$

6. $(0.000\ 183)(1670)(29.1) =$

7. $\dfrac{(0.001\ 99)(0.000\ 023\ 4)}{5670} =$

8. $\dfrac{(507)(142)(0.0112)}{60.1} =$

Unit analysis

All measurements are made by a direct or indirect comparison to some standard. Since for any given measurement there may be several standards available for comparison, the measurement must be expressed by means of a *number,* representing the numerical size, and a *unit,* telling which standard is being used. For example, a measurement of 10.5 cm indicates a length that is 10.5 times as long as the standard length of 1 cm. A measurement of $4^{5}\!/_{32}$ inches represents the same length. The numerical size is different because a different standard—and, therefore, a different unit—is being used.

Most sciences consider length, mass, and time to be fundamental quantities. The units related to these quantities are *fundamental units*. You are familiar with the set of units for the English system: foot, pound, and second. In the SI system, the combination metre, kilogram, and second is used. Other units are derived from these fundamental units on the basis of some physical relationship and are called *derived units*. For example, the term *density* involves the concept of mass per unit of volume and is expressed in the units of kg/m^3.

PRINCIPLES OF UNIT ANALYSIS

In working problems that involve units, you should treat them as if they were algebraic terms. This means that the laws governing fundamental mathematical operations also apply to the handling of units. The most important of these laws are

1. Addition and subtraction can be carried out on quantities only if they have the same units.

This is just another way of saying that you cannot add apples to oranges, or that 1.6 kg of copper + 1.6 mg of copper cannot be added until they are expressed in a common unit.

2. Multiplication and division may be carried out on quantities with the same or different units.

Example 1: A cube of metal 2.0 cm on a side has a mass of 88 g. What is its density?

The volume of a cube of side s is $V = s^3 = (2.0\ \text{cm})^3 = 8.0\ \text{cm}^3$. Density is the mass of a unit volume:

$$\frac{88\ \text{g}}{8.0\ \text{cm}^3} = 11\ \text{g/cm}^3$$

The units of the denominator and the numerator are *not* the same, and the answer is expressed in a combination of these units, g/cm^3.

Example 2: Compare the density of the metal cube of Example 1 to the density of water.

$$\frac{11 \text{ g/cm}^3}{1.0 \text{ g/cm}^3} = \left(\frac{11}{1.0}\right)\left(\frac{\cancel{g}}{\cancel{cm^3}} \times \frac{\cancel{cm^3}}{\cancel{g}}\right) = 11$$

In this case the units are the same for both quantities. Thus the answer is a pure number without units. It means that the metal has a density 11 times greater than that of water.

3. The same numerical value and the same units must exist on both sides of an equation.

From the above example,

$$\frac{88\text{g}}{8.0 \text{ cm}^3} = 11 \text{ g/cm}^3$$

Both sides of the equation have the same numerical value, 11, and the same units, g/cm³.

EXPRESSING QUANTITIES IN DIFFERENT UNITS

The problem of changing one expression for a quantity into an equivalent expression with different units is encountered frequently in science. For example, the lengths 91 cm, 0.91 m, and 9.1×10^2 mm cannot be added without first being expressed in a common unit.

Since the quantities 10.5 cm and 4⁵⁄₃₂ inches represent the same length, the process of changing from one expression to the other must preserve the equality of the two expressions. This fact should remind you of the mathematical rule that a quantity is unchanged when multiplied by 1. Thus, *to change the expression of a quantity to one with different units, multiply it by a ratio or series of ratios (called* conversion factors) *each of which has the value of 1.*

Let us start with the familiar equality 3 feet = 1 yard. If you divide both sides by 1 yd, you have

$$\frac{3 \text{ ft}}{1 \text{ yd}} = \frac{1 \cancel{\text{yd}}}{1 \cancel{\text{yd}}} = 1$$

Since the ratio 3 ft/1 yd is 1, we can use it to change the units of an expression for a measure of length. For example, if a rope is measured and found to be 5 yd long, we can express this same length in feet as

$$5 \cancel{\text{yd}} \times \frac{3 \text{ ft}}{1 \cancel{\text{yd}}} = 15 \text{ ft}$$

Note that the numerical value and the units have changed, but the length of the rope has not.

Suppose in the above example you had instead divided both sides of the equality by 3 ft. The result is still equal to 1:

$$\frac{3 \cancel{\text{ft}}}{3 \cancel{\text{ft}}} = \frac{1 \text{ yd}}{3 \text{ ft}} = 1$$

Thus two ratios, 3 ft/1 yd and 1 yd/3 ft, can express the relationship between feet and yards. How do you know which one to use? Unit analysis has a simple answer: *use the ratio that will eliminate the unwanted units, leaving only the new, desired units in your answer.*

This last ratio, 1 yd/3 ft, is not useful in changing the expression 5 yd into feet:

$$5 \text{ yd} \times \frac{1 \text{ yd}}{3 \text{ ft}} = ?$$

but could be used for the reverse change. If you originally had measured the rope in feet and wanted to know the length in yards, then

$$15 \cancel{\text{ft}} \times \frac{1 \text{ yd}}{3 \cancel{\text{ft}}} = 5 \text{ yd}$$

A more complex example is to express 17 mm/sec as the corresponding number of km/hr:

$$\frac{17 \cancel{\text{mm}}}{\cancel{\text{sec}}} \times \frac{1 \text{ km}}{10^6 \cancel{\text{mm}}} \times \frac{60 \cancel{\text{sec}}}{1 \cancel{\text{min}}} \times \frac{60 \cancel{\text{min}}}{1 \text{ hr}}$$

$$= 0.061 \text{ km/hr}$$

Note that the choice of ratios is made in such a manner that the units desired for the final answer remain and all unwanted units are eliminated. If any one of the ratios is inverted, this will no longer be true. For example, suppose the second conversion factor, 60 sec/1 min, is inverted. The answer is then

$$\frac{17 \cancel{\text{mm}}}{\text{sec}} \times \frac{1 \text{ km}}{10^6 \cancel{\text{mm}}} \times \frac{1 \text{ min}}{60 \text{ sec}} \times \frac{60 \text{ min}}{1 \text{ hr}}$$

$$= 1.7 \times 10^{-5} \frac{\text{km} \times \text{min}^2}{\text{sec}^2 \times \text{hr}}$$

Even though this is still a true equality, with the same numerical value and units on both sides, you have not answered the problem, and the answer has no physical significance.

Often working the problem both ways, once with a given ratio and once with the inverse of that ratio, will help you to decide which way is correct. For example, the density of alcohol is 0.79 g/ml; what is the density expressed as g/litre?

Trial 1: Using the ratio 1 litre/1000 ml,

$$\frac{0.79 \text{ g}}{\text{ml}} \times \frac{1 \text{ litre}}{1000 \text{ ml}} = 0.000\ 79\ \frac{\text{g} \times \text{litre}}{\text{ml}^2}$$

Trial 2: Using the ratio 1000 ml/1 litre,

$$\frac{0.79 \text{ g}}{\text{ml}} \times \frac{1000 \text{ ml}}{1 \text{ litre}} = 7.9 \times 10^2 \text{ g/litre}$$

Note that the desired answer is obtained only when the proper ratio is used.

Exercise 13

(Show cancellation of units in each of the following problems.)

1. A car is going 60 mph. What is its speed in (a) feet/sec, (b) km/hr, (c) cm/sec?
2. A fast runner can go a mile in 4.00 min. At that speed how fast can he run (a) 1500 m, (b) 440 yd, (c) 60 m?
3. An atom of oxygen has a mass of 2.68×10^{-23} g. How many atoms of oxygen are needed to make up 10 g of oxygen atoms?
4. The density of benzene is 0.88 g/cm^3 at 20 °C. What volume will be occupied by 1.0×10^2 g of benzene?
5. Rowboats rent for 50¢ per hour. What will it cost to rent one for 4 weeks?

Graphing

Many properties of substances are found to be interdependent. As the temperature of a gas increases, the volume increases (if other conditions are not changing). A relationship in which two values change in the same direction (one remains larger than the other by the same factor) is a *direct relationship*. A direct relationship may be expressed mathematically as $x = ky$ or $x/y = k$, where k is a constant.

Consider the following example of the direct relationship between the volume of a gas, V, and its absolute temperature, T, where $V = kT$. Note the straight line that results when the values are plotted (see Figure 78).

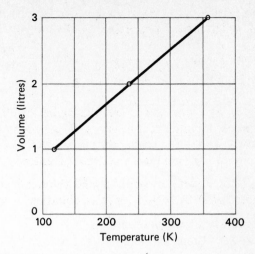

Figure 78 Graph for $V = kT$.

Volume (litres)	Temperature (K)
1	120
2	240
3	360

MORE EXAMPLES

Example 1: If $k = 1$, we find that $x = y$. As x increases in value, y also increases. Plotting these values on a graph with values of x along the horizontal axis and y along the vertical axis, we obtain Figure 79.

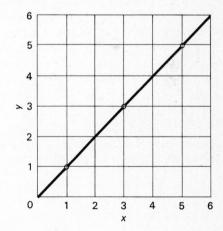

Figure 79 Graph for $x = y$.

x	y
1	1
3	3
5	5

Example 2: If $k = 2$, we find that $x = 2y$. Plotting these values, we obtain Figure 80.

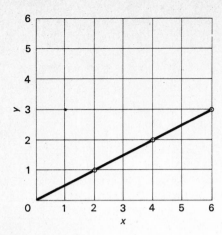

Figure 80   Graph for $x = 2y$.

x	y
2	1
4	2
6	3

Note that in either example the plot is a straight line passing through the origin where $x = y = 0$.

Consider now a second kind of interdependence. When one value becomes larger by a given factor and the other becomes smaller by the same factor, we have an *inverse relationship*. This can be expressed mathematically as $xy = k$ or $y = k/x$.

If $k = 6$, we find these values for x and y:

x	y
1	6
2	3
3	2
6	1

Plotting these values we obtain Figure 81.

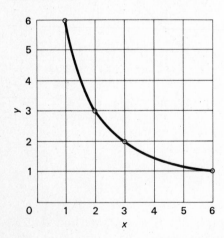

Figure 81   Graph for $xy = 6$.

The relationship between gas pressure and volume discussed in Chapter 2 of the textbook is an example of an inverse relationship in which $P = k/V$ or $PV = k$. Note the type of curve which results when the data for the pressure and volume of 32.0 g of oxygen are plotted in Figure 82.

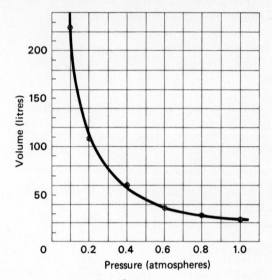

Figure 82   Graph for $PV = k$.

Pressure (atm)	Volume (litres)
0.100	224
0.200	109
0.400	57.5
0.600	38.0
0.800	27.7
1.00	22.4

Note that in an inverse relationship, as x becomes very large, y becomes very small and approaches but never reaches zero. When y becomes very large, x becomes very small but never reaches zero. (This is true except when $k = 0$.)

Exercise 14

1. Plot four values of x and y in which the ratio is direct and $k = 3$.
2. Plot six values of x and y in which the ratio is inverse and $k = 3$. Start with $x = 1$ and $y = 3$.
3. (a) What is the value of k in the following:

x	y
0.2	0.4
0.6	1.2
1.8	3.6

(b) Make a graph and plot these values.

4. The volume of a partially inflated rubber balloon varies inversely with the external pressure. (a) Write an equation to describe this relationship. Use P for pressure and V for volume. (b) It is found experimentally that when the pressure is 1.0 atm, the balloon has a volume of 22.4 litres. When the pressure is increased to 2.0 atm, the volume decreases to 11.2 litres. What is the value of k in the equation for exercise (a)? (c) What would the volume be under a pressure of 12 atm? (d) What would the volume be under a pressure of 0.50 atm?

Handling exponential notation

On page 135, we introduced exponential notation as an unambiguous, "shorthand" way of writing numbers. That section dealt only with the mechanics of writing numbers in exponential form. For the work that follows, we shall assume that you understand this process. (If necessary, review that earlier section *before* going on.)

In this section, we shall review the basic operations of addition, subtraction, multiplication, division, and square root using numbers in exponential form.

ADDITION AND SUBTRACTION

Express all numbers to the *same* power of 10, then add or subtract them. Since the exponential part of the number only locates the decimal point, it is retained unchanged in the answer.

Examples:

1.
$$\begin{array}{r} 2.3 \times 10^4 \\ + \ 1.4 \times 10^5 \end{array}$$

$$\begin{array}{r} 2.3 \times 10^4 \\ + \ 14 \times 10^5 \\ \hline 16 \times 10^4 \end{array} \quad \text{or} \quad \begin{array}{r} 0.23 \times 10^5 \\ + \ 1.4 \times 10^5 \\ \hline 1.6 \times 10^5 \end{array}$$

2.
$$\begin{array}{r} 3.2 \times 10^{-4} \\ - \ 9.6 \times 10^{-5} \end{array}$$

$$\begin{array}{r} 32 \times 10^{-5} \\ - \ 9.6 \times 10^{-5} \\ \hline 22 \times 10^{-5} \end{array} \quad \text{or} \quad \begin{array}{r} 3.2 \times 10^{-4} \\ - \ 0.96 \times 10^{-4} \\ \hline 2.2 \times 10^{-4} \end{array}$$

Exercise 15

1.
$$\begin{array}{r} 2.3 \times 10^4 \\ + \ 4.6 \times 10^4 \end{array}$$

2.
$$\begin{array}{r} 2.3 \times 10^4 \\ + \ 5.3 \times 10^5 \end{array}$$

3.
$$\begin{array}{r} 8.6 \times 10^{-6} \\ + \ 5.0 \times 10^{-5} \end{array}$$

4.
$$\begin{array}{r} 2.18 \times 10^{-2} \\ - \ 1.09 \times 10^{-2} \end{array}$$

5.
$$\begin{array}{r} 6.23 \times 10^{-9} \\ - \ 8.5 \times 10^{-10} \end{array}$$

6.
$$\begin{array}{r} 6.8 \times 10^7 \\ - \ 7.2 \times 10^6 \end{array}$$

MULTIPLICATION

Make separate groups of the non-exponential and exponential terms. Multiply the non-exponential terms. Then add the exponents, and express the answer as the product of these two groups.

Examples:

1. $(1.0 \times 10^2)(2.2 \times 10^3)(1.5 \times 10^4) =$
$(1.0 \times 2.2 \times 1.5)(10^2 \times 10^3 \times 10^4) =$
$(3.3)(10^{2+3+4}) = 3.3 \times 10^9$

2. $(2.0 \times 10^{-3})(7.1 \times 10^2) =$
$(2.0 \times 7.1)(10^{-3} \times 10^2) = (14)(10^{-3+2}) =$
$(14)(10^{-1})$ or 1.4×10^0 or 1.4

3. $(10^2)(6.3 \times 10^{-3})(10^7) =$
$(1 \times 6 \times 1)(10^2 \times 10^{-3} \times 10^7) =$
$(6)(10^{2-3+7}) = 6 \times 10^6$

Exercise 16

(Note in the above examples that multiplication by 1 is merely implied. Thus, $1 \times 10^2 = 10^2$.)

1. $(10^2)(10^3) =$
2. $(2 \times 10^7)(2 \times 10^4) =$
3. $(1.2 \times 10^{12})(8.0 \times 10^{-8}) =$
4. $(2.5 \times 10^6)(4.0 \times 10^{-3}) =$
5. $(1.3 \times 10^{-6})(3.0 \times 10^{-4}) =$
6. $(3.8 \times 10^{-3})(8.3 \times 10^3)(9.0 \times 10^{-7}) =$
7. $(10^{-4})(4 \times 10^3)(7 \times 10^8) =$
8. $(3.21 \times 10^{-16})(5.40 \times 10^{12}) =$
9. $(10^{-9})(10^{21})(10^{-45})(10^0) =$
10. $(2.4 \times 10^6)(2.4 \times 10^{-8})(2.4 \times 10^{-3}) =$

DIVISION

Make separate groups of the non-exponential and exponential terms. Divide the non-exponential terms. Subtract the exponents, and express the answer as the product of these two groups. When a problem involves both multiplication and division, the operations are combined.

Examples:

1. $(8 \times 10^6)/(2 \times 10^3) =$

$$\left(\frac{8}{2}\right)\left(\frac{10^6}{10^3}\right) = (4)(10^{6-3}) = 4 \times 10^3$$

2. $(5.0 \times 10^{-7})/(2.5 \times 10^2) =$

$$\left(\frac{5.0}{2.5}\right)\left(\frac{10^{-7}}{10^2}\right) = (2.0)(10^{-7-2}) = 2.0 \times 10^{-9}$$

3. $(6 \times 10^4)/(10^{-2}) =$

$$\left(\frac{6}{1}\right)\left(\frac{10^4}{10^{-2}}\right) = (6)[10^{4-(-2)}] = 6 \times 10^6$$

4. $\dfrac{(2 \times 10^3)(10^2)(3 \times 10^{-6})}{(6 \times 10^{-6})} =$

$$\left(\frac{2 \times 1 \times 3}{6}\right)\left(\frac{10^3 \times 10^2 \times 10^{-6}}{10^{-6}}\right) =$$

$$(1)[10^{3+2-6-(-6)}] = 1 \times 10^5$$

Exercise 17

1. $10^6/10^2 =$
2. $(2.7 \times 10^8)/(3.0 \times 10^5) =$
3. $(4.5 \times 10^{-9})/(5 \times 10^4) =$
4. $(1.77 \times 10^8)/(3.0 \times 10^{-3}) =$
5. $(1.45 \times 10^{-8})/(5.0 \times 10^{-12}) =$
6. $(6.7 \times 10^7)/(3.1 \times 10^{-8}) =$
7. $(4 \times 10^4)(5 \times 10^{-3})/(3 \times 10^{-6}) =$
8. $(3 \times 10^{-9})/(6 \times 10^7)(4 \times 10^{-3}) =$

SQUARE ROOT

If the exponent is not already divisible by two, rewrite the number so that the exponent is even. After grouping, find the square root of the non-exponential term, and multiply the exponent by $\frac{1}{2}$.

Examples:

1. $(16 \times 10^{12})^{1/2} = (16)^{1/2}(10^{12})^{1/2} = 4.0 \times 10^6$

2. $(8.1 \times 10^{-7})^{1/2} = (81 \times 10^{-8})^{1/2} =$

$$(81)^{1/2}(10^{-8})^{1/2} = 9.0 \times 10^{-4}$$

Exercise 18

(Note in the above examples that raising a quantity to the $\frac{1}{2}$-power is another way of indicating square root. Thus, $\sqrt{x} = x^{1/2}$.)

1. $\sqrt{10^8}$
2. $(2.5 \times 10^7)^{1/2} =$
3. $\sqrt{62.5 \times 10^{-5}} =$
4. $\sqrt{16} \times 10^{12} =$
5. $(10.0 \times 10^{-9})^{1/2} =$

6. $\sqrt{16.9 \times 10^{11}} =$
7. $[(2.0 \times 10^{-6})(4.5 \times 10^4)]^{1/2} =$
8. $[(7.5 \times 10^{-7})/(3.0 \times 10^{-12})]^{1/2} =$

Chemical equations vs. algebraic equations

Many of the fundamentals you have learned in algebra are extremely useful in chemistry. Some of the more commonly used manipulations are briefly reviewed here. Study each example as a means of refreshing your memory.

Example 1: Consider two pairs of equations. The first pair you will recognize from your experience in algebra, while the second pair makes use of symbols common to chemistry. They are otherwise identical.

$$2a + b = 2c \qquad 2C + O_2 = 2CO$$
$$2c + b = 2e \qquad 2CO + O_2 = 2CO_2$$

When we add the equations, we obtain

$$2a + 2b + 2c = 2c + 2e \qquad (1)$$

$$2C + 2O_2 + 2CO = 2CO + 2CO_2 \qquad (2)$$

The same quantity may be added or subtracted from each side of an equation without changing the equality. Subtracting $2c$ from both sides of equation *1*, we obtain

$$2a + 2b = 2e \qquad (3)$$

Subtracting 2CO from both sides of equation *2*, we obtain

$$2C + 2O_2 = 2CO_2 \qquad (4)$$

Each side of an equation may be divided by the same quantity without changing the equality. Dividing both sides of equations *3* and *4* by 2, we obtain

$$a + b = e \quad \text{and} \quad C + O_2 = CO_2$$

which are the simplified sums of the two sets of equations with which we started.

Example 2: Consider two more pairs of equations.

$$a + b = c + 26d$$
$$e + b = c + 24d$$

$$C(\textit{diamond}) + O_2(g) = CO_2(g) + 94.50 \text{ kcal}$$

$$C(\textit{graphite}) + O_2(g) = CO_2(g) + 94.05 \text{ kcal}$$

Subtracting one equation from the other, we obtain

$$a - e = 2d \qquad\qquad (5)$$

$$C(\textit{diamond}) - C(\textit{graphite}) = 0.45 \text{ kcal} \quad (6)$$

Adding e to both sides of equation 5, and $C(\textit{graphite})$ to both sides of equation 6, we obtain the final sums

$$a = e + 2d$$

and

$$C(\textit{diamond}) = C(\textit{graphite}) + 0.45 \text{ kcal}$$

Another way of doing the preceding example is the following: write the second equations in reverse order

$$a + b = c + 26d$$
$$c + 24d = e + b$$

$$C(\textit{diamond}) + O_2(g) = CO_2(g) + 94.50 \text{ kcal}$$

$$CO_2(g) + 94.05 \text{ kcal} = C(\textit{graphite}) + O_2(g)$$

Adding one equation to the other, we obtain

$$a = e + 2d$$

and

$$C(\textit{diamond}) = C(\textit{graphite}) + 0.45 \text{ kcal}$$

Note that the same results are obtained. There may be times when reversing one (or more) equations and adding them will be easier than doing the problem by the subtraction method.

Exercise 19

1. Given the following two steps for the production of SO_3, add these equations to get the equation for the production of SO_3 from S and O_2.

$$S(s) + O_2(g) = SO_2(g)$$

$$SO_2(g) + \tfrac{1}{2}O_2(g) = SO_3(g)$$

2. Add the following two reactions so the e^- cancels out.

$$Zn(s) = Zn^{++}(aq) + 2e^-$$

$$e^- + Ag^+(aq) = Ag(s)$$

3. Energy is required to evaporate water. The following equations indicate the amount of energy released when hydrogen and oxygen are burned to form water. Find the amount of energy needed to evaporate $H_2O(l)$. [Hint: ___ kcal + $H_2O(l)$ = $H_2O(g)$.]

$$H_2(g) + \tfrac{1}{2}O_2(g) = H_2O(g) + 57.80 \text{ kcal}$$

$$H_2(g) + \tfrac{1}{2}O_2(g) = H_2O(l) + 68.32 \text{ kcal}$$

Names, formulas, and charges of some common ions

Remember, in ionic compounds the relative number of positive and negative ions is such that the sum of their electric charges is zero.

POSITIVE IONS (CATIONS)

Name	Symbol	Name	Symbol
aluminum	Al^{+++}	lead	Pb^{++}
ammonium	NH_4^+	lithium	Li^+
barium	Ba^{++}	magnesium	Mg^{++}
calcium	Ca^{++}	manganese(II), manganous	Mn^{++}
chromium(II), chromous	Cr^{++}	mercury(I),* mercurous	Hg_2^{++}
chromium(III), chromic	Cr^{+++}	mercury(II), mercuric	Hg^{++}
cobalt	Co^{++}	potassium	K^+
copper(I),* cuprous	Cu^+	silver	Ag^+
copper(II), cupric	Cu^{++}	sodium	Na^+
hydrogen, hydronium	H^+, H_3O^+	tin(II),* stannous	Sn^{++}
iron(II),* ferrous	Fe^{++}	tin(IV), stannic	Sn^{++++}
iron(III), ferric	Fe^{+++}	zinc	Zn^{++}

NEGATIVE IONS (ANIONS)

Name	Symbol	Name	Symbol
acetate	CH_3COO^-	hydrogen oxalate ion, bioxalate	$HC_2O_4^-$
bromide	Br^-		
carbonate	CO_3^{--}	oxide	O^{--}
hydrogen carbonate ion, bicarbonate	HCO_3^-	perchlorate	ClO_4^-
		permanganate	MnO_4^-
chlorate	ClO_3^-	phosphate	PO_4^{---}
chloride	Cl^-	monohydrogen phosphate	HPO_4^{--}
chlorite	ClO_2^-	dihydrogen phosphate	$H_2PO_4^-$
chromate	CrO_4^{--}	sulfate	SO_4^{--}
dichromate	$Cr_2O_7^{--}$	hydrogen sulfate ion, bisulfate	HSO_4^-
fluoride	F^-		
hydroxide	OH^-	sulfide	S^{--}
hypochlorite	ClO^-	hydrogen sulfide ion, bisulfide	HS^-
iodide	I^-		
nitrate	NO_3^-	sulfite	SO_3^{--}
nitrite	NO_2^-	hydrogen sulfite ion, bisulfite	HSO_3^-
oxalate	$C_2O_4^{--}$		

*Aqueous solutions are readily oxidized by air.

The equation for the ionization is $HB(aq) \rightleftharpoons H^+(aq) + B^-(aq)$. Since all ions and molecules in water solution are aquated, the (aq) is assumed in the notation. We then write $K_A = [H^+][B^-]/[HB]$.

Acid	Strength	Reaction	K_A
perchloric acid	very strong	$HClO_4 \rightarrow H^+ + ClO_4^-$	very large
hydriodic acid		$HI \rightarrow H^+ + I^-$	very large
hydrobromic acid		$HBr \rightarrow H^+ + Br^-$	very large
hydrochloric acid		$HCl \rightarrow H^+ + Cl^-$	very large
nitric acid		$HNO_3 \rightarrow H^+ + NO_3^-$	very large
sulfuric acid	very strong	$H_2SO_4 \rightarrow H^+ + HSO_4^-$	very large
oxalic acid		$HOOCCOOH \rightarrow H^+ + HOOCCOO^-$	5.4×10^{-2}
sulfurous acid ($SO_2 + H_2O$)		$H_2SO_3 \rightarrow H^+ + HSO_3^-$	1.7×10^{-2}
hydrogen sulfate ion	strong	$HSO_4^- \rightarrow H^+ + SO_4^{--}$	1.3×10^{-2}
phosphoric acid		$H_3PO_4 \rightarrow H^+ + H_2PO_4^-$	7.1×10^{-3}
ferric ion		$Fe(H_2O)_6^{+++} \rightarrow H^+ + Fe(H_2O)_5(OH)^{++}$	6.0×10^{-3}
hydrogen telluride		$H_2Te \rightarrow H^+ + HTe^-$	2.3×10^{-3}
hydrofluoric acid	weak	$HF \rightarrow H^+ + F^-$	6.7×10^{-4}
nitrous acid		$HNO_2 \rightarrow H^+ + NO_2^-$	5.1×10^{-4}
hydrogen selenide		$H_2Se \rightarrow H^+ + HSe^-$	1.7×10^{-4}
chromic ion		$Cr(H_2O)_6^{+++} \rightarrow H^+ + Cr(H_2O)_5(OH)^{++}$	1.5×10^{-4}
benzoic acid		$C_6H_5COOH \rightarrow H^+ + C_6H_5COO^-$	6.6×10^{-5}
hydrogen oxalate ion		$HOOCCOO^- \rightarrow H^+ + OOCCOO^{--}$	5.4×10^{-5}
acetic acid	weak	$CH_3COOH \rightarrow H^+ + CH_3COO^-$	1.8×10^{-5}
aluminum ion		$Al(H_2O)_6^{+++} \rightarrow H^+ + Al(H_2O)_5(OH)^{++}$	1.4×10^{-5}
carbonic acid ($CO_2 + H_2O$)		$H_2CO_3 \rightarrow H^+ + HCO_3^-$	4.4×10^{-7}
hydrogen sulfide		$H_2S \rightarrow H^+ + HS^-$	1.0×10^{-7}
dihydrogen phosphate ion		$H_2PO_4^- \rightarrow H^+ + HPO_4^{--}$	6.3×10^{-8}
hydrogen sulfite ion		$HSO_3^- \rightarrow H^+ + SO_3^{--}$	6.2×10^{-8}
ammonium ion	weak	$NH_4^+ \rightarrow H^+ + NH_3$	5.7×10^{-10}
hydrogen carbonate ion		$HCO_3^- \rightarrow H^+ + CO_3^{--}$	4.7×10^{-11}
hydrogen telluride ion		$HTe^- \rightarrow H^+ + Te^{--}$	1.0×10^{-11}
hydrogen peroxide	very weak	$H_2O_2 \rightarrow H^+ + HO_2^-$	2.4×10^{-12}
monohydrogen phosphate ion		$HPO_4^{--} \rightarrow H^+ + PO_4^{---}$	4.4×10^{-13}
hydrogen sulfide ion		$HS^- \rightarrow H^+ + S^{--}$	1.2×10^{-15}
water		$H_2O \rightarrow H^+ + OH^-$	1.8×10^{16}*
hydroxide ion		$OH^- \rightarrow H^+ + O^{--}$	$< 10^{-36}$
ammonia	very weak	$NH_3 \rightarrow H^+ + NH_2^-$	very small

*The acid equilibrium constant, K_A, for water equals $1.00 \times 10^{-14}/55.6$.

Standard reduction potentials for half-reactions

All ions are in water. Ionic concentrations = 1 *M* in water. Temperature = 25 °C.

Strength as oxidizing agent	Half-reaction	E^0 (volts)	Strength as reducing agent
very strong oxidizing agents	$F_2(g) + 2e^- \rightarrow 2F^-$	+2.87	very weak reducing agents
	$H_2O_2 + 2H^+ + 2e^- \rightarrow 2H_2O$	+1.77	
	$MnO_4^- + 8H^+ + 5e^- \rightarrow Mn^{++} + 4H_2O^{--}$	+1.52	
	$Au^{+++} + 3e^- \rightarrow Au(s)$	+1.50	
	$Cl_2(g) + 2e^- \rightarrow 2Cl^-$	+1.36	increasing strength as reducing agent
	$Cr_2O_7^{--} + 14H^+ + 6e^- \rightarrow 2Cr^{+++} + 7H_2O^{+++}$	+1.33	
	$MnO_2(s) + 4H^+ + 2e^- \rightarrow Mn^{++} + 2H_2O^{++}$	+1.28	
	$\frac{1}{2}O_2(g) + 2H^+ + 2e^- \rightarrow H_2O$	+1.23	
	$Br_2(l) + 2e^- \rightarrow 2Br^-$	+1.06	
	$AuCl_4^- + 3e^- \rightarrow Au(s) + 4Cl^-$	+1.00	
	$NO_3^- + 4H^+ + 3e^- \rightarrow NO(g) + 2H_2O$	+0.96	
	$\frac{1}{2}O_2(g) + 2H^+(10^{-7}M) + 2e^- \rightarrow H_2O$	+0.82	
	$Ag^+ + e^- \rightarrow Ag(s)$	+0.80	
	$\frac{1}{2}Hg_2^{++} + e^- \rightarrow Hg(l)$	+0.79	
	$Hg^{++} + 2e^- \rightarrow Hg(l)$	+0.78	
	$NO_3^- + 2H^+ + e^- \rightarrow NO_2(g) + H_2O$	+0.78	
	$Fe^{+++} + e^- \rightarrow Fe^{++}$	+0.77	
	$O_2(g) + 2H^+ + 2e^- \rightarrow H_2O_2$	+0.68	
	$I_2(s) + 2e^- \rightarrow 2I^-$	+0.53	
	$Cu^+ + e^- \rightarrow Cu(s)$	+0.52	
	$Cu^{++} + 2e^- \rightarrow Cu(s)$	+0.34	
increasing strength as oxidizing agent	$SO_4^{--} + 4H^+ + 2e^- \rightarrow SO_2(g) + 2H_2O$	+0.17	
	$Cu^{++} + e^- \rightarrow Cu^+$	+0.15	
	$Sn^{++++} + 2e^- \rightarrow Sn^{++}$	+0.15	
	$S + 2H^+ + 2e^- \rightarrow H_2S(g)$	+0.14	
	$2H^+ + 2e^- \rightarrow H_2(g)$	0.00	
	$Pb^{++} + 2e^- \rightarrow Pb(s)$	−0.13	
	$Sn^{++} + 2e^- \rightarrow Sn(s)$	−0.14	
	$Ni^{++} + 2e^- \rightarrow Ni(s)$	−0.25	
	$Co^{++} + 2e^- \rightarrow Co(s)$	−0.28	
	$Se + 2H^+ + 2e^- \rightarrow H_2Se(g)$	−0.40	
	$Cr^{+++} + e^- \rightarrow Cr^{++}$	−0.41	
weak oxidizing agents	$2H^+(10^{-7}M) + 2e^- \rightarrow H_2(g)$	−0.41	
	$Fe^{++} + 2e^- \rightarrow Fe(s)$	−0.44	
	$Ag_2S + 2e^- \rightarrow 2Ag(s) + S^{--}$	−0.69	
	$Te + 2H^+ + 2e^- \rightarrow H_2Te(g)$	−0.72	
	$Cr^{+++} + 3e^- \rightarrow Cr(s)$	−0.74	
	$Zn^{++} + 2e^- \rightarrow Zn(s)$	−0.76	
	$2H_2O + 2e^- \rightarrow 2OH^- + H_2(g)$	−0.83	
	$Mn^{++} + 2e^- \rightarrow Mn(s)$	−1.18	
	$Al^{+++} + 3e^- \rightarrow Al(s)$	−1.66	
	$Mg^{++} + 2e^- \rightarrow Mg(s)$	−2.37	
	$Na^+ + e^- \rightarrow Na(s)$	−2.71	
	$Ca^{++} + 2e^- \rightarrow Ca(s)$	−2.87	
	$Sr^{++} + 2e^- \rightarrow Sr(s)$	−2.89	
	$Ba^{++} + 2e^- \rightarrow Ba(s)$	−2.90	
	$Cs^+ + e^- \rightarrow Cs(s)$	−2.92	
very weak oxidizing agents	$K^+ + e^- \rightarrow K(s)$	−2.92	very strong reducing agents
	$Rb^+ + e^- \rightarrow Rb(s)$	−2.92	
	$Li^+ + e^- \rightarrow Li(s)$	−3.00	

Solubility of common inorganic compounds in water

Negative ions (anions)	+	Positive ions (cations)	→	Compounds with the solubility
essentially all		alkali ions (Li⁺, Na⁺, K⁺, Rb⁺, Cs⁺, Fr⁺)		soluble
essentially all		hydrogen ion [H⁺ (*aq*)]		soluble
essentially all		ammonium ion (NH₄⁺)		soluble
nitrate, NO₃⁻		essentially all		soluble
acetate, CH₃COO⁻		essentially all		soluble
chloride, Cl⁻ bromide, Br⁻ iodide, I⁻		Ag⁺, Pb⁺⁺, Hg₂⁺⁺, Cu⁺, Tl⁺		low solubility
		all others		soluble
sulfate, SO₄⁻⁻		Ca⁺⁺, Sr⁺⁺, Ba⁺⁺, Pb⁺⁺, Ra⁺⁺, Ag⁺		low solubility
		all others		soluble
sulfide, ⁺⁺		alkali ions, H⁺ (*aq*), NH₄⁺, Be⁺⁺, Mg⁺⁺, Ca⁺⁺, Sr⁺⁺, Ba⁺⁺, Ra⁺⁺		soluble
		all others		low solubility
hydroxide, OH⁻		alkali ions, H⁺ (*aq*), NH₄⁺, Sr⁺⁺, Ba⁺⁺, Ra⁺⁺, Tl⁺		soluble
		all others		low solubility
phosphate, PO₄⁻⁻⁻ carbonate, CO₃⁻⁻ sulfite, SO₃⁻⁻		alkali ions, H⁺ (*aq*), NH₄⁺		soluble
		all others		low solubility

Exercise 1 (p. 132)

1. (a) mill   (d) mill   (g) $1,000,000
   (b) $1   (e) penny   (h) $100
   (c) $100   (f) $10

2. (a) $2\frac{1}{2}$¢   (d) $370   (g) $4,200
   (b) 73¢   (e) $1.61   (h) $254
   (c) 9.5¢   (f) 3.68¢

3. (a) nickel, quarter, 50¢ piece, $5 bill, $20 bill
   (b) 7.5 da$ (d) 1.027 k$ (f) 35.4 d$
   (c) 56 c$ (e) 2.08 M$ (g) 9.67 h$

Exercise 2 (p. 133)

1. (a) 1.3 cm; 0.013 m
   (b) 76 cm; 0.76 m
   (c) 4.1×10^2 cm; 4.1×10^3 mm
   (d) 83 m; 8.3×10^4 mm

2. (a) $P = (2 \times 12.1) + (2 \times 9.8) = 43.8$ cm
   (b) $A = (12.1 \text{ cm})(9.8 \text{ cm}) = 1.2 \times 10^2$ cm^2

Exercise 3 (p. 133)

1. (a) 0.454 kg
   (b) 3.2×10^3 g; 3.2×10^6 mg
   (c) 5.6×10^{-8} kg

Exercise 4 (p. 134)

1. (a) 1.51   (c) 1.3×10^3 ml
   (b) 0.2501   (d) 67,300 dm^3

2. $V = (12.1 \text{ cm})(9.8 \text{ cm})(6.4 \text{ cm})$
   $= 7.6 \times 10^2$ cm^3

Exercise 5 (p. 135)

1. $D = \dfrac{2.100 \text{ kg}}{7.6 \times 10^{-4} \text{ m}^3} = 2.8 \times 10^3$ kg/m^3

Exercise 6 (p. 136)

1. (a) 4   (e) 3   (i) 4
   (b) 5   (f) 3   (j) 4
   (c) 6   (g) 6
   (d) 3   (h) 2

Exercise 7 (p. 136)

1. (a) 3.00×10^2 (f) 9.40×10^{-6}
   (b) 8.50×10^4 (g) 1.83×10^{-4}
   (c) 1.86×10^5 (h) 1.55×10^{-2}
   (d) 1.61×10^7 (i) 8.05×10^{-3}
   (e) 5.13×10^{-3} (j) 8.01×10^1

2. (a) 0.000 007 64   (f) 944,000
   (b) 0.001 00   (g) 17.7
   (c) 50,500   (h) 0.000 462 8
   (d) 0.038   (i) 0.000 000 654
   (e) 2,190,000,000

Exercise 8 (p. 136)

1. (a) 21   (e) 2×10^3
   (b) 1.4×10^2 (f) 0.0200
   (c) 0.2   (g) 0.02
   (d) 5.8×10^2 (h) 5.00

Exercise 9 (p. 138)

1. ±0.4 °C   3. ±27 cm
2. ±0.02 g   4. ±0.03 g

Exercise 10 (p. 139)

1. $A = (10.0 \pm 0.1 \text{ cm})(2.5 \pm 0.1 \text{ cm}) =$
   $25 \pm ? $ cm^2
   Maximum-minimum method:
   $(10.1)(2.6) = 26.26$ cm^2
   uncertainty = 1.26 = 1 (rounded)
   % method: 1% + 4% = 5%
   uncertainty = 1.25 = 1 (rounded)
   Therefore, $A = 25 \pm 1$ cm^2

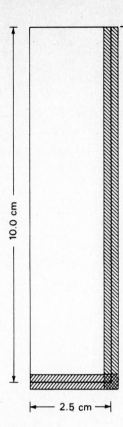

10.0 cm

2.5 cm

Area of uncertainty:
  $0.2 \text{ cm} \times 2.4 \text{ cm} = 0.48 \text{ cm}^2$
  $0.2 \text{ cm} \times 10.1 \text{ cm} = 2.02 \text{ cm}^2$
  Total $\overline{2.50 \text{ cm}^2}$
Uncertainty (maximum-minimum method):
  $2 \times 1.26 = 2.52 \text{ cm}$
Uncertainty (% method):
  $2 \times 1.25 = 2.50 \text{ cm}$

2. Heat =
  $(200 \pm 5 \text{ g})(5.0 \pm 0.2 \text{ °C})(1 \text{ cal/g} \cdot \text{°C}) =$
  $1000 \pm ? \text{ cal}$
  Maximum-minimum method:
  $(205 \text{ g})(5.2 \text{ °C})(1 \text{ cal/g} \cdot \text{°C}) =$
  $1066 \text{ cal};$
  uncertainty = 66 cal = 70 (rounded)
  % method: 2.5% + 4% = 6.5%
  uncertainty = 65 = 70 (rounded)
  Therefore, heat = 1000 ± 70 cal

3. $\dfrac{9600 \pm 200 \text{ cal}}{1.13 \pm 0.02 \text{ g}} = 8500 \pm ? \text{ cal/g}$
  Maximum-minimum method:
  $\dfrac{9800 \text{ cal}}{1.11 \text{ g}} = 8830 \text{ cal/g}$
  uncertainty = 330 cal/g = 300 (rounded)
  % method: 2.1% + 1.8% = 3.9%
  uncertainty = 340 cal/g = 300 (rounded)
  Therefore, heat of combustion =
  8500 ± 300 cal/g

4. $\dfrac{210 \pm 70 \text{ cal}}{10.3 \pm 0.2 \text{ g}} = 20.4 \pm ? \text{ cal/g}$
  Maximum-minimum method:
  $\dfrac{280 \text{ cal}}{10.1 \text{ g}} = 27.7 \text{ cal/g}$
  uncertainty = 7.3 cal/g = 7 (rounded)
  % method: 33% + 1.9% = 35%
  uncertainty = 7.1 cal/g = 7 (rounded)
  Therefore, heat of solidification =
  20 ± 7 cal/g

Exercise 11 (p. 140)

1. $2 \times 1 = 2$
2. $1600 \times 0.01 = 16$
3. $5 \times 0.3 = 1.5$
4. $1000 \times 50 = 50,000$
5. $15/750 = 0.02$
6. $6300/0.03 = 210,000$
7. $700/280 = 2.5$
8. $0.1/40 = 0.002$

Exercise 12 (p. 141)

1. $\dfrac{(9 \times 10^0)(5 \times 10^2)}{(6 \times 10^2)} = \left(\dfrac{9 \times 5}{6}\right)\left(\dfrac{(10^0 \times 10^2)}{10^2}\right)$
  ≈ 7

2. $\dfrac{(8 \times 10^{-3})(5 \times 10^4)}{(7 \times 10^1)(6 \times 10^{-4})} = \left(\dfrac{8 \times 5}{7 \times 6}\right)\left(\dfrac{10^{-3} \times 10^4}{10^1 \times 10^{-4}}\right)$
  $\approx 1 \times 10^4$ or 10,000

3. $\dfrac{(6 \times 10^1)(2 \times 10^{-1})}{(4 \times 10^{-5})} = \left(\dfrac{6 \times 2}{4}\right)\left(\dfrac{10^1 \times 10^{-1}}{10^{-5}}\right)$
  $\approx 3 \times 10^5$ or 300,000

4. $\dfrac{(7 \times 10^1)(2 \times 10^1)(9 \times 10^1)}{(2 \times 10^1)(9 \times 10^1)}$
  $\approx 7 \times 10^1$ or 70

5. $\dfrac{(2 \times 10^0)(2 \times 10^3)}{(4 \times 10^{-2})} = \left(\dfrac{2 \times 2}{4}\right)\left(\dfrac{10^0 \times 10^3}{10^{-2}}\right)$
  $\approx 1 \times 10^5$ or 100,000

6. $(2 \times 10^{-4})(2 \times 10^3)(3 \times 10^1) =$
  $(2 \times 2 \times 3)(10^{-4} \times 10^3 \times 10^1) \approx 12$

7. $\dfrac{(2 \times 10^{-3})(2 \times 10^{-5})}{(6 \times 10^3)} = \left(\dfrac{2 \times 2}{6}\right)\left(\dfrac{10^{-3} \times 10^{-5}}{10^3}\right)$
  $\approx 7 \times 10^{-12}$

8. $\dfrac{(5 \times 10^2)(1 \times 10^2)(1 \times 10^{-2})}{(6 \times 10^1)} =$

$\left(\dfrac{5 \times 1 \times 1}{6}\right)\left(\dfrac{10^2 \times 10^2 \times 10^{-2}}{10^1}\right) \approx 10$

Exercise 13 (p. 143)

1. (a) $\dfrac{60 \text{ miles}}{\text{hr}} \times \dfrac{1 \text{ hr}}{60 \text{ min}} \times \dfrac{1 \text{ min}}{60 \text{ sec}} \times \dfrac{5280 \text{ ft}}{1 \text{ mile}}$

   $= 88 \text{ ft/sec}$

   (b) $\dfrac{60 \text{ miles}}{\text{hr}} \times \dfrac{1.6 \text{ km}}{1 \text{ mile}} = 96 \text{ km/hr}$

   (c) $\dfrac{60 \text{ miles}}{\text{hr}} \times \dfrac{1 \text{ hr}}{60 \text{ min}} \times \dfrac{1 \text{ min}}{60 \text{ sec}} \times$

   $\dfrac{1.6 \text{ km}}{1 \text{ mile}} \times \dfrac{10^5 \text{ cm}}{1 \text{ km}}$

   $= 2.7 \times 10^3 \text{ cm/sec}$

2. (a) $\dfrac{4.00 \text{ min}}{\text{mile}} \times \dfrac{1 \text{ mile}}{1.6 \text{ km}} \times \dfrac{1 \text{ km}}{10^3 \text{ m}} \times \dfrac{1500 \text{ m}}{1 \text{ race}}$

   $= 3.8 \text{ min/race}$

   (b) $\dfrac{4.00 \text{ min}}{\text{mile}} \times \dfrac{1 \text{ mile}}{1760 \text{ yd}} \times \dfrac{440 \text{ yd}}{1 \text{ race}}$

   $= 1.00 \text{ min/race}$

   (c) $\dfrac{4.00 \text{ min}}{\text{mile}} \times \dfrac{1 \text{ mile}}{1.6 \text{ km}} \times \dfrac{1 \text{ km}}{10^3 \text{ m}} \times \dfrac{60 \text{ m}}{1 \text{ race}}$

   $= 0.15 \text{ min } (9.0 \text{ sec})/\text{race}$

3. $\dfrac{1 \text{ atom}}{2.68 \times 10^{-23} \text{ g}} \times \dfrac{10 \text{ g}}{\text{sample}}$

   $= 3.7 \times 10^{23} \text{ atoms/sample}$

4. $\dfrac{1.0 \times 10^2 \text{ g}}{\text{sample}} \times \dfrac{1 \text{ cm}^3}{0.88 \text{ g}}$

   $= 1.1 \times 10^2 \text{ cm}^3/\text{sample}$

5. $\dfrac{\$0.50}{\text{hr}} \times \dfrac{24 \text{ hr}}{1 \text{ day}} \times \dfrac{7 \text{ days}}{1 \text{ wk}} \times \dfrac{4 \text{ wk}}{\text{renting period}}$

   $= \$336/\text{renting period}$

Exercise 14 (pp. 144–145)

1. $x = 3y$

x	y
0	0
3	1
6	2
9	3

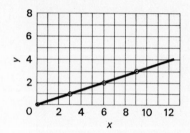

2. $xy = 3$

x	y
1	3
3	1
6	½
9	⅓
⅓	9
½	6

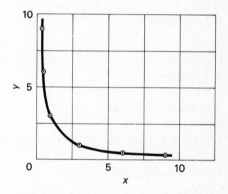

3. (a) $x = ky$
   $0.2 = k(0.4)$
   (b) $k = ½$

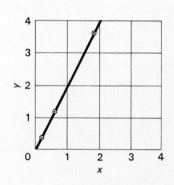

4. (a) $PV = k$
   (b) $(1)(22.4) = k$ $k = 22.4(1 \cdot atm)$
       $(2)(11.2) = k$
   (c) $(12 \; atm)(V) = 22.4 \; (1 \cdot atm)$
             $V = 1.9 \; 1$
   (d) $(0.50 \; atm)(V) = 22.4 \; (1 \cdot atm)$
               $V = 45 \; 1$

Exercise 15 (p. 145)

1. 6.9×10^4 4. 1.09×10^{-2}
2. 5.5×10^5 5. 5.38×10^{-9}
3. 5.9×10^{-5} 6. 6.1×10^7

Exercise 16 (p. 145)

1. 10^5 6. 2.8×10^{-5}
2. 4×10^{11} 7. 3×10^8
3. 9.6×10^4 8. 1.73×10^{-3}
4. 1.0×10^4 9. 10^{-33}
5. 3.9×10^{-10} 10. 1.4×10^{-4}

Exercise 17 (p. 146)

1. 10^4 3. 9×10^{-14}
2. 9.0×10^2 4. 5.9×10^{10}

5. 2.9×10^3 7. 7×10^7
6. 2.2×10^{15} 8. 1×10^{-14}

Exercise 18 (p. 146)

1. 10^4 5. 10.0×10^{-5}
2. 5.0×10^3 6. 13.0×10^5
3. 25.0×10^{-3} 7. 0.30
4. 4.0×10^{12} 8. 5.0×10^2

Exercise 19 (p. 147)

1. $S(s) + O_2(g) = \cancel{SO_2(g)}$
   $$\frac{\cancel{SO_2(g)} + \frac{1}{2}O_2(g) = SO_3(g)}{S(s) + \frac{3}{2}O_2(g) = SO_3(g)}$$

2. $Zn(s) = Zn^{++}(aq) + \cancel{2e^-}$
   $$\frac{\cancel{2e^-} + 2AG^+(aq) = 2Ag(s)}{Zn(s) \; 2Ag^+(aq) = Zn^{++}(aq) + 2Ag(s)}$$

3. $\cancel{H_2(g)} + \cancel{\frac{1}{2}O_2(g)} = H_2O(g) + 57.80 \; kcal$
   $$\frac{68.32 \; kcal + H_2O(l) = \cancel{H_2(g)} + \cancel{\frac{1}{2}O_2(g)}}{10.52 \; kcal + H_2O(l) = H_2O(g)}$$

Periodic table

KEY

Atomic number → 26	← Atomic weight 55.85
Symbol of element → **Fe**	
	Iron ← Name of element

* For those elements all of whose isotopes are radioactive, the parentheses indicate the isotope with the longest half-life.

IA	IIA		IIIB	IVB	VB	VIB	VIIB		VIII		IB	IIB	IIIA	IVA	VA	VIA	VIIA	VIIIA
1 1.0080 **H** Hydrogen																		**2** 4.003 **He** Helium
3 6.941 **Li** Lithium	**4** 9.012 **Be** Beryllium												**5** 10.81 **B** Boron	**6** 12.011 **C** Carbon	**7** 14.007 **N** Nitrogen	**8** 15.9994 **O** Oxygen	**9** 19.00 **F** Fluorine	**10** 20.179 **Ne** Neon
11 22.990 **Na** Sodium	**12** 24.30 **Mg** Magnesium												**13** 26.98 **Al** Aluminum	**14** 28.09 **Si** Silicon	**15** 30.974 **P** Phosphorus	**16** 32.064 **S** Sulfur	**17** 35.453 **Cl** Chlorine	**18** 39.948 **Ar** Argon
19 39.098 **K** Potassium	**20** 40.08 **Ca** Calcium	**21** 44.96 **Sc** Scandium	**22** 47.90 **Ti** Titanium	**23** 50.94 **V** Vanadium	**24** 52.00 **Cr** Chromium	**25** 54.94 **Mn** Manganese	**26** 55.85 **Fe** Iron	**27** 58.93 **Co** Cobalt	**28** 58.70 **Ni** Nickel	**29** 63.55 **Cu** Copper	**30** 65.38 **Zn** Zinc		**31** 69.72 **Ga** Gallium	**32** 72.59 **Ge** Germanium	**33** 74.92 **As** Arsenic	**34** 78.96 **Se** Selenium	**35** 79.904 **Br** Bromine	**36** 83.80 **Kr** Krypton
37 85.47 **Rb** Rubidium	**38** 87.62 **Sr** Strontium	**39** 88.91 **Y** Yttrium	**40** 91.22 **Zr** Zirconium	**41** 92.91 **Nb** Niobium	**42** 95.94 **Mo** Molybdenum	**43** (97) * **Tc** Technetium	**44** 101.1 **Ru** Ruthenium	**45** 102.91 **Rh** Rhodium	**46** 106.4 **Pd** Palladium	**47** 107.868 **Ag** Silver	**48** 112.40 **Cd** Cadmium		**49** 114.82 **In** Indium	**50** 118.69 **Sn** Tin	**51** 121.75 **Sb** Antimony	**52** 127.60 **Te** Tellurium	**53** 126.90 **I** Iodine	**54** 131.30 **Xe** Xenon
55 132.90 **Cs** Cesium	**56** 137.34 **Ba** Barium	**57–71** † see below	**72** 178.49 **Hf** Hafnium	**73** 180.95 **Ta** Tantalum	**74** 183.85 **W** Tungsten	**75** 186.2 **Re** Rhenium	**76** 190.2 **Os** Osmium	**77** 192.2 **Ir** Iridium	**78** 195.09 **Pt** Platinum	**79** 197.0 **Au** Gold	**80** 200.59 **Hg** Mercury		**81** 204.37 **Tl** Thallium	**82** 207.2 **Pb** Lead	**83** 208.98 **Bi** Bismuth	**84** (209) **Po** Polonium	**85** (210) **At** Astatine	**86** (222) **Rn** Radon
87 (223) **Fr** Francium	**88** (226) **Ra** Radium	**89–103** ‡ see below	**104** (261)	**105** (262)														

† LANTHANIDE SERIES

57 138.91 **La** Lanthanum	**58** 140.12 **Ce** Cerium	**59** 140.92 **Pr** Praseodymium	**60** 144.24 **Nd** Neodymium	**61** (145) **Pm** Promethium	**62** 150.35 **Sm** Samarium	**63** 152.0 **Eu** Europium	**64** 157.25 **Gd** Gadolinium	**65** 158.93 **Tb** Terbium	**66** 162.50 **Dy** Dysprosium	**67** 164.93 **Ho** Holmium	**68** 167.26 **Er** Erbium	**69** 168.93 **Tm** Thulium	**70** 173.04 **Yb** Ytterbium	**71** 174.97 **Lu** Lutetium

‡ ACTINIDE SERIES

89 (227) **Ac** Actinium	**90** 232.04 **Th** Thorium	**91** (231) **Pa** Protactinium	**92** 238.03 **U** Uranium	**93** (237) **Np** Neptunium	**94** (244) **Pu** Plutonium	**95** (243) **Am** Americium	**96** (247) **Cm** Curium	**97** (247) **Bk** Berkelium	**98** (251) **Cf** Californium	**99** (254) **Es** Einsteinium	**100** (257) **Fm** Fermium	**101** (258) **Md** Mendelevium	**102** (259) **No** Nobelium	**103** (260) **Lr** Lawrencium